Seven Basic Steps
to
Total Health
Study Guide

Dr. Keith and Laurie Nemec

www.totalhealthinstitute.com

Seven Basic Steps to Total Health Study Guide

Medical Disclaimer
The medical and health information in this book is based on the training, experience, and research of the authors. Because each person and situation is unique, the reader should check with a qualified health professional before following this program. Therefore, the authors, and Total Health Institute specifically disclaim any liability, loss, or risk, personal or otherwise, which is incurred as a consequence, directly or indirectly, of the use and application of the contents of this book.

Published by **Total Health Institute**
by arrangement with Hosanna Publications, Inc.

Printed in the United States of America

Contents

Foreword

Are you listening to your body? It will talk to you. It starts with symptoms like tiredness, fatigue, bloating, gas, pain etc. These symptoms when not addressed turn into conditions, which then eventually turn into "dis-ease," which we call health challenges. These are the people who come through the doors everyday at Total Health Institute. People with everything from major health challenges, to those whose bodies are just beginning to talk to them. Why do they come to Total Health Institute? The one common ingredient we find in the hundreds of individuals that get healed from major health challenges is that they are led by their hearts, not their heads. Dr. Nemec and I ask them to make sure that wherever they go, whatever treatment they get, they make sure they are being led by the *knowing* in the heart. The knowing doesn't come from the head; knowledge that is based on facts, figures and statistics does. The knowing comes from a pure heart not covered with fear. From the "knowing" the person now takes the action steps. It doesn't take a lot of faith because faith comes from the knowing that God puts in your heart. These are the action steps that are taken from the knowing: doing what God has put in your heart at 100% and keeping your focus on the Truth that God has revealed in your heart. There will at times be a feeling of a war going on inside you. This war is the battle between the spirit and the flesh, the heart and the head. You will always win this war if you live in the moment, staying very present and not getting caught up in the future or past. Future thoughts include "who will get me out of this?" or "when will I get out of this?" These future thoughts of anxiety and panic bring with them emotions of fear, hopelessness, depression and worry. Past thoughts of "why did this happen to me?" or "I have tried everything and nothing works" and "I should have done this or that," bring with them emotions of bitterness, resentment and anger. The answer is "let go"; let it all go, people! This concept of "letting it go" is not passive but very proactive. It doesn't mean sit back in your chair, but let go of the future and past thinking and stay in the moment. This is where God is. He is the I AM present. This is where He speaks to your heart and gives you direction in your life; with His directions placed in your heart you begin to take your action steps. Faith without action steps is dead. You must always be letting go of the outcome. You are not responsible for the outcome, that's God's job; you are only responsible to still your mind so you can hear the direction, the action steps He has put in your heart – the *knowing*. Once you can accomplish this, step aside and watch – this is the place of miracles, what we call heaven coming to earth. I have two people in my life who have given this awareness to me; the first was the Living God who gave it to my husband, then my husband who has empowered me with this awareness. I am in love with them both.

Laurie Nemec

Foreword

The message of the moment is twofold:

First, this is the time the people of the world must learn to be led by a deep inner knowing of Truth in their heart, their spirit instead of more superficial knowledge filling their head, their mind.

Second, it is time to enter into two covenant relationships: one with the Living God, the God who speaks to us today with the answers to our real life situations, who isn't buried with religion (which is a product of our old lie-filled mind), but who is alive and gives us all the wisdom, all the power, all the love, all the joy, all the peace, all the hope, all the knowing we need, when we need it, when we are in a partnership with Him, a covenant relationship with Him; One with Him in body, in mind, and in spirit. The second is the body, mind and spirit covenant with yourself, where each part takes care of the other two, each part is willing to die for the other two. Each part loves unconditionally the other two.

The only way we can save our world is to let the Spirit of the Living God reign supreme in our hearts where we are led by the all-knowing He provides. He has the answer for every question, concern and situation that will arise in your life journey, but to access the answer, it is only found in the *knowing* in your heart. This is the place where God speaks. The True answer is never found in the knowledge of the mind, because the mind is clouded and blocked. The mind is filled and programmed with the world system, the ego, the flesh, the 5 senses, religion, time future and past and physicality. The mind is filled and programmed with the lie. The heart is filled and programmed with the Truth. When one tries to access the answer from the mind, the heart/spirit is suppressed. Likewise when one tries to access the answer from the heart/spirit, the mind is stilled. So how can you know the answers, know the Truth, know God's perfect wisdom to all your life situations? "Be still and know that I AM." I AM the answer to every question, I AM the Way and I will show it to you, I AM the Truth and I will place it in your heart, I AM the Life and I will bring it into your body, your mind and your spirit. The first step is to learn to still your mind. This means to stop thinking and start knowing. To stop the raging waves of the ocean of thoughts and start listening to the drops on the still pond of your heart as they spread to touch every part of your being, every part of your body, mind and spirit. To "know" you must learn to listen to the soft, quiet voice of Truth spoken into your heart. To access this "knowing" you must begin on a journey, a journey into total health of body, mind and spirit, and the first steps of this journey are the:

SEVEN BASIC STEPS TO TOTAL HEALTH

In closing I would like to dedicate this book to the two who have taught me every thing I know in my heart about total health: to my covenant partner in my life journey, the love of my life – my wife Laurie, whose name means victory and freedom, and to the one and only Living God with whom I am covenanted with for all eternity.

Dr. Keith Nemec

Introduction

This study guide was compiled from our recorded live series at Total Health Institute: The Seven Basic Steps to Total Health. It has been put in study guide form to deepen your revelation of these life-changing Truths. As we tell all the people who come to Total Health Institute, you must listen to the tape series at least seven times to get a complete revelation of the Truths presented. This would also apply to the reading of this study guide. As you read, pray and meditate over the words of Truth, God brings them to light for you. How many times have you read a Truth over and over until all at once it all becomes clear, the cloud has lifted and you can see the Truth so clearly and how it fits into the grand scheme of life? The same will happen with the tape series and study guide.

Listen and read, listen and read. God will turn the light on the Truth that is for you at that point of your life journey. Do not listen and read with your mind, because you will feed it and block the Truth from filling your heart, your spirit. As the mind is fed the spirit will be suppressed or quenched. Instead listen and read with your spiritual ears and eyes, and the hidden gems and treasure will shine like the Morning Star, so bright will it be that it will illuminate the Truth so that you will know it in your heart, not in your mind.

"You will know the Truth and the Truth will set you free."

This study guide has additional notes and remarks placed in each section, they are listed as **MORE**, also a "go deeper" section is found at the end of each section to give you questions to pray and meditate about along your total health journey.

The Journey into Total Health in Body, Mind, and Spirit

Are You Ready?

Let's begin with a few pertinent questions:

- *Are you ready to restore your total health?*
- *Do you need to be healed today?*
- *Do you want to be healed today?*
- *Do you want more energy?*
- *Do you want more vitality, like you had in your youth?*
- *Do you want to feel better?*
- *Do you want to look better?*
- *Do you want to start living instead of merely existing day by day?*
- *Are you sick and tired of being sick and tired?*
- *Do you want to live life with a passion and a purpose?*
- *Do you want to go deeper in your relationship with God?*

If the answer to any of these is YES! You are about to begin a journey that will change your life forever. It will change not only your life, but also the lives of your children and other family members.

Are you well or are you sick? Most people in America assume because they feel all right and they do not have any major symptoms that they are healthy. Few things can be further from the truth than that statement. Let me ask, how do you know you do not have cancer or are not about ready to drop dead from a heart attack? The answer is not "I just had a checkup and the doctor said I am in great shape" because tests cannot pick up disease until it reaches a certain stage of development. For example, a thyroid gland has to be over 40% out of function before it can be picked up on blood tests. How many people just had a normal EKG and drop dead of a heart attack that very day? How many people look like the picture of health, jog five miles a day and work out at the health club and are dead in six months from metastasized cancer? Even top medical sources state that 80% of disease can already be present before your first symptoms begin. So what's the answer?

Become proactive with your health and your life, because your total health of body, mind and spirit is your life!

Proactive vs. Reactive

A proactive person chooses to make changes in his life because he **knows** in his heart that he is supposed to. A reactive person makes changes in his life only if he has to. A proactive person cherishes the gift of health and guards it with the proper action steps that God has put in his heart. A proactive person thinks about his family, how he can impart to them the highest quality of life, and meets any challenge (health or otherwise) with the intent to overcome and grow better from the experience. A reactive person is quite the opposite. He thinks he is healthy and does not have to do anything for his health unless his symptoms or conditions start to interfere with his lifestyle ('if it isn't broke don't fix it' mentality). When health challenges come his way he sees them as work and questions "why did this happen to me?" Fear and doubt make their home in his mind. Is it easier to catch a ball when you first drop it and it is six inches from your hand or to wait until it six inches from the floor? *The choice is up to you, to choose health or eventual disease, to choose life or death, but remember; no choice is to choose eventual disease.*

Dis-ease

Disease means lack of ease, lack of balance, of harmony and homeostasis. Have you ever seen a top spin so perfectly that it appears to be still? This is balance. This is how God created us to function, in perfect balance, harmony and homeostasis. So what is throwing us out of balance? The answer can be many reasons but here are a few of them:

Lack of oxygen
Lack of proper water intake
Toxic, dead, deficient food
Lack of deep sleep
Lack of exercise
Electromagnetic radiation (EMFs)
Mental/emotional stress

What is this lack of balance, harmony and homeostasis turning into?

- 9 out of 10 people in America will die from heart disease, cancer or diabetes.
- You have a 50% chance of dying of a heart attack.
- 1 out of every 2 Americans will develop cancer in their lifetime.
- Cancer is the number one disease that causes death in American children.
- Diabetes rate in the world is expected to double in the next 10 years.
- 60 million Americans have heartburn.
- 35 million Americans have Irritable Bowel Syndrome.
- Asthma afflicts over 17 million Americans, with 5 million of them children.

- Asthma has increased by 75% from 1980 to 1994.
- Pain - 26 billion + over the counter pain pills are consumed each year.
- Never in the history of the world has one nation (United States) had more people with high blood pressure, high cholesterol, and obesity in adults and children.
- Depression is projected to become the second leading cause of disability worldwide by the year 2020.
- Over 28 million Americans take anti-depressant and anti-anxiety agents.

Symptoms

Symptoms are the beautiful way our body talks to us to tell us that something is not right inside us and that we have to make changes. Unfortunately most people do not listen to their symptoms, they cover them up with drugs so they can keep doing whatever they want to do without listening to their body. The problems begin to arise when you do not learn to listen to your symptoms and make appropriate changes in your total health. If these symptoms are suppressed too long they turn into conditions, and if those are not addressed by getting to the causes instead of covering up the effects, they turn into the diseases that steal and destroy your life. So how do you know you are going out of balance? Just look at the symptoms that ALWAYS turn into disease if they are not addressed at the root causes, and/or are covered up with more pills:

- Fatigue
- Constipation
- Diarrhea
- Bloating
- Heartburn, reflux
- Gas
- Pain, numbness, weakness, tingling
- Recurrent infections
- Allergies/sensitivities
- Insomnia
- Joint problems
- Tachycardia/palpitations of the heart
- Weight problems either high or low
- Emotional highs and lows
- Anxiety/depression
- Malaise – the blahs
- Not looking forward to something – no hope

If these symptoms are not addressed and the root causes eliminated, it is just a matter of time until the body will talk louder, much louder with disease so you will no longer be able to cover it up.

Who Wants to Be Cured Today?

What is curing? It is something done outside of you to you to affect a change.

An example is a woman who has breast cancer and has her breast cut off, has 30 treatments of chemotherapy and radiation and has lived two years since that procedure, and is pronounced cured. This is the place of temporary cures.

What is healed? Take another woman with breast cancer. This woman looks at the breast tumor and asks her body and her heart, "What are you telling me?" She stills her mind and learns to listen to the voice of God, the voice of Truth spoken into her heart. Her heart shows her the path to her healing of not only her body, but her body, mind, emotions, and spirit, seeing them all as one. She obeys the peace and actions steps her heart has shown her, she walks them out in faith (believing, trusting and relying upon the Truth that was spoken to her heart) and this produces life, health and healing.

Cause and Effect

Sickness and disease do not just happen. It is always a cause and effect relationship even though you might not know all the causes. The seeds you planted yesterday are bearing fruit today; the problem is it is bad fruit. But the seeds you learn how to plant today can bear awesome fruit of total health tomorrow, four months from now, one year from now. Always remember if you sow corn you will always reap corn. You always know what you are going to harvest by what you planted in the ground. The same law holds true with your health. If you sow the 7 basic steps to total health day in and day out, that is exactly what you are going to reap – TOTAL HEALTH of body, mind and spirit.

The effect we call dis-ease has many causes, many roots that blocked the flow of life, of health and of healing. These roots are spiritual, mental, emotional, and physical, in that order. The spiritual roots are the most powerful, being the hundredfold loss or block; this is a loss of the love, joy, peace and hope that God fills your heart with. This is a loss of the knowing in your heart that you are healed because you cannot hear what God is speaking into your heart, the action steps you are to take in faith (believing the Truth He has revealed into your heart). Then the mind and emotion, counting as a tenfold loss or block; this is believing the lies the world system tells you, the word of men who tell you "it is impossible" or "you cannot overcome it." These negative thought patterns lead to the production of negative emotions, most often fear, which will shut down the immune system, shut down the body from healing. The physical factors are a one fold loss; this is the negative effects of low oxygen, toxic air, dehydration, toxic water, dead, deficient, and toxic food, lack of 9.5 hours of dark, deep sleep, lack of exercise. You cannot cut the 100X loss (of lack of love, joy, peace, hope and knowing in your heart) out with a knife in surgery. No drug will remove the 10X loss of a lie-filled mind causing toxic, deadly negative emotions which are negative energy that destroy organs, glands, tissues, and body parts. No medicine will remove the 1X loss of breathing, drinking, and eating toxic air, water, and food, along with not getting enough dark, deep sleep and exercise. This is why the only way to rid yourself of dis-ease is not by surgery, drugs, or medicines (these are temporary band-aids, for temporary cures, not forever healing – run over the dandelions with the lawn mower and they are temporarily fixed, but you have even more of them to deal with next week), but to heal the body, mind and spirit as one. *Restore the body, mind and spirit covenant partnership, which means all are one, helping each other to maintain total health, maintain wholeness.*

Prerequisites to Healing

There are some basic concepts that must be understood before you begin your healing journey; they include:

- Responsibility
- Mind of a Child
- Attitude
- Thinking vs. Knowing
- Focus
- Perseverance
- Letting Go

Responsibility

Whose responsibility is your health? Is it your spouse's, your mother's, your father's, your pastor's, priest's, rabbi's, spiritual mentor's, is it your doctor's? No, it is yours and yours alone. *So whatever is in the past is finished, let go of it and move on to the present moment of health and healing.*

Mind of a Child

The mind of a young child is open because it has nothing in it. It goes by the heart, by the spirit. I have seen people who say that their grand babies cry whenever they try to hold them. Why? Because a little baby has no past memory, no established thought patterns from which to analyze the world; so he follows his heart, his spirit, and when he is held by someone who is very out of balance in body, mind and emotions, he can feel it and it does not feel good, so he cries. What a beautiful demonstration of total health. The baby's heart/spirit told the baby's body that this is not a good energy to be in contact with, and because the baby is so pure and unblocked, its awareness of imbalances around it are very keen, designed by God to be like that to keep him healthy throughout his life. The problem begins as the baby grows and is given toxic, dead, deficient food, sugar filled drinks instead of water, as it is exposed to EMFs that weaken the nervous and immune systems, as it is exposed to a world system of lies and absorbs those lies into its mind, emotions and body. This causes the flesh to grow, the ego to grow, false beliefs are programmed into the system, personality or masks are developed to cope and prevent mental/emotional hurt and pain, all this progressively replacing the inborn Truth that the baby was meant to live, grow and develop in. The end result is an out-of-balance creation of God. *It's disease just waiting to happen*!

Attitude

Attitude is how we see everything in our life. There are three types: negative, positive and God. A *negative* attitude is seeing everything as negative, seeing life as what is going to go wrong, it is too good to be true, it is always cloudy, or even if it is sunny, don't get used to it because the clouds are coming, why did it happen to me? A *positive* attitude appears on the surface as one that promotes health, but when one looks deeper beyond the superficial layer we see that, what is good today can easily become bad tomorrow. People with good attitudes use their minds to try to convince themselves that everything is going to be all right, "don't worry about it, I can handle it, I am strong". The problem is a positive attitude is still a product of the mind and if it is pushed or stressed enough it will swing from positive to negative, from good to bad. The "God" attitude is the only one that truly promotes total health, healing and life because it is a product of the heart, and of the spirit, not of the mind. The God attitude see everything from the heart, it sees everything through God's eyes. It sees "all are one", it sees everyone and everything as a creation of God. No matter how bad or negative someone might appear, he/she is still God's creation with a lot of built-up and passed-down blockages and imbalances. It sees everything in life as a gift from God and although some packages (like disease) come in a very unappealing outer wrap, those are the very ones that have the greatest blessings inside. It has only these desires, to "*Love the Lord your God with all your heart and with all your soul and with all your mind and with all your strength,*" and to "*Love your neighbor as yourself.*" This is not work, this is out of the love, joy and peace that God has filled his/her heart with that this attitude flows from.

Thinking vs. Knowing

The journey into total health, healing and life is not a journey of the mind but one of the heart/spirit. Question. Do you think you are healed or do you *know* you are healed? Thinking is a product of the mind; knowing is a product of the heart. If you only *think* you are healed, you are easily swayed by the thinking process once the healing journey gets a little rough and rocky. Your typical response to stress and pressure in the healing journey is "I didn't think it was going to be this difficult" and you quit the journey because your mind talks you out of it. If you *know* you are healed, you are not shaken no matter what tomorrow brings because you know God is in it. God has put the knowing in your heart and all you have to do is listen to your heart, obey it, and never quit, stop or give up on the journey because you do not walk alone, God is walking with you every step of the way and at times, when needed, carrying you. This again can be illustrated with the young baby. Does the baby think that the person holding her is her mother or does she know that she is her mother? The baby has not developed the mental concepts of mother, but just try to take that baby out of her mother's arms and you will quickly hear her response, loud crying. The baby knows that their two hearts beat as one, and only one can calm and soothe, it is the one from which she came from. She knows her mother. This is how we know God. *This is how we know we are healed.*

Focus

This is keeping your eyes on the target. Keeping your eyes fixed on what God has put in your heart as your path to total health. It's not looking to the left or to the right or comparing your journey to anyone else's. It is only seeing, hearing and speaking the Truth that God has filled your heart, your spirit with. It's keeping your eyes on Him, on His Words of Truth spoken into your heart, and faithfully walking out that Truth to completion.

Perseverance

It's not those who start the race strong who receive all the blessings, the victory and freedom, but those who finish strong who receive them. Perseverance means endurance, patience, patient waiting, and steadfastness. The concept of never giving up, never stopping, never quitting, and not shrinking or falling back all are implied, to keep choosing the Truth each moment.

> *"Consider it pure joy… whenever you face trials of many kinds, because you know that the testing of your faith develops perseverance. Perseverance must finish its work so that you may be mature and complete, not lacking anything."* (NIV)

Letting Go

In order to become the new you, the *you* that God created to be in total health of body, mind, and spirit, you must let go of the old you. The old you is the old world/ego/flesh/religion/5 sense bound/time past and future bound/physical limitation bound, lie-filled mind. So how do you let go? First you become balanced physically, living the 7 basic steps to total health; this causes the healing energy to be redirected inwardly to heal (let go or release) the stored negative energy (emotions) from your past and those that were generationally passed to you. Next the wrong mind patterns (stored lies) start to heal (let go or release) and the conscious thinking mind begins to be reprogrammed with the Truth; once this is sufficiently renewed with Truth, the stored memory in the unconscious mind heals (lets go or releases all stored lies). Once the physical body is balanced, the emotional toxins have been released, the conscious and unconscious mind has been reprogrammed with Truth, then it is time to put the old mind completely to death, to let go of ALL the lies that were programmed into the human race since Adam broke the first covenant with God and ate (became one with) the tree of the knowledge of good and evil, the tree of lies. How can we put the old mind to death? After balancing body, mind and spirit we always follow the Truth God places in our heart instead of the lies that fill our mind. We let go of the mind way (thinking, calculating, knowledge, remembering from our past), and we hold on to the heart/spirit way (knowing in our heart, following only what brings love, joy and peace). To let go means to let go of being ruled by the mind, and to begin being ruled by the heart/spirit. God's ways (the knowing of the heart/spirit) are not man's ways (the knowledge of the mind). A powerful tool in letting go (of the old mind) is to break the mind barrier by doing the exact opposite of what your mind tells you to. When you do this the mind barrier begins to shatter and the Spirit is empowered in you. An example is a woman who has a fear of flying (fear is a product of the old, lie-filled mind, and one of its most powerful chains to keep us imprisoned, and under its rule). Fear is not of the Spirit; love, joy, peace and hope are. This woman is on a plane as it starts to taxi down the runway, when it stops and the pilot says there is engine trouble, the mechanic has been called to repair it. The old mind tells her with fear, "You better get off this plane," but her heart has a peace. She remains and the plane takes off. Halfway through the flight the plane hits severe turbulence and her old mind says, "See you should have gotten off the plane, now you are in big trouble." The fear rises higher and higher, causing anxiety, and bringing her to the verge of panic, when she is so overwhelmed she **lets go** of her mind completely and goes into the fear. She amazingly finds a tremendous peace in the midst of the storm. She has let go of her mind, broken the mind barrier and entered the presence of God.

Are You Ready to Run the Race?

The race is your total health journey. Let us look at it as an actual race on a track in a stadium, with people in the stands. As you get in the starting blocks to run the race you must remember the four rules of the race:

1. Keep your eyes fixed on the target, the finish line.
2. Never stop, or quit
3. Never look back
4. Never look to the right or left

These rules apply to running the race of total health:

1. Your eyes are fixed only on the Truth, the Way that God has put into your heart. You see nothing else but this Truth and Him. There is no other way but the one He has shown you in your heart and confirmed with His love, joy and peace.

2. There is only one thing that can stop your healing on this planet, only one thing under heaven. It is YOU! Who heals you? God heals you and you heal you. Does God want me healed? Cut your finger and watch the miracle of God, watch your finger heal. It does it naturally without effort or thought. This is God's part in healing, it is a given. Then who is the only other one that can stop the healing? The other half of the partnership—YOU. So keep going, following your heart. If the race seems at times impossible, just keep pressing forward, because God is the God of impossibilities. With Him all things are possible as long as you do not quit, stop or give up.

3. There is nothing in your past that is going to bring healing, only letting go of it and living in the infinite present moment where God is. You must burn your bridges behind you and press on forward living every moment to the full, no longer living from the past, or living for the future, only living in the I AM presence of God. This is the only place of total health, the only place of healing, the only place of life.

4. In the Olympics many a race has been lost at the last moment when the runner in the lead took his eyes off the target to see who was on his right or left. In the total health race it is very important to never compare yourself and your race to anyone else's except yours. Everyone in life is running a different race, a different course with different obstacles. No two races are the same so to compare races is just to feed the ego mind and block the flow of Truth from the heart. The only one running your race in the entire world is you and God.

Climbing the Mountain

What is the mountain that you have to climb to live in total health? Is it a life-threatening disease, a relationship breakup, or is it financial ruin? Whatever comes in the path of your life, you were designed by God to overcome and grow in the overcoming. Yes, your cancer can truly be your second greatest blessing after your covenant relationship with God, your marriage to God. You ask, "How can that be"? Very simply it is because to overcome that health challenge you will be forced to grow physically, mentally, emotionally and spiritually. It cannot be overcome unless you balance every part of your being: your body, soul (mind/will/emotions) and spirit. All are one; all must work together as one to climb the mountain. Always remember, God is the God of Truth and His Truth states:

By knowing God is in everything, and everything is designed to strengthen you in your journey so that you become complete, mature, not lacking anything, also knowing God is faithful; He will not let you be tempted (tested) beyond what you can bear. But when you are tempted (tested), He will also provide a way out (up) so that you can stand up under it. (NIV) The way out is the way up to the top of the mountain. When you reach the top of the mountain of your health or life challenge that is where you find victory and freedom. The path to this freedom is first to crawl, then to walk, then to run, then to climb, and once you have climbed the mountain then you can fly, and once you can fly then you will be all that He created you to be.

What is Total Health?

It is when the body, mind and spirit are in harmony and balance. The three have become one. This isn't only the three being apparently healthy as individual parts: my body feels good, my mind is clear, sharp, focused, and creative, my emotions are balanced and my spirit is one with God. No, total health means the three have become ONE. They look out for and take care of each other with all their ability and strength. An example is total health in regards to eating toxic, processed, deficient, cooked food. If you were to be confronted with this choice your spirit knows it will not add life into the body, but instead will take it away, so it tells your heart you do not want it. Your body, once it becomes balanced, knows that if you were to eat it you would feel symptoms immediately, so it is one with your spirit/heart. Then comes your mind which consciously has the knowledge of what promotes true health and what takes it away and also remembers what happened the last time you ate that food, how you felt sick for days. Your mind also knows that this is not the type of fuel that should be brought into the temple of God's Spirit –your body. So the mind becomes one with the will or free choice to choose not to eat this food. The body, mind, will and spirit are all in agreement. They are all one. This is total health, and this is the way the three become one in every area of your life, whether it is eating, and making decisions or having relationships, all are one. To make a decision we must understand that the Spirit always knows what is Right and puts the "knowing the Right decision" in your heart. The body knows the Right choice because it speaks with relaxation, ease and decreasing tension. It also speaks with the "gut feeling". The mind's purpose in decision-making is to simply listen to the heart and the body and willfully choose what they have filled you with, instead of following the programmed stored lies that have accumulated in the conscious and unconscious mind. To clarify this, where does God speak to, your head (mind) or your heart (spirit)? The answer is always the heart because the mind is too filled with the things of this world, the self (ego), gratification, the desires of the flesh, the lies. So He fills your heart with what is Right, with that which is True, and this then fills your *supremeconscious mind* (the mind of God in us, which is the "knowing of the heart" filling the mind, rather than the knowledge of the world and lies filling the mind). This Truth then reprograms the conscious (thinking) mind and the unconscious (stored memory) mind, if our will is free enough and open enough to follow this inspiration or "knowing from the heart."

Balanced

When a person is balanced without blockages (in the body, or mind); when they are in total health of body, mind, and spirit, the body and spirit are extremely aware of ALL negative energies and wrong information (lies) that try to enter their being. This includes not only food, water and air that are chemical filled, toxic, dead, or deficient, but also high electromagnetic fields (EMFs), toxic emotion-filled people, ego/world/ flesh/religion/time bound/physical limitation bound, lie-filled, old mind people (even if they are smiling and appearing very friendly). When you are balanced and in total health, this extreme awareness to the physical, emotional, mental and spiritual atmosphere around you serves two purposes:

1. To maintain your total health of body, mind, and spirit – you are less likely to become sick with a major dis-ease when your body, your will and your spirit are in agreement to separate from negative energy, and lie-filled environments.

2. It allows you to become extremely aware of the Spirit of God's voice because He speaks to your spirit, your mind, and your body because "all are one," all listening to the other, all doing what the other needs, all in covenant with one another. The Spirit of God speaks to your spirit, letting it know of potentially harmful (or needful) situations that are arising. Your spirit in turn speaks to your body, and your body produces symptoms strong enough so that your free will chooses to stay out of harm's way (or you operate in the spiritual gifts to help those God has directed you to).

Example A: *A man is going to board his scheduled plane flight, suddenly he feel nauseous and starts to vomit, so he misses the plane flight.* Once the flight has taken off, his nausea and vomiting stop and he feels amazingly better. He later finds out that the plane crashed. This is God's Spirit speaking to his spirit, which spoke to his body, which produced symptoms strong enough to keep him off the plane (these symptoms were strong enough so the mind could not talk him out of it, he had no choice). This man has balanced his body with the 7 basic steps to total health and has released many emotional toxins, along with beginning to reprogram the old conscious and unconscious mind with Truth. He has not put the old, lie-filled mind to death completely yet, this is why his body needed to give him strong enough symptoms so his mind could not talk him into getting on the plane.

Example B: *A woman who has put the old mind to death, so much so that she listens only to the Truth God speaks to her heart and follows it no matter what.* She is running late to catch her flight, and if she misses it she will not only miss a critical business meeting, but will also miss her son's first school play which she had told him she would not miss. As she boards, the still quiet voice of God's Spirit speaks with a soft "do not get on the plane." This woman knows that voice very well, she is so balanced that she has trained herself to hear that voice and she has heard it often, so whenever God speaks to her, she knows His voice and obeys. She comes off the plane in obedience to the voice of God spoken into her heart (not questioning or thinking about it), just knowing the Truth that has always set her free. She later finds out the plane has crashed. She needed no symptoms, *she had already put the world/ego/flesh/religion/time bound/physical limitation bound, old lie-filled mind to death.* Her "will" obeyed the voice of Truth spoken into her heart. This woman has balanced her body with the 7 basic steps to total health and has released all emotional toxins, and also has completely reprogrammed the old conscious and unconscious mind with Truth. She has put the old, lie-filled mind to death completely. Her body did not need to give her symptoms to override a debate between the mind and the heart/spirit. There is never a debate because she will always listen to her heart, and only her heart no matter what the cost is. She is free from her old mind. It's dead, and it has no hold on her.

Example C: *A woman who is balanced in body, mind, and spirit goes to hug an old friend she hasn't seen for years and suddenly feels intense pain in her stomach, and an overwhelming sense of fear.* She stills her mind, listens to her heart and knows that God is telling her that her friend has major emotional toxins of fear that are causing stomach problems. She then shares with her friend the 7 steps to total health and the friend breaks down and cries, saying, "I have been praying that God would show me how to heal my stomach problems and overcome the fear I have lived with all my life, and He sent you!" God's miracle has occurred and the healing has begun. This woman is so balanced after living the 7 basic steps to total health for years that she is a pure vessel through which God's love, God's power, and God's gifts can flow through with no blockages at all. Her spirit and her body instantly tell her what is wrong with her friend, because the Spirit of God wanted to use her as a vessel to heal the woman. By speaking the Truth she knows in her heart and what the Spirit is telling her with symptoms, she knows exactly what area of the friend's life God wants to heal, the miracle of God has truly occurred and the healing has truly begun. This is heaven coming to earth.

What then is total health? It is to be in a covenant partner relationship with the Living God so you can hear and know His voice. It is to be in a covenant partner relationship with your body, mind, and spirit so all can work together to allow you to do all that God has created you to do and be all that God has created you to be. It is to be in a covenant partner relationship with your spouse so you can love him/her unconditionally and help him/her do and be all that God created him/her to do and be. *It is to be in a covenant partner relationship with all humanity so you can be the True Light to the world to receive from God and pour out to those He directs you to with His love, His joy, His peace, His hope*. This produces miracles and transforms the world so that His kingdom will come.

_____
_____
_____
_____
_____
_____
_____
_____
_____
_____
_____
_____
_____
_____
_____
_____
_____
_____
_____
_____
_____
_____
_____
_____
_____
_____
_____
_____
_____
_____

Empty

The Body, Mind, and Spirit Covenant

There is no more important Truth to come to know in your heart in the journey of life, health, healing, and wholeness of body, mind, and spirit than **covenant**. This means we have become one with whoever we covenant with. In the journey of life, there are four essential covenants that must be **known** in order to live life to the full, to be all that we were created to be, to fulfill our purpose on this planet. They are collectively called the covenant of life, which is made of the covenant with God, the covenant with yourself, the covenant with your spouse, and the covenant with all humanity. It is out of this "covenant of life" that everything good in life flows. All blessings of love, joy, peace, hope, passion, compassion, purpose, wholeness, healing, total health of body, mind, and spirit, and of life are found once the "covenant of life" has been partaken of in all its parts. To enter into the "covenant of life" you must come to **know** it in your heart, in your spirit, in your soul, and in your body. Every part of your being must **KNOW** the "covenant of life" and be willing to fulfill the terms of the covenant in its entirety.

What is Covenant?

Covenant is the strongest bond any individuals or groups can have between each other. A covenant includes giving your body, your mind, your heart/spirit, your very life, if necessary, to another to help them be all they were created to be, complete, whole in body, mind, and spirit. To help them grow and mature spiritually, mentally, and physically. The first covenant relationship was between God and man in the Garden of Eden. Covenant - binding relationships have been passed on from the Garden, through ancient times, even up to today. Covenants in ancient times were made between two tribes, where the two tribes essentially became one in every way. Tribes with different strengths would covenant together to become more complete or whole. An example would be if Tribe A was a strong warrior tribe, and Tribe B was a tribe of great wisdom and understanding; when they became covenant partners, they took on each other's strengths, minimizing any weaknesses. This made them more balanced, more whole, more complete than they ever could have been on their own.

Modern day covenant is defined as an agreement between two parties, each binding himself to specific obligations, a legal contract.

In ancient times covenant was defined as a compact made by the passing between pieces of flesh – cutting a covenant.

- Two tribes decide to covenant together. They essentially decide to become one tribe, each receive the other's strengths, eliminating their own weaknesses (promise of blessings). The wise covenanted with the strong. This agreement lasted at least 8 generations; so one would make sure they took this partnership/relationship very seriously.
- A covenant was always a bond for life or death. Covenant terms are agreed upon, each other's strengths are stated, a reminder that there is no breaking the covenant, if one tribe breaks the covenant the other tribe must fulfill the covenant agreement by killing them (shedding of blood, promise of cursing).
- Acknowledgement that those who are in covenant have a closer bond than natural brothers hence the terms blood brothers, "blood is thicker than water," "blood is thicker than milk."
- Always accompanied by the shedding of blood, cutting the hand or forearm, hence the term "blood brothers."
- Taking of oaths. This is stating verbally all that you will be, do, and give to your covenant partner.
- If covenant is broken one party MUST kill the other party as payment for the breaking of the covenant, there is no choice in this, it must be done or the covenant has no power. The covenant's greatest strength is that the two have become one and will give everything they have to meet the need of the covenant partner, even to the giving of one's life for the other.

Making of a Covenant

- They choose a covenant representative, a person that embodies all that tribe is (if the tribe were great warriors, he would be the greatest of all the warriors). In essence that person is "the tribe" and as a tribe (nation) they are all "in him."
- Exchange of weapons and gifts (pledging strengths, loyalty, life to the covenant brother).
- Sacrifice a young bull, split in half down the middle.
- The two covenant representatives walk between the bloody halves in a figure eight pattern.
- Symbolic meaning of sacrifices: I will become your protection, I will assume your responsibility, I will take your place, I will in essence become "you," I will keep this covenant even if it kills me, if I break this covenant may I be killed and cut to pieces as this animal has been.
- Representatives give their oath that the terms of the covenant will be kept while they are standing between the bloody halves. Once stated, the oaths can never be revoked or gone back on.
- Terms of the covenant are then put into writing, signed and sealed before witness, and read publicly.

- An incision is made on each representative's right forearm or palm and the two bloods flow together as one. Blood always represents life. The lives become one. The scar is a visible reminder of the covenant.
- Exchange of names: Tribe A becomes tribe BA, Tribe B becomes tribe AB. The two tribes are now essentially one.
- Each tribe cannot wait to help the other, they think, plan, and pray how to bless the other tribe. This is the desire of their heart. The covenant is very proactive, not reactive at all.
- Covenant Meal – final act of the covenant is an eating of bread and drinking of wine. Symbolic meaning that as you eat this bread, my body and all that is contained in it is "yours." As you drink this wine, my life (my blood) is yours even if it kills me.
- A memorial is set up: stones, or a tree is planted.
- Covenant brothers actively seek and plan ways they can fulfill the covenant. They are constantly praying, and thinking how they can bless their covenant partner. This is not a passive agreement.

Marriage: A Covenant Relationship

- Exchange of marriage vows – terms of the covenant: for richer or poorer, in sickness and in health until death do us part.
- Ring – the visible sign of the covenant instead of cutting the hand or forearm.
- Woman takes on the husband's name.
- The two become one, each eagerly waits to rush and meet the others needs, while praying and planning to give to the other.

Marriage – Two Becoming One

If you are looking for someone to complete you, do you look for someone who is just like you, or someone who is the opposite of you?

You look for your opposite so that your weaknesses are their strengths and their weaknesses are your strengths.

The two become a greater more complete one, rather than each other by himself/herself. This covenant works only if the two are one with God; otherwise, instead of looking to help the other's weakness, one just sees the weaknesses as burdens.

Key Ingredient to the Power of the Covenant

One covenant partner has no right to receive his promises of blessings from his covenant partner unless he has done all he himself can do, before receiving from his covenant partner. **The greatest insult to a covenant relationship is to ask for something you yourself can provide.** This at very least makes the covenant relationship null, and void, and at most costs you your life for breaking the covenant agreement. **So our covenant partner is willing to do and give all that they are, all that they have, only**

after you have done, and given all that you are and all that you have first.

Partners in Covenant

■ Partner **A** desires to purchase a piece of property valued at $100,000. Partner **A** asks partner **B** for the $100,000 when he has $50,000 in the bank.

■ This is an abomination to the covenant – asking for something from your covenant partner that you yourself have.

■ You must get to the end of yourself before your covenant partner gives from himself.

■ Abomination – Most of the Hebrew words translated "abomination" have the meaning of "impure," "filthy," and "unclean" – that which is foul smelling and objectionable.

Covenant -Marriage

How would a woman feel and what would she say if her husband sat on the couch watching TV and said:

■ Honey, change the channel for me.

■ Honey, get me my glass of water on the counter.

■ Honey, pick up my coat on the floor.

She would say, "I can do those things for you but why can't you do them yourself?"

Now if her husband is on the couch lying there sick, she rushes to do those things and meet all his needs because where he is weak, she is strong, where he cannot do for himself, she does for him. This is love; this is the covenant.

Covenant with God

How do you think God feels and what would He say if His covenant partner sat passively asking:

■ *God, heal my body.*

■ *God, take away all these problems.*

■ *God, heal my marriage.*

■ *God, make me prosper.*

He would say I can do for you and give to you all that I AM once you have given all that you have and all that you are. Now if you are listening to His voice of peace spoken into your heart and are in faith obediently taking the action steps He has shown you to 100% of your ability, that's when He meets you with the rest, with all that He IS. This is the place of miracles, the place of healing. This is love. This is the covenant.

There are four covenants that can be called "The Covenant of Life." *These four covenants are what all life, wholeness, healing, and total health of body, mind, and spirit are built upon. They are the very foundation of life.*

The Covenant of Life

- **Covenant with God** – this is becoming one with your creator and sustainer, restoring the relationship that was lost in the Garden, and even making it better, because not only do you become "one with Him," but His Spirit comes and lives in you to guide, teach, strengthen, empower, help and enable you to "know all things." His Spirit is what makes "all things possible," and is what makes miracles become the norm.

- **Covenant with one's self** – this is the body/mind/spirit covenant of loving yourself. This is your body willing to die for your heart's desire, this is your mind being willing to be put to death so the heart/spirit can rule supreme over the body/mind/spirit covenant, this is your heart/spirit knowing the Truth and your mind, your will, and your body obeying and walking out that Truth to completion; never quitting, stopping, or giving up no matter what the cost. *This is the Way and the Truth that brings Life. This is the Truth that will set you free, free from bondage to the old lie-filled mind, free to follow the Truth in your heart and see the miracles of life in every moment.*

- **Covenant with one's spouse** – this is marriage the way God created it to be. The two have become one in every way. Each one always praying, thinking, and planning ways to bless the other in his/her life journey of growth and maturity, in becoming the person God created him/her to be in every way. Complete and whole, not lacking anything, and able to freely receive and freely give the love, joy, peace, and hope of God. *This is the unconditional love of God in action.*

- **Covenant with others** – once the other three covenants have been partaken in, this covenant naturally flows from them. In this covenant you see "**all as one**" or "**all are one**." This is the covenant relationship that sees everyone part of the same whole – humanity. As with the other three covenants, one is praying (listening to the voice of God, the voice of Truth spoken into your heart) to see how to bless those around us, those He has led into our path, our journey of life.

Covenant with the Living God

This is the first and greatest of all the covenants because it is out of this covenant that the other three flow. This covenant is when we ask the Living God to become our covenant partner, our blood brother, and our marriage partner. This can only be done from the heart, never from the head or mind. Things that are from the heart are unchangeable, immoveable. Things that are from the head or mind are very changeable (here today, gone tomorrow, happy today, sad tomorrow), and are very moveable, being built on sinking sand. Covenant means you are binding yourself WILLFULLY to another to dedicate your life to lifting him/her up, to being and doing whatever he/she needs. You will be there to meet his/her needs no matter what. Covenant is not "I have to," but "I love to" and "I live to."

When we enter the covenant with the Living God, we dedicate our lives to being His physical representation on earth. We are His body, He is our heart, our spirit, the two have become one never ever to separate or be separated. This means no matter what life situation arises, He is there with you and will lift you up once you have done all that He has shown you in your heart. He does the rest to empower you to climb the mountain of your life challenge. *This brings love, joy, peace and hope in your journey of life that strengthens and matures you, so you will be complete, not lacking anything, and whole in body, mind, and spirit.*

Covenant with One's Self –Body/Mind/Spirit Covenant.

This is loving yourself. Love is the strongest covenant word. This means your body, your mind, your heart/spirit are all one, all looking out for each other, all taking care of each other, all willing to die, if necessary, to ensure the life and health of the others.

Your body is a powerful covenant partner. It will do whatever your mind, or your heart asks it to, no matter what, it will lay down its life if necessary if either your mind or your heart asks it to.

Your heart/spirit receives the Truth from God and carries out that Truth. It is the most powerful covenant partner because it will never quit, stop or give up on the Truth that it has received from God.

Your mind is the weakest covenant partner. It is the one that believes lies instead of the Truth. It is the only covenant partner that is not willing to die for the other two, so it must be renewed and reprogrammed with the Truth that has been placed in the heart. Only once the mind has been renewed with Truth will it be willing to die to ensure the life and health of the whole being. What areas of the mind need to die to ensure total health of your whole being? The following nine are:

1. World system
2. Ego
3. Flesh
4. Personality
5. False belief systems
6. Religion
7. 5 senses bound thinking
8. Time past, time future bound thinking
9. Physical Bound Thinking

Once the mind dies (meaning it has separated from, and has no part in) to all these nine areas, it now can become a powerful partner in the body/mind/spirit covenant.

To live a life to the full in body, mind, and spirit, to heal, to be whole, you must always look at everything in your life as connected to the body/mind/spirit covenant. For example you did not get cancer, heart disease, diabetes, or any other disease because of just physical causes. **Everything in life is connected to the body/mind/spirit hundredfold principle**. This states that the physical, which includes air/breathing, water, food, sleep, and exercise, has a one fold or 1X effect on your total health, whether adding 1X if you are living these basic steps or subtracting 1X if you are breaking these natural laws of health and healing.

The mind and emotions have much more influence on your total health, causing a tenfold or 10X increase or decrease depending on if you are renewing your mind with Truth (this is the 10X increase in total health), or believing the programmed lies that you have been taught your whole life and were passed down to you *generationally* (this is the 10X decrease in total health).

The heart/spirit is where the Truth of God is received, it has the most powerful influence or affect on your total health, a hundredfold or 100X either increase or decrease. The 100X increase comes when we freely receive the Truth spoken into our heart. The Truth brings with it love, joy, peace, and hope. Where these are, there can be no fear, no negative emotions. *Love is the strongest covenant word.* It means that you have entered covenant with God and you will do what He has put in your heart, never quitting, stopping or giving up until it is accomplished. In this quest of fulfilling what God has placed in your heart you eventually come to the end of your strength and ability. This is where your covenant partner God steps in and gives you ALL that HE IS. This is the place where "all things are possible" because you and God are an inseparable "one." You have become His physical body; He is your Spirit. This is the place of miracles. So if someone has cancer or any other major health challenge, you cannot cut out, radiate out, or medicate out the 10X decrease in total health because of the lies stored in the mind and negative emotions (negative energy stored in the organs, glands, tissues, and body parts) which were caused by these believed lies. You cannot cut out the 100X decrease in total health because of the lack of love, joy, peace, and hope in the heart. All you can do is temporarily cut out the effect (the tumor), never ever getting to the deep underlying causes of the hundredfold principle, the physical, mental, emotional, and spiritual causes of dis-ease. Only the body/mind/spirit covenant operating in true covenant partnership can heal all the causes so the effect becomes healing, health, and wholeness of body, mind, and spirit.

Who Are You?

You are a spirit being who has a mind, will, and emotions, who lives in a physical house we call your body.

Spirit

You were created by God as a spirit being, He breathed the breath (His breath) into you that gave you life. First spirit life, then soul (mind, will, and emotions) life and then physical life. Your spirit has four functions that keep you whole, that keep you in total health in body, mind, and spirit. They are consciousness or awareness, communion with God, intuition, and executor of the body/mind/spirit covenant.

Consciousness/Awareness

This is the knowing the Truth in your heart, not your head or mind. This function of your spirit knows the Truth when it hears or sees it, and it also knows the lies. It knows the Truth because your spirit is God's breath in you, it is God in you and God is only Truth, there is no lie, so your spirit hears, sees, and knows only Truth. The problem today is that most people are ruled by their old world, ego, flesh, lie-filled minds instead of their Truth-filled hearts/spirits. Their spirits tell them the Truth in their hearts but they cannot hear the still, small voice of the Spirit (like drops of Truth on the still pond of your heart) amidst the raging waves of the ocean of the old minds. *If one can train himself/herself to still the raging waves of the ocean of his/her mind, then he/she will indeed hear the drops of Truth that are always falling on the Truth-filled pond of his/her heart.*

Communion

This is the most awesome function of our spirit, it is the part that talks and listens to God. It is the part that communes with Him, our creator and sustainer. This intimate communication line was interrupted when Adam broke the original covenant partnership with God by eating from the tree of the knowledge of good and evil. From this broken covenant – humankind empowered the lie-filled mind to rule their beings. They quenched the Truth-filled heart/spirit (the knowing in the heart) and enthroned the mind (the knowledge of the mind which is based in the lie). Then God in His infinite love and wisdom made the Way, so the communication line could be permanently restored. This was a new and everlasting and unbreakable covenant that would be made between Himself, His Son, and all human beings. This covenant is entered into when you recognize, have the consciousness/awareness of the Truth, that you cannot live life from your lie-filled old mind but instead must live from your Truth-filled heart/spirit. When you ask the Living God into your heart in essence you are saying "NO" to the world, ego, flesh, lie-filled old mind and "YES" to the Truth-filled heart where God lives. This is grace, which is another powerful covenant word which means *"I am personally entering into a covenant with the Living God, I will do all that He places in my heart, with all my strength and ability no matter what the outcome, because I know in my heart that when I give all that I have in following my Truth-filled heart, He (the Living God), my covenant partner will meet me with all that He IS to carry the action steps to completion.* When I enter this covenant, I have committed my life to following only my Truth-filled heart and not my lie-filled old mind. I will follow this Truth no matter what the outcome, no matter what it costs me – even if I have to put everything I have ever been taught or learned to death with my old knowledge lie-filled mind, even if it costs me my physical life, because I know, that I know, *that I know* when I live a life solely from a Truth-filled heart I will be blessed with ALL the covenant blessings my covenant partner (the Living God) is just waiting to pour upon me – so much so that I cannot even think or imagine. When I enter this covenant relationship I realize that I am committing my body, my mind, and my spirit to following the Truth placed in my heart. I will follow this Truth never quitting, stopping, or giving up, no matter what the price demands. I also realize that if I choose to go back into the thinking of the world, ego, flesh, religion, time past, time future or physical bound old mind, I am breaking the covenant, I am voiding the covenant of its power to bless me with ALL God's love, joy, peace, and hope. I realize that I have become one with the Living God, I am His body, He is my Spirit, we are one in every way and I will do and be all that He has placed in my heart – for all eternity."

Intuition

This function of your spirit just "knows." It is a mother who knows her child is in danger, even though she cannot see her. It is the man who "knows" he is not supposed to get on that plane, and the plane crashes. It is the business man who "knows" that it will be a good investment. It is the "gut feeling," the inner knowing that leads and guides us. It is our 6th sense. We all have this function of the spirit, although many times it is clouded by feeding our old lie-filled mind, and living from our old minds so much that ALL functions of the spirit become suppressed, even our 6th sense – *our intuition.*

Body/Mind/Spirit Covenant Executor

This function of your spirit purpose is to maintain wholeness or total health of your body, your mind, and your spirit. The body, mind, and spirit were created by God to work in harmony and balance as "one." This means if you are in balance and keeping the body/mind/spirit covenant, the three communicate to each other, keeping you whole, in total health, living God's kind of life – *eternal life.* Eternal life doesn't just mean living forever with God in heaven, it also means living God's designed life right now on this planet. It means living life to the full in body, mind, and spirit. The function of your spirit as body/mind/spirit executor is to receive the Truth from God for any situation that arises in your life journey. This is the "knowing" the

Truth in your heart. Next the body willingly obeys all the desires of your heart of Truth. Then comes the mind that has been filled with lies, and has been trained from a generational and personal past of the world system, ego, flesh, religion, past and future bound thinking, and physical limitation bound thinking. The mind has to be willing to "let it go" and die to all it has been programmed with in order to be reprogrammed and renewed with Truth. This is the greatest blockage to all of humankind's total health of body, mind, and spirit. This is the greatest blockage that prevents the Spirit of God from flowing unhindered in our lives and the world today. The key deciding factor is found in a part of your soul (mind, will, and emotions). It is your WILL. Your will is either free, and will always choose the Truth, or it is bound and will always choose the lie of the old mind. The choice is yours – choose life or death, blessing or cursing. Life and blessing are receiving everything from God, your covenant partner, once you have given all you have in following the action steps He has revealed to your heart. Death and cursing are choosing to separate from God, from the Truth revealed in your heart. This means that you live life from yourself, from your old mind. This means it is you, and you alone against the world, against the prince of the world, against the father of lies. You will **NEVER** have true love, joy, peace, and hope (knowing) if you choose to follow the old lie-filled mind.

Mind

The mind can be seen as three parts although they still come together to form the whole – the mind. They are the supremeconscious mind, the conscious mind, and the unconscious mind.

Supremeconscious Mind

This is the mind of Truth, the mind of God living in man. This is only accessed when one stills the conscious, thinking mind enough to follow the Truth-filled heart/spirit. All great inspirations, creations, inventions come from the supremeconscious mind. This is the idea that "just appeared," it was not thought out or calculated. It was a revelation, a light that went off inside you, an "I got it" moment. The supremeconscious mind is where the Truth of God, the "all knowing" of God (which is in your heart/spirit) enters your mind. It is where the answer to every question is found. It is the mind of God in you.

Conscious Mind

This is the thinking, figuring, calculating, planning mind. This is the mind most people live in and from. This mind is where the lie, from the first broken covenant between God and man, when Adam ate of the tree of the knowledge of good and evil, entered. This is the old preprogrammed mind that does what it does because of what it has been taught by a world system of lies, by family and friends that also have been trained in lies, in false belief systems, which have been passed down through the generations.

Unfortunately 95% of our lives are lived from this part of our mind when only 5% should be. The 5% is how much is needed to do the basic activities of daily living, which become almost automatic. The other 95% should be lived from the Truth-filled heart/spirit flowing into the supremeconscious mind. The reason the conscious thinking mind is the greatest blockage to our total health and wholeness is because it has been preprogrammed with the lies. The lies says, "You can do it all by yourself, you are the ruler of your universe, there is no God outside of yourself, the physical world is all there is, physical laws cannot be broken, all things are not possible, it must be right if everyone else believes it and does it." That is why it is the conscious thinking mind that must be stilled. It is the old lie-filled conscious mind that must be put to death, so that it can come back to life programmed with Truth and Life, programmed with what is Right, what is Truth, with Love, with what is the Way, with Life. In life one must die to the old lie-filled mind, still the never ending chatter of the thinking mind (raging waves in the ocean of the thinking mind), to hear the drops of Truth that are always falling upon the Truth-filled pond of your heart/spirit. *Those drops of Truth radiate and touch every part of your being, and once they have touched your being, you radiate and resonate as a shining light, as a frequency of love, to touch the entire world with that Truth that has been placed in you.*

Unconscious Mind

This is the stored memory, the recording tape of your entire life. This contains every event that has ever happened to you, the ones you remember and mostly the ones you do not. These are still stored in the unconscious mind – all the lies, all the stored memories—held inside, negative emotions (which are negative energy that actually takes up residence in your organs, glands, tissues, and body parts). All your life experiences are stored here and if they were negative, toxic emotions (which are generated from the lie-filled old mind) they are buried in the unconscious mind and also in the organs, glands, tissues, and body parts of the entire body. To heal, to become whole in body, mind, and spirit one must first reprogram the conscious thinking mind with Truth, then the unconscious mind will begin to "let go of" or release the stored lies and the stored emotions (negative energy) that were created by those lies, and begin to reprogram and renew with Truth. This happens when the supremeconscious mind that is filled with Truth, starts to reprogram the conscious thinking mind with that Truth. When two of the three parts of the mind are filled with Truth, they naturally start to reprogram the unconscious mind to let go of the lies and fill up with the Truth that they are filled with. This is like running distilled water through the mineral clogged water pipes in your house. Eventually all these mineral deposits will dissolve, as they are absorbed into the mineral free distilled water. The distilled water is the Truth; in time all the blockages in the pipes (the stored lies in your body, in your unconscious mind and in your conscious mind) will "let go of" those mineral deposits, those stored lies, and negative energy, and the pure water (the Truth) will flow freely and fill all the pipes in your house (your organs, glands, tissues, and body parts). No more blockages because all have been "let go of" to the Truth which flows through the house – *which is you.*

Body

What is the body? It is energy manifested in physical, 5 sense, form.

What is Your Body?

- A collection of organs, glands, tissues.
- Organs, glands and tissues are made of cells.
- Cells are made of molecules.
- Molecules are made of atoms.
- Atoms are made of proton, neutron, and electrons whirling in 99.9% empty space held together by ENERGY.
- Subatomic particles are not point-like but strings that vibrate at specific frequencies. Frequency is ENERGY.
- Your body is ENERGY.

Energy and Information

- **Everything in your life consists of energy and information.**
- Energy can be negative, positive, or spirit.
- Information can be right or wrong.
- Positive energy is energy of life, health and healing.
- Spirit energy is the energy of love, joy, peace and hope.
- Negative energy - dead, deficient, toxic food, water, air, negative thoughts and emotions.
- Information - Right or wrong, based on the knowing in the heart = Truth, or based on the world system of knowledge = lie.

To understand how health is restored and maintained in the physical body, three Truths must be known.

1. Health flows from spirit, to soul (mind, will, and emotions), to physical body.
2. Health is accessed most easily from physical, to soul, to spirit.
3. The physical is made up of energy and information.

These Truths are vital to the healing and total health of not only the physical body, but to the mind and spirit as well.

1. The spirit has the 100X effect on total health; it flows to the mind, will, and emotions that have a 10X effect, which flows to the physical that has a 1X effect on total health. The true blockage of this flow of life is in the mind, will, and emotions. The reason this path (from spirit to soul to body) to total health is a more difficult one is because

the mind is filled with the lies, and those lies produced stored negative energy (emotions) in the organs, glands, and tissues of the body. Because of the mind, the heart/spirit is blocked from receiving the Truth from God. This blockage in the old, lie-filled mind causes a person to think there is no God, or that they are their own God (ego mind), or they do not want to come back into a covenant relationship with God because they think God is angry with them, or is going to punish them, or they would have to join a religious group and work for God (religion mind). They also think they do not have time for God, they are too busy climbing the ladder of success and working to be the best (world/ego mind), or they have just decided that pleasure in life consists of eating, drinking, being entertained, having more sex, or getting more physical "things" (flesh mind). They can also be too busy planning their futures or running away from their pasts (time bound mind). All these old, lie-filled mind blockages of the heart/spirit prevent the Truth from penetrating the spirit, mind, will, emotions, and body.

2. If a person starts to access total health with the physical action steps, this is tolerated by the old mind much more than giving one's life to God in a covenant relationship. Why? Because to give your whole being to God means your old mind has to die, your world, ego, flesh, 5 sense bound, personality, religion, time future and past bound, and physical limitation bound old, lie-filled mind has to die. It will not go down without a fight. This is the battle between the heart/spirit and the old mind. Unless a person has a supernatural spiritual awakening to the Truth, the heart/spirit and body are imprisoned by the old mind. So if one cannot access total health through the front door (the spiritual awakening by the Truth), because the gatekeeper (the old, lie-filled mind) is guarding it too closely, then one can go in the back door with the first 5 steps of the 7 basic steps to total health. The old world, ego, flesh, lied-filled mind might allow you to start breathing deeper, drinking more pure water, eating more energy-containing food, getting to sleep earlier, and exercising because it knows if it does not do some maintenance care, the physical body will start having too many symptoms or develop dis-ease. This would not be good for the old, lie-filled mind because it could potentially decrease or even lose its authority over the body, mind, spirit covenant. When do people get spiritual? When they suffer or develop disease. The old mind wants to avoid these at all costs, so it allows the 5 basic steps in the back door. This is like opening the gates to the Trojan horse. The old mind, not knowing, has opened the door to the very thing that will put it to death. How? Once your physical body becomes balanced with

the first 5 of the 7 basic steps to total health, then the life energy used for health and healing no longer has to be used to just get you out of bed and get you through your day. This energy can be turned inward to start releasing stored emotional toxins (stored negative energy). As these emotional toxins are "let go of," more energy is available to dislodge the foundational lies that they were attached to. As the stored emotions release and the negative mind patterns are uncovered, the Truth can now be seen, even if it is very faint, shining through the coated heart/spirit light. This is when your supremeconscious mind and will come together to choose to keep uncovering the light/Truth buried. As more foundational stones of lies are removed, as more and more emotional toxins are released (because the physical is staying balanced), more Truth shines through the heart/spirit until enough is revealed so that the heart/spirit, the supremeconscious mind, the conscious thinking mind, and the will, all align in agreement and choose Life, the choice to come back to their long lost covenant partner – God. They choose to enter the covenant of Life with Him, with themselves (the body/mind/spirit covenant), with their spouse, and with all humanity. They have become a new creation, the old, lie-filled mind has gone (been put to death), the new Truth-filled heart/spirit, and supremeconscious mind has come.

3. The physical body is made of energy and information. Everything in life is energy and information. If one is living in bondage, enslaved by the old mind, the energy is negative and the information is wrong (the lie). If one is in covenant with the Living God and is taking care of the temple of His spirit, which is your body, the energy is spirit and the information is Right (Truth). There are different degrees of health on the journey to total health.

What Energy and Information is Your Body built with?

- Negative energy + wrong information (the lies): eating, drinking and breathing dead, deficient, toxic food, water and air, and believing the lies.
- Positive energy + wrong information (the lies): eating, drinking and breathing living food, pure water and pure air, but believing the lie.
- Negative energy + Right information (the Truth): eating, drinking and breathing dead, deficient, toxic food, water and air while knowing the Truth in the heart.
- Positive energy + Right information (the Truth): eating, drinking and breathing pure living food, water and air and knowing and following the Truth in your heart. This enables healing to occur on all levels of body, mind, and spirit.

■ Spirit energy + Right information (the Truth): transcending all natural laws by receiving and flowing in the energy from God and only knowing and following the Truth in your heart. This is the Spirit of God flowing through you to bring the people of the world back to being led by the Truth-filled heart instead of the lie-filled, old mind. This is the Spirit of God touching the world around you to lead them back into a covenant relationship with Him.

Covenant with One's Spouse – One's Other Half

This is natural once you have entered covenant with the Living God (love God), and have entered the body/mind/spirit covenant (love yourself). Loving yourself includes your other half, your spouse. When you are one with God, receiving and giving in a covenant relationship, and you are one with yourself (balanced in the body/mind/spirit covenant), then that love, life, and light shines into your other half – your covenant marriage partner. The strength of the covenant with your spouse is only as strong as the covenants that preceded it: your covenant with God, and the body/mind/spirit covenant. As with the other covenants, you constantly keep your covenant partner on your heart, and in your thoughts. You pray to see how you can bless her/him in her/his life journey, how to help her/him grow and mature to be all that God created her/him to be. You love her/him unconditionally which means you give to her/him as the Spirit directs you without ever expecting to receive back. This is God's kind of love, this is grace, this is covenant, but this giving of gifts never expecting to receive back can only operate if you are first being filled up by your first love, your first covenant partner – the Living God. If you are not receiving from Him, and you are not balanced in the body, mind, and spirit covenant with yourself, you can never pour out His love, His light, His life, His Spirit into their life, being the vessel or channel that God's love flows through. But if you are so "one" with the Living God, your first covenant partner, and you are so balanced (you have removed all the physical blockages, let go of the stored emotional toxins, put the old world/ego/flesh/lie-filled mind to death, and have reprogrammed the conscious and unconscious mind with Truth) without any blockages, you can now let the Spirit flow through you unhindered to your spouse. You can now love her/him with the purest, and truest love. You will lift her/him up on a pedestal always. She/He is and always will be the "diamond of your eye." You are two hearts that beat as one for all eternity.

Covenant with Others

"Love your neighbor as yourself," means you must balance the body/mind/spirit covenant first before you can be a True covenant partner with all humanity – "all are one." We have all been created by God to be "one," everyone receiving and giving, all flowing in their gifts to one another, all looking out to bless, help, to lift up one another, all seen as covenant partners. Not a "me against you" mindset, but a "we can do it together" heart. The key factor in covenanting or loving your fellow human being, your neighbor, is the word "yourself." This means that to be in covenant with one another, to love one another, you must first love yourself; you must first become balanced in the body/mind/spirit covenant. The meaning is once you, yourself, have balanced your physical body (by following the 7 basic steps to total health), balanced your mind (by letting go of the emotional toxins, and reprogramming your old mind with Truth), and balanced your heart/spirit (by listening to, and obeying the Word of Truth placed in your heart, taking the actions steps shown in faith, never quitting, stopping or giving up no matter what the outcome or cost to you), now you are the TRUE LIGHT of the world, not only in spirit, but also in mind and body. This means that you have the pure energy pulsing through your body (from following the 7 basic steps to total health), and you know the Right information (you follow the Truth-filled heart, not the world/ego/flesh/lie-filled old mind). *When you are balanced, whole, in total health in body, mind and spirit, you are a beacon of light that shines so all the world can see, and none can deny.* Everyone will be attracted to this balanced body/mind/spirit covenant LIGHT, and you will positively entrain the whole world to the frequency of love, joy, peace, hope, Truth, Life, and the Way. Many who have entered into the covenant relationship with the Living God are a light to the world around them but a light in spirit only, not in mind or body. This is why not many of the world, of your neighbors, are attracted to this light. Who wants a partial light these days? To tell someone how awesome your relationship is with the Living God, when you are an emotional roller coaster, tend to become depressed, and are sick, let's those seeking know that you might have something, but that is definitely not what they want. The people in this world want it all – total health in body, mind, and spirit because that is what God created us for – to be whole, healed, set free from all bondages of the old mind, to be in total health in body, mind, and spirit. All humanity is seeking this complete message and the one who loves themselves first – balancing their body, mind, and spirit with the 7 basic step to total health, can then entrain those around them, your neighbor, your world, to a higher level of Truth awareness and the Right energy (entrain upward) and information (open to the Truth in the heart once the physical is balanced, the negative emotional toxins, negative stored energy, have been released or "let go of" and negative mind patterns, the old mind, have been reprogrammed and renewed with Truth so the heart of Truth can rule over the body/mind/spirit covenant relationship, and then the Spirit of God can flow unhindered to pour out gifts to one another). We will "all be one." Your Kingdom has come.

Seven Basics Steps to Total Health Overview

Seven Basics to Total Health

1. Air/Oxygen/Breathing
2. Water
3. Food
4. Sleep
5. Exercise
6. Fasting
7. Prayer

Why do so many people not heal?

- Not doing the 7 basics to total health on a daily basis.
- Looking at a part instead of the whole (breast, liver, colon, lung).
- Looking at the dis-ease as physical more than physical, mental, and spiritual all combined as one, all needing to be addressed as one.
- Addressing effects instead of causes (dandelion flower vs. root).
- Seeking a cure instead of a healing (outside of yourself instead of inside yourself).
- **MORE** - Do not know about the flow of life, what blocks that flow and how to remove these blocks (in a person with advanced cancer who has four weeks to live, if they cut their finger it will heal, this shows that life is still flowing in the body, why then does it not flow to the tumor and heal it? The answer is blockage in the flow of life, which needs to be removed).
- **MORE** - Whole vs. individual parts must be stressed in healing. It is what you consistently do everyday of your life that makes you who you are. You can never ever heal when you look at the effects instead of removing the causes. Mow the dandelions down with the lawnmower and what have you done? Temporarily removed the dandelions, but in actuality you only spread more dandelion seeds to grow. The only way to remove the dandelion so it never comes back is pull it out by the root, the cause, so there can be no more effect.
- **MORE** - Too much pressure in the bag. If we looked at our health as a plastic bag, and our symptoms, conditions and dis-eases as a popping of the bag in a specific area, how can one possibly heal and live in total health unless they remove all the pressure in the bag? This is addressing all the causes of the pressure or imbalance (all the physical, mental, emotional, and spiritual causes) instead of just trying to mend the "pops" in the bag. If you mend this pop, which is cancer

but do not remove the pressure then it just pops somewhere else, you either get cancer somewhere else or you get another dis-ease somewhere else. Why? Because you never removed the cause, never removed the pressure, never removed the imbalance that caused the "pop" in the first place.

- **MORE -** The River of life flows to every cell in your body. Let us look at this river as an actual river. If we dam up the river with boulders what happens? Upstream from the dammed area it produces a flood, downstream from the blocked area it produces a drought. Two problems produced by the same blockage. Now let's say this river is the river of life to your immune system. If you put blockages in this river it produces two situations: a flood in the immune system that is known as autoimmune disease (multiple sclerosis, rheumatoid arthritis, Crohns colitis, thyroiditis-Graves, Hasimoto, adrenalitis-Addisons, diabetes, hepatitis, nephritis, lupus, scleroderma), and allergies and sensitivities. It also produces a drought in the immune system that is known as recurrent infections of all types (bacterial, viral, fungal, parasitic) and cancer. So what is the answer? Is it to bomb the body with chemotherapy, radiation and surgery for the cancer or is it to take high doses of steroid medication, for the autoimmune disease, until it destroys other organs, glands and tissues? Or is it simply removing the blockages in the river of life so the low immune function increases to normal and the hyperimmune function decreases to normal, and then learning how not to put any more boulders in the river to block it up.

How is health and healing accessed?

Two ways.

First

- From the Spirit of God filling the spirit (heart) of the person with Truth. This Truth then flows into his supremeconscious mind (mind of God). This Truth also begins to set him free from both conscious (thinking) and unconscious (stored memory) negative mind patterns and emotional toxins. This supremeconscious mind then leads the person into specific action steps to restore his physical health.

Second

- From doing the easiest things to change first-breathing properly to increase oxygen intake, proper daily water intake, proper diet, proper daily amount and onset of sleep, proper daily exercise, learning how to say no to what negative mental, emotional and physical activities are slowly killing you (fasting), learning how to hear the voice of God spoken into your heart and mind (the Truth, the Way, the Life).

■ From taking these action steps you can then begin to use energy that was being used to keep you alive in survival mode, for deeper inner healing (letting go) of stored negative mind patterns and emotional toxins from your past and those that were generationally passed to you. As you become freer in mind and emotions you begin to open spiritually to the love of God and seek to intimately know Him in your heart.

Health / Healing flow from:

Spirit of God – the Truth, the Way, the Life,
into
Spirit of Man – knowing God, being filled with His Spirit, and partaking of the tree of life,
into
Mind – Supremeconscious - filled with all Truth;
    Conscious - willfully choosing Truth and reprogramming with Truth;
    Unconscious - releasing stored lies, reprogramming with Truth;
into
Emotions – replaced with spiritual states of being: love, joy, peace, hope;
into
Body – bringing health and healing.

Health / Healing is accessed from

Body – 7 basics to total health,
which when balanced starts to balance
Emotions – releasing stored emotional toxins from organs, glands, tissues and body parts,
which when balanced opens the mind up to Truth.
Mind – Supremeconscious - Truth flowing from the heart,
    Conscious - willfully choosing Truth, and reprogramming Truth,
    Unconscious - releasing stored lies, reprogramming Truth,
    which when reprogrammed and renewed with Truth, become open and allows the
Spirit of Man – knowing God in your heart, partaking of the tree of life,
to be filled with
Spirit of God – the Truth, the Way, the Life,
and flow God's Spirit unhindered to bring the kingdom of God, the Spirit of God into the hearts and minds of men, women and children. This is heaven (Spirit) come to earth (body/physical), God's creations living as He created them to.
MORE - Why is total health of body, mind and spirit more easily accessed from the physical first? Because all of humanity has old mental thought patterns (lies) and emotional toxins (stored negative energies) that have been passed from Adam and Eve all the way down through the generations. Also,

all have the lies and stored negative energies that they themselves have accumulated in their life. All these combine to block the heart from receiving the Truth. Once the physical body is balanced with the 7 basic steps, the energy that was being used to just keep you going in survival mode can now be turned inward into deep inner healing and the release of the lies (old mind) and stored negative energies (toxic emotions). These release naturally without effort or counseling. The body, soul and spirit just let them go at the right time. Now once the body is balanced and the mind and emotions have been balanced, the heart is open to receive the Truth. **MORE -** What is an emotional toxin, and how can it store in the body? Emotional toxins are negative energies that can store in any gland, organ, tissue, or body part causing either rapid progressive damage or dis-ease of that area of the body or slow progressing damage that fully manifests years later with dis-ease. They occur when someone who has been programmed from birth and even before (generational) with lies spoken into their mind, and believes them. This gives rise to the negative emotions. Also when someone is at a weak point (vulnerable) and is hit with too many negative energies at one time, the system is on overload and its defenses temporarily break down, opening the door to these negative toxic emotional energies that take up residence in organs, glands, tissues and body parts, either rapidly or, more commonly, slowing destroying them.

An example: If you accidentally hit your child in the face while playing around, it produces a lot of pain but because it was done by the person he loves and no harm was meant, the pain quickly goes and healing is rapid. Now a different scenario occurs: the parent walks into the room after receiving the report card of the child and seeing average grades, so the parent hits the child and screams, "You will never amount to anything," along with "if your grades aren't better next time you are going to be severely punished!" This trauma of being hit now has a whole different negative energy to it. It becomes the 10 fold, even 100 fold, loss or block in his total health, causing storage in the body. The dis-ease has been born not to fully manifest until forty years later with cancer of the liver, which was the organ most susceptible to the fear, or even unresolved TMJ (jaw joint imbalance), facial muscle paralysis, or skin cancer. These are on the side of the face that was struck many years ago, but struck with devastating negative energy that caused a 100 fold decrease or block in the flow of life, opening the door to eventual dis-ease. These toxic emotions and toxic lies can store in any area in the body and progressively destroy it if not released. But they are released progressively, when we make the seven basic steps to total health a lifestyle for our body, mind and spirit.

The Path to Healing

- 1st step physical, 2nd step mental/ emotional, 3rd step spiritual
- Your body only has so much life-maintaining/ sustaining energy. But if you eat dead, deficient, toxic food. You drink dead, depleting, toxic drinks. You breathe toxic air. You do not sleep enough and do not exercise, do not fast to break addictions, do not learn to listen to His voice in prayer. Too much of this life sustaining energy is going into the present just to keep you alive.

Energy - The Flow of Life, Health

- Your body has so much energy that it uses to sustain and maintain your health in the present.
- If you do not daily practice the 7 steps to total health then the body begins to become depleted of its energy to maintain health. This eventually will result in symptoms, conditions and dis-ease.
- If you master the 7 steps, then the body can redirect the energy it has been using in the present (just to keep you alive) to where the blockages in energy flow began - your past and the negative information that was passed to you generationally. When this occurs deep inner healing begins and the body/mind retraces back to the origin of the blockage/imbalances.

Retracing - The hallmark of healing

Retracing is the path of restoring health back from dis-ease. As one retraces he passes through, in reverse order, from dis-ease to conditions to symptoms to blockages to where there are no more blockages. Complete healing can never be attained unless one retraces back to the origin of the blockage of energy flow.

A 53 year old man has cancer. As he starts on the 7 basic steps to total health he starts to feel better, his energy greatly increases, his strength and stamina begin to improve, his digestion improves, his constipation and bloating leaves, his sleep becomes more sound and increased, his skin starts to clear and his brain fog lifts. He also feels more joyful and more at peace. He knows he is healing. After eight weeks doing the 7 steps he starts to experience headaches that he had not had since he was 12 years old; these last for one week then are gone. One month later he starts to have stomach pains which were identical to the ones he had when he was 6 years old, but have had not had since that time. These last for ten days and then are gone.

MORE - Retracing is seen in everyone who attains total health. It goes back to where the body just temporarily patched itself to get by. It then releases and rebalances, so the condition is totally gone, not just in dormancy awaiting for the time to erupt with a full-blown disease. How does one know if they are retracing or actually getting worse? If you are doing the 7 basic steps to total health daily, you are retracing; if you are living the standard American lifestyle you are getting worse.

MORE - retracing is not just seen with physical symptoms but also with emotions, mind patterns, attitudes and even cravings.

Example: A person starts doing the seven basic steps to total health and initially feels great but after about one month he starts to have cravings for pizza. He has no idea why he is craving pizza because he has not had pizza in years and does not really like it. This demonstrates one of two possible healing/retracing scenarios: First, he used to eat pizza when he was a child at the family get-togethers, and whenever he used to eat relatives would tell him that he was never going to amount to anything and that cancer runs in the family. These lies filled the child with low self esteem and fear, both stored in that young impressionable body, mind, spirit being. Now 30 years later the boy is a man who is following the seven basic steps to total health and has balanced his physical body, so next up on the list is to turn the energy for healing inward to the mind and emotions both in his past and the generational mental/emotional toxins passed to him. This is why, as he releases the stored mindsets of low self esteem and the negative emotions of fear, he all of a sudden has a craving for pizza.

These negative energies were attached to the memory of pizza. This also can be a generational mental/emotional toxin that was initially caused by his mother becoming extremely fearful while eating pizza for dinner one night while hearing the news that the stock market just crashed and all their investments were gone. Fear attached to the food. As the emotion of fear detoxes and leaves the system sometimes the image of the food, or anything else can arise that was attached to the negative energy (the emotion or stored lie) when it first happened, hence craving pizza.

The Anatomy of Dis-ease
- At age 1 a boy develops a decreased appetite.
- At age 6 he develops stomach pains.
- At age 12 he develops headaches.
- At age 17 he develops allergies.
- At age 28 he develops regular constipation/bloating.
- At age 36 he develops chronic fatigue.
- At age 44 he develops anxiety and depression.
- At age 53 he is diagnosed with cancer.

Why do we address healing from the body first then the emotions and then the mind?

- It takes energy to heal, and the least amount needed is for the physical body.
- Once you have balanced the physical body through the 7 basic steps, then more energy is available to be used to heal the stored emotional toxins (blockages). As these release, once again more energy is available to heal the most energy-demanding part of your being: your negative stored mental patterns that you developed in your lifetime and those that were passed to you generationally. As these are released we become open to the love of God, to the awesomeness of His creation, and we seek to know Him intimately.
- Once we come to know Him intimately His Spirit fills us and flows to every part of our being: mind, will, emotion and body.
    - **Mind** - our conscious mind becomes renewed with Truth, our unconscious mind releases all old stored negative mind patterns (the old you is going, going, gone), we begin to operate in the supremeconscious mind - the unhindered mind of God that flows from His Spirit living in our heart. The knowing in the heart is flowing directly into our God mind.
    - **Emotion** - all emotions both negative and positive are released from future, past and generational, being replaced with the spiritual states of being: Love, joy, peace and hope.
    - **Will** - your will is no longer self-centered, ego, flesh driven. It has become an extension of the love, joy and peace that fill your heart. Your will and God's will have become one.
    - **Body** - All blockages have been removed so the flow of energy and life is restored to every cell, tissue, gland, organ and system. Health and vitality are regained.

Health Flow Switch

There is a built in switch, which is a function of your spirit, which keeps your body, mind and emotions in health. This switch monitors the flow of life in the body and mind. When the flow is decreased to an area the switch is triggered and the spirit sends messages to the mind and body to self-regulate, to self-adjust. This happens automatically, you are usually aware of it by symptoms. This switch is set high in a newborn baby, but as they start down the path of breaking the 7 basic steps to total health, the normal American life, the switch has to be set lower and lower because of the constant abuse from diet, and other physical and mental/emotional stresses and toxins in the environment. This switch wonderfully alerts you of any block of energy flow from outside and on the inside of you.

As a child grows, more and more imbalances occur in the system so to adapt, the switch is set lower and lower until by the time he becomes an adult the switch has been lowered to the lowest level. How do you know how high your health switch is set? The more symptoms you have when you break the 7 steps and are exposed to physical/mental/emotional stresses and toxins the higher the switch is set. **The absence of symptoms in the presence of breaking the 7 steps, and in being exposed to physical/mental/emotional stresses and toxins, the lower the switch is set.**

This switch is simply the ability of your spirit to communicate to your mind and your body. It is a wonderful creation of God because it always lets you know if you are doing anything or being in any environment that would cause a blockage of the flow of life in your body/mind/emotions. Simply stated, it helps you stay on the path to total health, because once you step off that path you experience significant symptoms in your body or mind or emotions. In restoring your health your first desire is to reset the health switch to a high level so you are notified (by symptoms) of anything that would slow or stop your healing. Once operating at a high level the chances of getting sick again are extremely low because your symptoms are so strong you cannot continue breaking the 7 steps or living in physical/mental stresses and toxins in your environment.

Who is healthier?

■ The person who eats at a fast food restaurant and feels great

or

■ The person who takes one bite of fast food and is sick for a day?

■ The person who feels great after eating a big meal at a fast food restaurant has no health. His health flow switch has been set so low it does not even communicate to his body anymore because his body is not listening (in actuality it is his mind that is not listening and his body that has to pay the price of the abuse. This starts a break in the "all are one" relationship between the body, mind and spirit - the body/mind/spirit covenant). Because he has no symptoms when breaking the 7 steps, he also has no symptoms when he exposes his body to physical toxins, chemicals, and mental/emotional toxins. This person will feel great today and drop dead of a heart attack tomorrow. This person will feel great today and be diagnosed with terminal cancer tomorrow.

■ A person who is sick for a day after taking one bite of fast food has a very high level of health (if they are balanced, having taken the 7 basic steps to total health). Their health flow switch is set high so as to alert them of anything that would block the flow of life to any gland, organ, tissue, or body part. Eating this food sets off an alarm to the body/mind health flow (an insult to the body/mind/spirit covenant) and in response the body is notified that this has happened, thus eliciting symptoms significant enough not to be ignored. This helps in teaching the mind the proper choices to stay on the path of total health.

A Lesson from Nature

■ Feed something that we would serve at a fast food restaurant to a wild animal that eats the purest living food, and it can die. This is health. Animals have an instinct to know what to eat. They eat only what their bodies require to stay healthy. Living food. The only animals that deviate from this are domesticated animals, dogs and cats, and they develop all the same diseases that humans do.

> *Your body is the temple of God's Spirit.*
> *Honor God with your body.*

What is your body?

■ Your body is millions of cells and each one of those cells is a little you. They all talk to each other via chemical messages called neuropeptides. Your nervous system talks back and forth with your immune system (which acts like a circulating nervous system). Your stomach can talk to your immune system. Your liver can talk to your pancreas. Your intestines can talk to your heart. Each one of these cells is a little you. *They are all the people in your kingdom - which is you.*

Kingdom, Prophet, King

■ In the kingdom called "you," live all the people called your cells. These people are under the rule of the king. The king receives the Word of God, the Way, the Truth, and the Life for his kingdom from the prophet, who directly hears the voice of God and gives the Word to the king for the people. The king is your mind. Your mind tells the cells what to do. The prophet is your heart. Your heart hears the voice of God and tells your mind the direction, the Way, the Truth, the path to Life and total health.

What kind of a king are you?

■ Are you a loving, wise and strong ruler who wants what is best for his kingdom?

■ Are you a tyrant - a cruel selfish dictator who is only out for himself, a power hungry king?

■ Are you a cold and weak ruler who is looking out only for his own survival, just trying to stay king?

■ Are you a king who does not want to be king? One who does not care what happens to the kingdom? One who wants no responsibility?

The loving, strong, wise king

■ He wants what is best for the individual as well as the group. He knows that all are one. If part of his kingdom is hurting then he is hurting. He is one with God; he is one with himself. He is one with all others and he knows that all are one. He listens intently to the voice of the prophet. He carries out the words of the prophet with great care and commitment. He knows he is accountable to God and to the people.

The cold, cruel, dictator king

■ He has a power or control type of personality. He is insecure so he tries to prove he is somebody. He seeks to control, to dominate. He does not care about the welfare of the kingdom, only that they see him as somebody of power, somebody to be feared. He is self-centered to the highest degree. He is not one with God or one with himself. He wants to be separate from all others and definitely does not see all as one, instead all for him. He pays no attention to the prophet or the words of the prophet.

The weak, insecure king

■ He can't control but is controlled by others who are stronger than he. He is codependent on others. He is just trying to survive, trying to have some security, just trying to stay king. He is trying to prove he is a good king but is too fearful and insecure to look out for the wellbeing of others. He can barely take care of himself. He is not one with God or himself. He is not one with others but needs from them. He does not see all are one because he can only see himself and his own needs. He doesn't listen to the prophet because everyone else in his world in authority speaks much louder than the quiet, soft voice of the prophet.

The "I don't want to be king" king

■ He wants no responsibility for the kingdom and its people. He wants to live his life his own way, doing what he wants when he wants to. He sees his world as just himself and wants to keep it that way. He is not one with God; he wants to be only one with himself. He wants to separate from all others and cannot see all are one because, to him, he is the only one. He will listen to the prophet only if the prophet tells him something useful about himself.

How will the cells of your body respond?

■ If all the cells in your body are little versions of you then how will they respond to you the king?

■ Will they lovingly serve and obey you because they feel the love and strength of the king - your mind - being led by the prophet - your heart? Do they feel that all are truly one?

■ Will they feel abused and rejected so they will rise up in rebellion and start their own colony? This is cancer.

■ Will they get so tired of the abuse and punishment that they strike back at innocent others in the kingdom? This is autoimmune dis-ease and allergies.

■ Will they feel so much rejection and repression from the king that they just give up the will to live? This is a weakened immune system, recurrent bacteria, viral, parasitic, fungal infections along with other forms of cancer.

■ Do they feel betrayed instead of loved, do they feel they have been abandoned for another love-success, power, career, money, flesh? This is heart dis-ease, cardiovascular dis-ease.

■ Has the lack of love has taken their breath of life away? This is lung dis-ease, respiratory dis-ease.

■ Do they feel like they are in slavery working 18 hours a day with no appreciation, no thanks, so they just start to break down and die? This is pancreatic, liver, gall bladder, stomach, intestine, kidney and bladder dis-ease.

■ Do they feel the king (mind) is not being led by the prophet (heart/spirit)? Instead he is making wrong decisions, changing his mind, confused, doubtful, and fearful? This is tremendous stress to the people. This is nervous system and hormonal system dis-ease.

How do you bring your body into an "all are one" state of total health?

■ Change the king's heart - remove all the blockages of the heart (the strongholds of the old unrenewed mind): world, flesh, ego, personality, 5 senses, false belief systems, religion, time and space, so the *Truth in the heart can flow freely into the supremeconscious mind, the mind of God in you.*

■ Listen and obey the prophet (heart/spirit) - learn to listen to the voice of God that speaks love, joy, peace and hope into the heart. This voice will speak the Truth that will show you the Way to the Life of total health in body, mind and spirit. *Faith with action steps leads to life, health and healing.*

■ Change your mind (a renewed and reprogrammed mind filled with Truth instead of the old mind filled with lies), change your perception (how you see things from the Truth-filled heart and supremeconscious mind) and you change your reality, your life and your health.

■ Forgive each other - if all are one then the king must forgive the people and the people the king. The king must ask for forgiveness from his people for any wrongs he has done them and vow a renewed relationship. I'm okay with my stomach and my stomach is okay with me, I'm okay with my breasts and my breasts are okay with me.

■ Restore the "love one another" relationship between you and your body. Enter into a covenant relationship with your body, a marriage of the mind and body (the body/mind/spirit covenant). "I will love you, I will take the best care of you, I will protect you, I will keep you always in my mind. I will help you in every way and I will do anything I can for you. You will also do all this for me. We are partners." The mind and the body have become one. "All are one" becomes reality.

■ Learn to listen to the people of your kingdom- your cells, tissues, glands, organs and body parts. Take time to listen. The higher you set your health switch the more you will hear them talking (the turtle is starting to come out of its shell). What do they usually say? That something is not right; there is a block in the flow of life starting in the body/mind complex. Your body will talk so your mind can make the correction in food, water, sleep, exercise, change environment, reduce a stress, fast, listen to the voice of God spoken into your heart. Sometimes the body will say it's time to go to the next level in your journey - you need to improve your diet even more, need to sleep even more, need to listen to God's voice even more. Initially the body and mind talk when they release stored physical, mental and emotional toxins - these are the symptoms of body/mind/emotion detoxification.

■ After listening to the people of the kingdom (your cells, tissues, glands, organs and body parts), the king (your mind) presents what they (your kingdom- the cells of your body) have told the king (your mind) to the prophet (your heart/spirit) and lets God speak to the heart, which in turn speaks this Truth to the king (your mind) so you best know how to take care of your kingdom (your body). When the mind listens to the heart he becomes wise and takes the Right action steps to keep harmony and balance in the kingdom (the body).

■ Take only the actions steps spoken from God into the heart (prophet) and then into the mind (king). Do not listen to the mind (king) by itself. The mind must have received the Way, the path, the Truth to restore Life from the heart/spirit. This is the supremeconscious mind, the mind of God, being filled from the Spirit of God spoken into the heart/spirit of the man.

- Learn how to make your kingdom (your body) work most efficiently with the least amount of effort. This is done when you follow the 7 basic steps to total health.
- Let the people of your kingdom (cells, tissues, glands, organs and body parts) know you need each and every one of them. The eye needs the foot, the liver needs the pancreas, and the colon needs the thyroid.
- Be a loving, strong and wise king over your kingdom. Always do what is best for the whole and not the individual. Remember to always listen to the prophet (heart/spirit), this is where the Truth, the Way to Life and health is found.

How to restore the body-mind break (break in the body/mind/spirit covenant).

- Let your body know you have changed. You are being led by your heart (a part of your whole being) instead of by your old mind that is filled with the world, ego, flesh, 5 senses, religion, time, and physicality. You are going to fill your supremeconscious mind from your Truth-filled heart, which then will fill your conscious (thinking) mind. You are going to renew your conscious (thinking) mind to the Truth, the Way to Life and health that the spirit/heart has revealed.
- Renewing or reprogramming your mind with Truth. Thinking about what (is in your Truth-filled heart, not what is in your old lie-filled mind) is true, lovely, right, pure, of good report, excellent or praiseworthy. As he thinks in his heart (not his mind) so is he, (NKJV) but it must be the Right Word at the Right time to bring victory, freedom, healing and total health of body, mind and spirit. The Right Word at the wrong time is like having the key to the door but you came at the wrong time and you have no access to the door to use the key. The Right Word at the Right time is the one God fills your heart with at that moment, not the one that you have stored in your conscious mind.
- Let go and forgive your body and ask forgiveness from your body.
- Prove yourself to your body by a consistent change in character. Actions speak louder than words.
- The turtle (your body) will come out of its shell when it knows you have truly changed.
- Time will tell. As tests arise, when stress comes, when you are offered your old lifestyle, when you face your old food, when you are confronted with your old habits. If you say "NO!" you pass the tests and your body sees this and knows you really have changed.

■ Your body knows you are not perfect but can see that you are committed to total health, to "all are one," to the body/mind/spirit covenant of life.

Healing is a contract, a covenant between your spirit, your mind and your body. This is why if you eat something wrong you will have significant symptoms. It is not the food, but the break in the covenant (partnership) that causes the body, mind and spirit to produce the symptoms.

At the highest level of health (unblocked flow of life at all levels) God speaks to the heart/spirit with love, joy, peace and hope.
He speaks to the mind through the supremeconsciousness and He speaks to the body through symptoms.
God is now being felt in your heart/spirit, your mind and your body.

What messages are you the king giving the people of your kingdom?

■ "I have cancer and I am going to die in 6 months"
(your cells obey you the king).
■ "We have a health challenge that we are going to overcome together"-"all are one," all are for each other, all are in covenant with each other.

When you take drugs or hormones what message are you giving your body?

You are not doing your job very well so I am going to bring in something else to take over your job. This gives the gland or organ the message to just shut down, wither and die.

What messages are you the king giving the people of your kingdom?

- I don't like my skin.
- I don't like my breasts.
- I don't like my body.
- I have a bad heart.
- I have a bad stomach.
- I have a bad leg.
- You are a pain in my neck.
- I wish I would die.
- You are killing me.
- This is too much for me to handle.
- The me is you - your conscious mind (thinking, calculating mind)
- The we is: God's Spirit, your spirit/heart, your supremeconscious mind (the mind of God in you) and every cell in your body working together for the overcoming of all things, for the victory and freedom, for total health of body, mind and spirit.

How does your body talk?

Symptoms, conditions and dis-ease
Symptoms mean:

- Getting worse

  or
- Getting better

It depends on what you are doing, the 7 basic steps or the standard American diet (SAD) and lifestyle.

Referral Symptoms

When there is an imbalance in this organ or gland, the symptom or place it can be felt in the body is the referral area.

- Heart - left shoulder and/or shoulder blade, chest, left arm, left jaw
- Pancreas-left shoulder and/or shoulder blade, center of back, left side abdomen
- Liver - right shoulder and/or shoulder blade, right abdomen
- Stomach-center of the back, between shoulder blades
- Lungs - midback, upper back, chest
- Intestines - periumbilical area (around navel), lateral thigh, low back
- Kidney - flank, inguinal (groin), low back
- Ovaries, uterus, prostate, testicle - lower back, lower abdomen, inner thigh

90% of all back pain is visceral in origin (meaning it originates from an organ/gland imbalance/dysfunction).

MORE - Referral symptoms are wonderful ways you can listen to your body speak. The pain, discomfort, and tightness in these areas are the associated organs and glands talking to you saying "help me!" So many people ignore these symptoms of back pain, discomfort, and tightness, setting the stage for full-blown dis-ease. Don't pop a pill—instead learn to listen to your body talking. Is your left shoulder and shoulder blade pain digestive overload from eating too many sugars and starches that the pancreas cannot handle? Is your right shoulder and shoulder blade pain just your body saying that you are eating, drinking and breathing too many toxins that are overloading your liver? Is stiffness and tightness between your shoulder blades and in your mid back just your stomach saying, "I can't handle this toxic, dead, deficient food that you are dumping in me!"

How closely connected are body, mind and spirit? In a balanced person, living in total health, the three become one, each helping the others to remove blockages to the flow of life.

MORE - the following chart will help you to understand how the body, mind, emotions, and spirit are one. When one part is out of balance they all start to go out of balance, and exhibit symptoms. An example would be that if you throw your heart out of balance with the SAD (standard American diet), then the cholesterol not only has a physical effect on the body but also spirit, mind, and emotion effects as well. Those who physically imbalance their heart are more prone to emotional imbalances of hate, hopelessness, and the emotional roller coaster of happy one moment then sad the next. They are also prone to the mental imbalances of depression, and looking for love from the world, and from people instead of from God. Spiritually they are not feeling God's love, joy and peace and they also have difficulty knowing God's voice and patiently waiting in the moment. The reverse also applies. If you see your situation in life as hopeless, if you willfully open the door to hate, if you allow your thought patterns to dip into depression, then these mental, emotional imbalances cause the physical heart to go out of balance, to become dysfunctional and open the door to dis-ease. Also the willfully allowed mind (believing the lie) and emotional (the negative energy the lie has produced) imbalances block the flow of the Spirit and block the ability to receive the love, joy and peace of God, and block the hearing and knowing of His voice.

Body/Emotion/Mind/ Spirit

Body	Spirit	Mind-Body	Mind	Emotion
Heart	Knowing Love Joy Peace Patience Block leads to lack of knowing, lack of love	Looking for love from the world, from people instead of from God Broken heart Animal fat/ cholesterol, sugar, artificial man made food lack of exercise	Awareness Centered Self love Love of others Respect Depression Protection	Happy/Sad Hopelessness Hate
Body	**Spirit**	**Mind-Body**	**Mind**	**Emotion**
Lungs	Flow of life Breath of life Receiving from God to give to others Block leads to lack of receiving /giving	Suffocating from the stresses of life Smoking Breathing toxins, fumes	Vitality Release Holding on Reactive Respon- sive	Grief Grieving

Body	Spirit	Mind-Body	Mind	Emotion
Colon	Letting go Forgiveness	Eating a high cooked animal fat/protein diet High processed sugar or starches Lack of fiber	Self poisoning Release Control Compulsive-ness	Unforgive-ness Blame Guilt

Body	Spirit	Mind-Body	Mind	Emotion
Stomach	Peace Truth	World mind Emotional stress manifesting Eating rushed Eating a high cooked animal fat/ protein diet High processed sugar or starches Lack of fiber	Intolerance Rejection Change Thinking	Low self esteem Overly sympath-etic Emotional

Body	Spirit	Mind-Body	Mind	Emotion
Liver	Grace Kindness	Future mind World mind Ego (self centered) mind Religion mind Eating a high cooked animal fat/ protein diet toxins, chemical Caffeine High processed sugar / starches	Planning Organizing Processing Storage	Anger Resent-ment Fear

Body	Spirit	Mind-Body	Mind	Emotion
Gall Bladder	Grace Kindness	World mind Ego (self centered) mind Religion mind Eating a high cooked animal fat/ protein diet toxins, chemical Caffeine High processed sugar / starches	Decisions Motivation Release Mobility Flexibility	Anger Resent-ment Fear

Body	Spirit	Mind-Body	Mind	Emotion
Small intestine	Power	World mind Ego (self centered) mind Flesh minded Eating a high cooked animal fat/ protein diet Fiber High processed sugar / starches	Intellect Separation Self poisoning Nourish-ment	Vulner-able Lost

Body	Spirit	Mind-Body	Mind	Emotion
Kidneys	Faith Power	Future mind 5 senses mind Ego (self centered) mind Flesh minded Cooked animal protein diet Toxins Heavy metals Lack of water High processed sugar / starches	Will power Overwhelm Paranoia Sensuality	Fear Fear of coping

Body	Spirit	Mind-Body	Mind	Emotion
Bladder	Faith Power Letting go Forgiving	Future mind 5 senses mind Ego (self centered) mind Flesh minded Eating a high cooked animal protein diet Lack of water High processed sugar / starches	Will power Release Control Sexuality	Fear Resentment

Body	Spirit	Mind-Body	Mind	Emotion
Spleen	Peace Grace Letting go Forgiving	Future mind 5 senses mind Ego (self centered) mind Flesh minded Eating a high cooked animal protein diet Lack of water High processed sugar / starches	Cleansing Purifying Unconscious thinking	Worry Low self esteem

Body	Spirit	Mind-Body	Mind	Emotion
Thyroid	God's will Grace	World mind Ego (self centered) mind Lack of sleep Eating a high cooked animal fat/ protein diet Caffeine High processed sugar /starches	Commun-ication Strong willed Activity Choked by life Suffocating Cloudy thinking Paranoia	Emotional instability

Body	Spirit	Mind-Body	Mind	Emotion
Pancreas	Peace Grace	Future mind Ego (self centered) mind High processed sugar/starches Eating a high cooked animal fat/ protein diet Caffeine	Adaptability	Worry Low self esteem Anxiety

Body	Spirit	Mind-Body	Mind	Emotion
Thymus	Love Joy Peace Hope	World Mind Ego (self centered) mind High processed sugar/starches Lack of sleep Eating a high cooked animal fat/protein diet	Self acceptance Defensive Heart protective	Low self esteem

Body	Spirit	Mind-Body	Mind	Emotion
Adrenal	Faith Foundation in the Truth	Future Mind World Mind Ego (self centered) mind High processed sugar/starches Lack of sleep Caffeine Eating a high cooked animal fat/protein diet	Drive Motivation Will power Strength Obsession Paranoia Exhaustion Survival	Emotional instability Fear

Body	Spirit	Mind-Body	Mind	Emotion
Ovaries Testes	Receiving from God to give to others	5 Sense Mind World Mind Ego (self) mind Eating a high cooked animal fat, protein diet High processed sugar/starches Lack of sleep	Reproduction Sensuality Sexuality Self preservation Life acceptance Release-O Drive-T Strength-T	Loneliness

_____
_____
_____
_____
_____
_____
_____
_____
_____
_____

Heart connection to the 7 basics

Air	Water	Food	Sleep	Exercise	Fasting	Prayer
Lack of proper breathing decreases oxygen to the heart and all other cells of the body	Low water intake causes the blood to become sludge, heart works to hard Decrease oxygen and increase toxins	cooked animal fat, protein choles-terol	Heart over-worked no time to rest and heal	Decreased blood flow, decreased oxygen increased toxins	Physical Mental Spiritual	Cannot hear the Truth spoken into your heart to know the Way

This is how breaking the 7 basic steps to total health negatively affects the organs/glands and total health of body mind and spirit.

Enter into a marriage agreement today, a covenant between your body, your mind, and your spirit.
All are you.
All are one.

_____
_____
_____
_____
_____
_____
_____
_____
_____
_____

Go Deeper

1. Why are stored negative mind patterns and stored negative emotions more detrimental to your total health than physical chemicals, toxins and imbalances?
2. Why can cancer or any other disease never be healed using the methods of modern medicine and science?
3. Can one be in total health if one is reactive instead of being proactive?
4. Why is cause and effect so critical in restoring and maintaining total health?
5. What is the difference between being cured and being healed?
6. Do you fully understand the "pressure in the bag" analogy of health and disease?
7. Where does the river of life begin from and chart its course in bringing total health to wherever it flows?
8. Why is it easier to lead an average person to total health of body, mind and spirit from the 7 basic physical steps first rather than from a spiritual awakening?
9. How do you know if the increased symptoms you are having are the condition getting worse, retracing, or your health switch talking to you?
10. What kind of king or queen are you (are you operating in the supremeconscious, the conscious or unconscious mind) as you rule over your kingdom (the cells of your body)? Do you listen to and obey the voice of the prophet (the Truth-filled heart) each moment?
11. Do you understand how referral symptoms are just another way your body talks to your mind to get it to make changes before dis-ease appears, and by ignoring or covering up symptoms you are breaking the body/mind/spirit covenant?
12. Do you understand how anger, resentment or fear can throw your liver out of balance? Also by being self-centered, always thinking about the future and being filled up with the world system - this too can throw the liver out of balance and lead to dis-ease.
13. Do you understand how low self-esteem, anxiety, and sugar in the diet not only throws the pancreas out of balance but also blocks the flow of peace into your heart?
14. Why do you think the power and gifts of God can flow freer in a person who lives the 7 basic steps to total health and is balanced, than in a person who leads an average American lifestyle?

_____

_____

_____

_____

Air/Oxygen/Breathing

**The 1st Basic of Total Health is
Air/Oxygen/Breathing**
Who heals you?
**God heals you and you heal you!
Do you want to see God heal you?**

**Cut your finger and watch the miracle of God as healing energy flows through your body to heal your finger.
If God's healing life energy flows to your finger to heal it, why doesn't it flow to your malignant tumor, to your diseased heart, lung, liver, pancreas, colon, thyroid etc.?
The answer is** *blockage.*
The flow of life is flowing to the finger, but is blocked from flowing to the tumor, the organ, the gland, the tissue, or the body part.

Flow of Life, River of Life/Health
- If the flow of life/health and healing is a river then any blocks in the river will cause two conditions: one of excess, one of deficiency.
- The river of life of the immune system. If one puts blocks in the river two conditions occur:
  - Flood: this is the overactive immune system that manifests with autoimmune dis-ease (multiple sclerosis, rheumatoid arthritis, colitis, diabetes, thyroiditis, adrenalitis, liver disease, kidney disease) and allergies, sensitivities.
  - Drought: this is the under active immune system which manifests as recurrent bacterial, viral, parasitic, fungal infections and cancer.

_____
_____
_____
_____
_____

What are the blocks in the river?

Stresses: Physical, mental, emotional, spiritual.

Physical: Decreased oxygen, decreased water, wrong food choices (animal, cooked, processed, preserved), decreased sleep, decreased exercise, temperature, overdoing, structural. A one fold decrease (-1X) in your total health.

Mental: Lie vs. Truth, knowledge vs. knowing, wrong perception of God, self, others, the world. A tenfold decrease (-10X) in your total health.

Emotional: All emotions whether positive or negative instead of spiritual states of being - love, joy, peace and hope. A tenfold decrease (-10X) in your total health.

Spiritual: not knowing God, not knowing yourself, not knowing your purpose/mission. A one hundredfold decrease (-100X) in your total health.

How do you remove the blocks in the river?

- 7 basic steps to total health done daily.
- SEMB.
- Learn how to not only remove the blocks but also keep them removed. This is a forever changed lifestyle; this is a total health in body, mind and spirit lifestyle.

Energy - The Flow of Life, Health

- Your body has so much energy that it uses to sustain and maintain your health in the present.
- If you do not daily practice the 7 steps to total health then the body begins to become depleted of its energy to maintain health. This eventually will result in symptoms, conditions and dis-ease.
- If you master the 7 steps, then the body can redirect the energy it has been using in the present (just keep you alive), to where the blockages in energy flow began - your past and the negative information that was passed to you generationally. When this occurs, deep inner healing begins and the body/mind retraces back to the origin of the blockage/imbalances.

Body, Mind, Emotions and Spirit as One

- Once you balance the physical body, the energy for healing is directed deeper to the stored emotional toxins (blockages). As they release, the negative mind patterns (that produced the emotional toxins) start to release from the unconscious mind (stored memory). We then willfully choose to change our conscious perceptions (I can heal, I will not die, I have not fulfilled my call), renewing our conscious thinking mind. Once the stored negative mind patterns are released (both consciously and unconsciously), the stored negative emotional toxins have been released, and the body is balanced with the 7 steps, then the spirit can flow unhindered to heal and maintain health of the whole being.

Air - Oxygen

- The most important component of air that every cell in our body needs to maintain life is oxygen.
- Oxygen is the most crucial nutrient our body needs to maintain health.
- Up to 96% of our nutritional need comes from oxygen; the other 4% comes from food.
- 30 day+ without food, 3 days without water, only 3 minutes without oxygen and you die.

Oxygen Facts

- You need about 1 cup of oxygen per minute while resting and 2 gallons per minute while exercising vigorously.
- Your brain which makes up 2% of the body mass requires over 20% of the body's oxygen needs.
- Oxygen makes up 21% of the air we breathe. Polluted indoor and outdoor environments consist of less, even as low as 7%.
- You breathe in about 2800 gallons of air each day.
- The average man consumes 8 lbs. of oxygen, 4 lbs. of food and 2 lbs. of water per day.

Why is oxygen so important?

- The food we eat, starches, complex carbohydrates, and fats are turned into simple sugars and then combined with oxygen, and a form of combustion (fire) produces byproducts of energy, carbon dioxide and water. This energy is stored in a compound called adenosine triphosphate or ATP. ATP is our fuel to live, to think, to breathe and to move.

> *"ATP is the basic currency of life. Without it, we are literally dead. Imbalance or interruption in the production and flow of this substance results in fatigue, disease, and disorder, including immune imbalance, cancer, heart disease and all of the degenerative processes we associate with aging".*
> **Sheldon Saul Hendler, M.D.,**
> **from his book *The Oxygen Breakthrough***

Oxygen destroys pathogens
(bacteria, virus, parasites, fungus and cancer)

- Most pathogens are anaerobic which mean they grow best in low oxygen environments.
- Nobel prize winner for physiology and medicine, Dr. Otto Warburg demonstrated that the key ingredient for the formation of cancer is a decrease of oxygen at the cellular level.[1]
- Dr. Warburg showed that when oxygen supply is decreased as little as 30%, our excess protein-filled cells (from our high protein diets) could become malignant cancer cells.
- Dr. Warburg also stated that, with a steady supply of oxygen to all the cells, cancer could be prevented indefinitely.

Oxygen

- As the amount of sugar/protein/fat increases in the body the amount of oxygen decreases inversely.
- As oxygen increases endorphins increase (natural pain killer, and mood balancer), neuropeptides (cell to cell communicators) increase, insulin levels increase, blood pH balances, hypertension decreases, toxins are removed quicker, lymphatic drainage increases, blood flow increases, immune system balances, energy improves, metabolism balances, anxiety lifts, mind/emotion balances, memory improves and brain chemistry balances.[2]

The Physical Environment for Healing (See Appendix)

How do we become oxygen deficient?[3]

- Polluted air.
- Eating dead/cooked, devitalized, processed, or preserved food.
- Poor breathing technique.

Polluted Air

- Biggest sources are smoke filled air, automobile exhaust, factory emissions, and garbage burning.
- Indoor air pollution is 10 times worse than outdoor air pollution.
- Oxygen level in normal fresh air is 21%. Some major air-polluted cities are only 10%. Some smoke filled rooms drop to as low as 7%. Oxygen content of air bubbles trapped in amber and core samples of ice from Polar Regions show twice the oxygen level of our air today, close to 40 %.[4]

Dead/Cooked, Devitalized Food

■ The lowest oxygen content is found in cooked, processed, preserved foods. This is 80-90% of the average American diet. Meat, chicken, fish, dairy and eggs are very low in oxygen. Microwaved foods and refined sugars are at the bottom of the oxygen content list.

Poor Breathing Technique

■ This is the greatest source of oxygen deficiency.

■ On average we use less than 20% of our lung capacity because of our restricted breathing patterns.

■ Most people are chest breathers never fully using the diaphragm to fully inhale and fully oxygenate the body.

Oxygen examples

■ The average person **A** living in a major city is breathing only 20% of the 10% oxygen in the air - this is 2% oxygen daily.

■ The average person **B** who smokes inside is breathing 20% of the 7% oxygen in the air - this is less than 1.5% oxygen daily.

■ One should be breathing 80% of the 21% oxygen in the air - this is 17% oxygen daily. This is 850% more oxygen than person **A** and 1100% more oxygen than person **B**.

How Can You Increase Your Oxygen Content?

■ Decrease air pollution.

■ Increase living/raw green foods.

■ Improve breathing technique.

■ Open the windows of your house 30 minutes each day even in the winter to get more oxygen in the house and remove the pollutants: fumes, out gasing, chemicals and toxins.

■ Get outside each day and breathe the air. The more the better.

■ Purchase an ozonator/ionizer for your house to increase the oxygen content in the air and to remove the chemical and toxins in the air.

Increase the Living/Raw Green Foods

■ Highest oxygen content is found in living green food: sprouts, especially wheatgrass, sunflower, and buckwheat.

■ Next comes algaes: chlorella, spirulina.

■ Next come raw green vegetables such as kale, collards, spinach, dandelion, broccoli, and other dark green vegetables.

Improve Breathing Technique

■ Regular deep and full diaphragmatic breathing fully oxygenates the blood, and energizes every cell in the body.

Benefits of Deep Breathing

- Single most important way to increase the oxygen content of the body.
- The most important way to generate electrical charge and energy to the body. This is critical to every system, organ, gland and tissues health and maintenance.
- The greatest mover of lymphatic fluid, 10-15 times more than any other, even intense exercise. Lymphatic fluid is the foundation of the immune system, 2/3 of your white blood cells are in the lymphatic system. The lymphatic system is also the major sewer system to rid the body of waste products produced from the cellular metabolism.
- Detoxifies/eliminate waste products from the body. 70% leave through breathing, 20% through skin, 7% through urine and 3% through the bowel.
- The primary conductor of the life energy in our bodies is the cerebrospinal fluid (CSF). Deep breathing ionizes this fluid. Deep breathing is the most important factor in maintaining the flow of the cerebrospinal fluid. The CSF is one of the highest energetically-charged elements in the body. The CSF bathes the brain and spinal cord and feeds it the glucose it needs to function, and removes wastes.
- Maintains movement of all internal organs and glands. Without this movement the organs and glands would become dysfunctional and eventually dis-eased.

Baby's First Breath

- Baby grows in a compacted state.
- Baby's first breath expands the cranial bones along with all the bones of the body. The first breath in essence decompacts the baby's body and brings motion = life.[5]
- If the breath or cry is not strong the cranial bones don't full expand. This causes a decrease in the pumping of the cerebrospinal fluid (CSF), one of the most energetically charged substances in the body, which not only oxygenates and feeds the brain and spinal cord, but most critically generates and sends the bioelectrical energy throughout the body to every cell via the nervous system.

Benefits of Deep Breathing

- Energizes every cell in the body both electrically and biochemically.
- Every cell, tissue, organ, gland is electrical in nature. This electrical energy or charge is greatest in the fascia around the heart

(pericardium) and the fascia around the brain and spinal cord (meninges). The fascia surrounds every organ, gland and tissue and maintains their health by keeping this energy flowing. A block in this energy will cause dysfunction and dis-ease of the area. Deep breathing generates this electrical energy.

Fascia

■ The fascia is a thin "wrap" like tissue that covers every organ, gland, nerve, muscle, tissue and system in the body. The fascia and bones have electrical properties that allow them to conduct electrical current.

■ The fascia carries these electrical charges from the heart and nervous system to every part of the body.

Heart

■ The heart is much more than a pump to circulate blood; it is a generator of electrical energy.

■ The fascia around the heart is called the pericardium. It is the main storage bank of electrical energy in the body.

■ Both the heart and the brain (CSF) produce the electrical energy that maintains the health and life of every cell of every organ, gland and tissue in your body.

Driving Down the Fascial Highway

■ The flow of life, of health, of healing is by nature energetic/electric.

■ The primary generators of this energy/electricity are breathing (lungs, diaphragm), the heart and the brain (CSF).

■ The path that this energy flows is from the 7 energetic generator/storage areas to the organs, gland, tissues and systems of the body via the fascia or fascial highway.

Blockage on the Fascial Highway

■ The energy of life is flowing along the fascia like cars traveling at high speed down a highway. The speed of the cars is likened to the frequency of the energy traveling along the fascia. The frequency = 700 mph is the speed the cars are driving when one is at a very high state of total health, total balance of body, mind and spirit. Now let us introduce a few low frequency energies along the fascia (dead, toxic food, negative emotions - fear, negative mindsets). These low frequencies are like cars driving between 30 to 60 mph on a 700 mph highway. The result? Traffic back up - BLOCKAGES in the flow.

Stress, Trauma and the Energy Block

■ Any stress whether it is physical (-1X), emotional (-10X), mental (-10X) or spiritual (-100X) is an energetically charged event. This can block the flow of energy, the flow of life along the fascial highway. According to Wolff and Davis's law our bones and tissues grow and regenerate according to the demands (stresses) placed upon them. According to these laws, **stresses and traumas are recorded events in the tissues of the body**.

■ **MORE** -stresses both physical and mental/emotional, are energetically charged events that actually do store in the body. They store in the organs, glands, tissues - muscles, ligaments, joints, bones, nerves, blood vessels, skin and body parts. They do not release until the body is balanced enough (following the 7 basics) to direct enough energy inward to cause them to release.

Benefits of Deep Breathing

■ **Releases stored emotional toxins** (negative energy that have locked into the fascia of organs, glands or tissues causing an energy block). In order to remove the blockage, quantum physics shows us we need to raise the energy of the blockage higher so it can essentially flow again. This is called **entrainment**. When a high frequency energy pattern maintains close contact with a low frequency for a period of time the lower frequency will be caused to permanently increase its rate of vibration to match or very closely resemble the higher frequency.

■ **Helps clear unconscious mind patterns**[6]. As the emotional toxins (negative charged stored energies that block the flow of life energy) are released they are connected to the unconscious mind patterns that are stored. When the emotional toxin clears, the body/mind/spirit covenant directs the life energy, the healing energy, to the source of the emotional toxin—the stored unconscious negative mind pattern. In essence if both are connected then when one burns up (releases), the energy increases to set the other on fire and burn the other one up (releases) also.

Entrainment[7]

■ Pendulum clocks when put together will within a short time swing in unison.

■ Mother nursing her baby. Their heartbeats will beat in a synchronous pattern.

■ Women living together in time will have their menstrual cycles at the same time.

Positive Entrainment

■ Breaking the 7 basic steps to total health, and negative mind/emotions all cause negative energy that lock into the fascia of organs, glands or tissues causing an energy block. In order to remove the blockage, quantum physics shows us we need to raise the energy of the blockage higher so it can essentially flow again. This is called positive entrainment. When a high frequency energy pattern maintains close contact with a low frequency for a period of time the lower frequency will be caused to permanently increase its rate of vibration to match or very closely resemble the higher frequency.

Negative Entrainment

■ Breaking the 7 basic steps to total health, and negative mind/emotions all cause low frequency negative energy patterns that lock into the fascia of the organs, glands or tissues causing an energy block. When a low frequency energy pattern maintains close contact with a medium frequency for a period of time the medium frequency will be caused to permanently decrease its rate of vibration to match or very closely resemble the low frequency.

People Entrainment

■ When an average person is around people who are negative in mind, emotions and body they start to negatively entrain and they themselves start to become negative in mind, emotions and body. Negative produces more negative.

■ When an average person is around people who are positive in mind, emotions and body they start to positively entrain and they themselves start to become more positive in mind emotions and body.

■ When a dis-eased person is around anyone but positive people in spirit, mind and body they negatively entrain.

Cell Entrainment

■ The cells of every organ, gland and tissue are like average people, they will entrain positively if you are positive in spirit, mind and body. They will also entrain negatively if you are negative in spirit, mind and body.

■ The cells of your body will also entrain positively or negatively depending on the people you surround yourself with.

■ The cells of your body will also entrain positively or negatively depending how much of the world system you either separate from or stay connected to. (It's okay to be in the world system as long as the world system is not in you - is not negatively entraining you).

The doctor says you have cancer and have 3 months to live. If you believe him you have opened the door of your house (heart/spirit) to the lie and every cell of your body negatively entrains.

The doctor says the same thing but this time you do not believe him, you do not open the door of your house (heart/spirit) to him, instead you know the Truth in your heart that says "all things are possible" and that God heals you and you heal you. You take the action steps in faith as He leads you in your heart and you give all that you have into the journey and He meets you with all that He has. This is the place of healing; this is the place of miracles. This is the place of *total health*.

Energy and Frequency

- The denser (heavier) the object, thought, emotion, the lower the frequency. The lighter the object, thought or emotion the higher the frequency. Gases are higher frequency than liquid or solids. The highest frequencies belong to the spiritual realm, next the mind and emotion realm and last the physical realm. The human breath has the highest frequency possible because it is not only a gas, but spirit as well.
- Everything is always moving, because all matter, whether gas, liquid or solid, is made up of atomic and subatomic particles that vibrate in space. Over 99.9% of matter is empty space, just these particles vibrating in space. The rate of vibration is called frequency. Everything in our world is composed of frequency. Sounds, colors, thoughts, actions, things. These are all made of the same energy, protons, neutrons and electrons. The only difference is their frequency

Entrainment Frequencies

Highest frequencies to positively entrain to higher states of health and healing are:

- Spirit states of being – love, joy, peace, and hope.
- The breath of God = the breath of man = spirit.
- Supremeconscious mind – this flows from an unblocked heart/spirit. It is the mind of God in man.
- Living water, living food especially when connected to the spiritual state of praise, and thanksgiving.
- Exercise when it is combined with praise, thanksgiving and prayer.

Lowest frequencies to negatively entrain to lower states of health and dis-ease are:

- Negative Mind Patterns – based in lies instead of Truth, the world system (knowledge vs. knowing), ego (self), flesh (negative mind/emotion/body energy), religion, time, and space bound old mind.
- Negative Emotions – fear, anxiety, worry, frustration, self-criticism, boredom, resentment, bitterness, loneliness, hopelessness, guilt, grief, anger, and hate.
- Lack of breathing.
- Toxic water; dead, deficient, toxic, preserved or processed food.
- Lack of sleep.
- Lack of exercise.

Who Opens the Door to Negative Entrainment?

You do!

If someone does not bring the truth (but instead the lie from the old mind), do not invite, accept or admit him into your house (body) or encourage him in any way. Anyone who **encourages** him becomes a partner (covenanted) in his lie. (NLT/AMP)

Encourage means to feed the feeling or thought: to assist something to occur or increase.

You have the free will to open the door or close it to the lies, the world, the negative mindsets and negative emotions around you, to your flesh, to your ego, to past or future thinking. *The choice is up to you.*

Retracing and the Fascial Highway

- These stresses and traumas are recorded events in the tissues of the body. They are not only traffic backups, blockages. *They damage the road itself.* If these blockages are not removed then the ever growing, ever renewing body lays new roads down over the old ones. These are the new fascial highways. The problem is that the new roads are built right on top of collapsed, damaged roads that have not been repaired. This is like building on sinking sand instead of solid ground; the result is a very weak road that cannot support any stress or trauma. One that can be driven on slowly but cannot tolerate any stress or it starts to break apart and again block traffic flow, energy flow.
- Retracing is the act of peeling away all the layers of highway over the years until you get to the original damage, the original trauma, or the original stress. Once you get there symptoms might start again temporarily until you positively entrain the original blockage. Once you have done this, then the symptoms, conditions and dis-eases are

gone and can never come back because you have removed the blockage at its source. The only way it could come back is if you open the door to negative spirit, mind, emotion and body frequencies/energies all over again. This is very unlikely after you have fulfilled the prerequisites to retrace.

Retracing Prerequisites

■ You must balance the physical body with the daily actions steps of the 7 basics steps to total health - air, water, food, sleep, exercise, fasting and prayer (listening and breathing).

■ Next you must let your heart rule over your head, go with knowing rather than knowledge, Truth rather than lies. You must renew and reprogram your conscious mind with the Truth.

■ Next you must use your free will to choose the path to life and health (narrow road) instead of the path to blockages, imbalances, dis-ease and death (wide road).

■ You must choose to let go of your past and your future and live with God, the "I AM" in the present moment.

■ You must follow the path your heart tells you at 100% of your ability, you must give all of yourself to the journey. This is when God gives all of Himself to you, His covenant partner. This is the place of miracles. This is the place of God.

How to Turn Lower Frequencies into Higher Frequencies

■ Whenever we take a physical act and connect it to a spiritual act we raise its frequency to that of the spirit (highest level of positive entrainment is spiritual).

■ The breath of God = the breath of man = spirit. Let everything that has breath praise the LORD. (NIV)

■ Supremeconscious mind – this flows from a Truth-filled, unblocked heart/spirit. It is the mind of God in man.

■ Living water, living food, especially when connected to the spiritual state of praise, and thanksgiving.

■ Exercise when it is combined with praise, thanksgiving and prayer.

What is breathing?

■ It is the only visceral (organ/gland) function of the body that can be controlled both consciously and unconsciously that can be voluntary or involuntary. This is in contrast to the heart beating, the nerve transmissions flowing, digestion, and assimilation. Because of its dual nature, breathing has the ability to connect body/emotions/ mind and spirit.

What is breath?

- Latin word for breath is *spiritus*
- The LORD God formed the man from the dust of the ground and breathed into his nostrils the **breath** of life, and the man became a living being. (NIV)
- But there is a spirit in man: and the *inspiration* of the Almighty giveth them understanding. (KJV) – knowing the Truth in the heart and the supremeconscious mind flowing into you through the Spirit of God - the *inspiration.*
- Our breath, our respiration is how we receive our life energy, our breath of life.

Types of Breathing

- Physical life sustaining
- Physical blockage clearing
- Emotional clearing
- Mental pattern clearing
    - *Conscious mind clearing*
    - *Unconscious mind clearing*
- Spirit refilling
- Spirit of God - receiving to give, infilling to outpour.

Four Phases of Breathing[8]

- Lower abdomen filling
- Solar plexus filling
- Middle chest filling
- Upper chest filling

Each breath filling area corresponds to a body, mind, emotion, and spirit covenant connection.

MORE - As was previously shown, organs and glands have mind, emotion and spirit correlations; so also does each part of a full breath have physical, mental, emotional and spiritual correlations. This is because as the breath is taken in, it energizes different organs, glands, and mind and emotion patterns as it rises higher and higher. If you fail to take a full breath, you fail to energize these organ, gland, mind, emotion and spirit centers. Also the reverse holds true. If you throw the corresponding organ, gland, emotion, mind pattern out of balance and/or block the spirit, it causes you to be unable to fully inhale, causing a never- ending cycle of decreasing total health of body, mind, emotions and spirit. You can see this cycle in effect when you are fearful or mentally stressed, you say that you have shortness of breath or cannot get enough oxygen. It is also seen when you eat toxic, dead, deficient food, which throws the entire digestive tract out of balance, which in turn throws the breathing mechanism out of balance; the result is the same, shortness of breath, tightness in the chest, tightness in the throat, and feeling like you are not able to take a deep breath and get enough oxygen.

Lower Abdomen Filling

- **Physical** - large intestine, bladder, sexual organs, lower spine, pelvis, hip.
- **Emotional** - fear, unforgiveness, resentment, inability to let go.
- **Mental** - not "one with another," one-on-one relationships imbalance (codependent, control), needing something from another.
- **Spiritual** - receiving to give, flowing.

Solar Plexus Filling

- **Physical** - stomach, pancreas, liver, gall bladder, small intestine, kidneys, adrenal glands, spleen, middle spine, abdomen.
- **Emotional** - fear, anger, resentment, worry, anxiety.
- **Mental** - not "one with yourself," ego driven (whether great or lowly), power seeking, needing yourself to be something or someone, paranoia, obsession rejection, depression, frustration.
- **Spiritual** - loving yourself, being at peace with yourself, knowing whom you are, knowing what your purpose is.

Middle Chest Filling

- **Physical** - heart, lungs, bronchial tubes, thymus, breasts, ribs, diaphragm, shoulders, arms.
- **Emotional** - grieving, not releasing, holding on instead of letting go, hate, lack of love.
- **Mental** - not "one with God" (wrong perception of God), do not feel loved, depression.
- **Spiritual** - knowing God, being one with God, receiving from Him, being filled with Him.

Upper Chest Filling

- **Physical** - thyroid gland, parathyroid glands, hypothalamus, esophagus, trachea, larynx, mouth, teeth, gums, neck.
- **Emotional** - suffocating, choked by life.
- **Mental** - imbalances in your will, your choices, suppressed will, weak will, wrong choices, suppressed choices, no choices, inability to communicate.

■ **Spiritual** - doing God's will instead of your own, walking the path He has shown you no matter what happens, once the action step has been revealed to your heart you do it no matter what.

How to Breathe

■ Inhale through the nose, exhale through the nose is most preferred. This energizes the centers of heart, will, mind and purpose.

■ Pull breath into the lower abdomen first. This is critical to fill all four areas. Put one of your hands just below your navel and make sure as you pull the breath in, your hand starts to lift up as the abdomen pushes out. You might initially have to consciously "push your stomach out" to train yourself to breathe in to this area.

■ Next step is to put your other hand on the middle of your chest (heart area). As the breath is first pulled into the lower abdomen (hand below navel rises up first) it then proceeds to fill the solar plexus and then up to the middle chest. When the breath starts to fill the mid chest your upper hand should begin to lift up (as your lungs expand further). As the lungs fully fill, the upper chest will also rise but more up toward your head than out from your body. This is the complete cycle of taking in the breath. You should consciously draw the breath in from the lower abdomen to the solar plexus to the mid chest to the upper chest. You can check yourself by making sure the lower hand below your navel rises before your upper hand on your chest does.

Inhale -Exhale

■ Your inhale should be long and smooth

■ Your exhale should be just letting the breath go, it should not be forced, pushed or controlled any way. Similar to filling a balloon with air and just letting it go, no energy or effort should be used.

■ The breathing ratio is ideally 3:1 inhalation time to exhalation time. Pulling in the deepest inhale leads to a relaxed, natural, short exhale.

Breathing Analysis

In analyzing our breathing we must remember that blocked breath filling has a body-emotion-mind-spirit covenant connection. When one area is out of balance all four are being stressed to help that stressed area rebalance.

■ Lack of lower abdomen filling
■ Lack of solar plexus filling
■ Lack of mid chest filling
■ Lack of upper chest filling
■ Lack of all filling

Lower Abdomen Block

■ **Physical** - large intestine, bladder, sexual organs, lower spine, pelvis, and hip imbalances, conditions and dis-ease.

■ **Emotional** - fear, unforgiveness, resentment, inability to let go.

■ **Mental** - not "one with another," one-on-one relationships imbalance (codependent, control), needing something from another.

■ **Spiritual** - receiving to give, flowing.

Solar Plexus Block

■ **Physical** - stomach, pancreas, liver, gall bladder, small intestine, kidneys, adrenal glands, spleen, middle spine, and abdomen imbalances, conditions and dis-ease..

■ **Emotional** - fear, anger, resentment, worry, anxiety.

■ **Mental** - not "one with yourself," ego driven (whether great or lowly), power seeking, needing yourself to be something or someone, paranoia, obsession rejection, depression, frustration.

■ **Spiritual** - loving yourself, being at peace with yourself, knowing whom you are, knowing what your purpose is.

Middle Chest Block

■ **Physical** - heart, lungs, bronchial tubes, thymus, breasts, ribs, diaphragm, shoulder, and arm imbalances, conditions and dis-ease.

■ **Emotional** - grieving, not releasing, holding on instead of letting go, hate, lack of love.

■ **Mental** - not "one with God" (wrong perception of God), do not feel loved, depression.

■ **Spiritual** - knowing God, being one with God, receiving from Him, being filled with Him.

Upper Chest Block

■ **Physical** - thyroid gland, parathyroid glands, hypothalamus, esophagus, trachea, larynx, mouth, teeth, gum, and neck imbalances, conditions and dis-ease.

■ **Emotional** - suffocating, choked by life.

■ **Mental** - imbalances in your will, your choices, suppressed will, weak will, wrong choices, suppressed choices, no choices, inability to communicate.

■ **Spiritual** - doing God's will instead of your own, walking the path He has shown you no matter what happens, once the action step has been revealed to your heart you do it no matter what.

Restrictions to Proper Breathing

- Holding in your stomach, trying to keep your stomach flat is taught as proper for women.
- Pushing chest out and holding stomach in together is seen in men who want to appear strong.
- Tight pants or clothes that restrict movement in all areas.

Types of Breathing

- Physical life sustaining
- Physical blockage clearing
- Emotional blockage clearing
- Mental pattern clearing
    - *Conscious mind clearing*
    - *Unconscious mind clearing*
- Spirit refilling
- Spirit of God - receiving to give, infilling to outpour.

Physical Life Sustaining

- This is the basic type of breathing that everyone does every second of his or her life. This is the primary source of oxygen and energy for the body. This is the first type of breathing that must be mastered before one progresses to the other types of breathing. This is done as was previous stated: fill lower abdomen, then solar plexus, then mid chest, then upper chest. The ratio is 3:1 inhale to exhale. Use your hands to teach you initially. Lower hand below navel, upper hand on mid chest - heart area.

Physical Blockage Clearing

- Once you have mastered the physical life sustaining type of breathing you can now direct that life energy, that healing energy into a specific part of the body through the physical blockage clearing type of breathing.
- This is done by first putting your hand on the organ, gland, tissue or body part that has the symptoms or dis-ease. (SEMB)
- Next you see that area healed in your mind as you deep breath through all four phases.
- Next you say out of your mouth as you exhale, "I thank God for my life and for my healing."
- Next you breathe until there is a release in the flow of the exhale. This can be described as a lightness, an ease, a smooth, unrestricted relaxed exhale. (This is opposed to tight restricted breathing that most people have - similar to the breathing after something has alarmed you, this is tight and restrictive. After the alarm has been resolved the relaxed deep sigh is released and breathing becomes free and lighter.)

Sometimes it is accompanied by deep relaxation or other sign of release in the physical body.

■ As you breathe you might start to tone or sound. This is a release in the energy blockage of the area. This is not done consciously but released via the unconscious mind that is connected to the stored emotional blockage that has made the area of symptoms or dis-ease its home. Continue to breathe until there is a smooth unrestricted exhale, deep relaxation or other release is felt in your body, or the toning has either stopped or turned into a uniform constant tone.

Emotional Blockage Clearing

■ This is used to clear any conscious or unconscious emotional blockages.

■ You do this type of breathing like the physical blockage clearing with a few changes.

■ Put your hand on the solar plexus area, right below the sternum or breastbone. (SEMB)

■ You see in your mind the negative emotion being released as a darkness or heaviness being lifted right out of your stomach - solar plexus. You then visualize the light, love, joy, and peace of God filling the void the emotion left after it came out. Some people envision a brilliant white light filling the dark hole that the emotion left.

■ Next you say, "I thank God for my life and my healing."

■ Next you breathe until there is a release in the flow of the exhale. This can be described as a lightness, an ease, a smooth, unrestricted, relaxed exhale. Sometimes it is accompanied by deep relaxation or other sign of release in the physical body.

■ As you breathe you might start to tone or sound. This is a release in the energy blockage of the area. This is not done consciously but released via the unconscious mind that is connected to the stored emotional blockages. Continue to breathe until there is a smooth unrestricted exhale, deep relaxation or other release is felt in your body, or the toning has either stopped or turned into a uniform constant tone.

Mental Pattern Clearing

■ This is used to clear any conscious or unconscious negative mind patterns that caused negative emotions to store in the physical body.

■ You do this type of breathing like the physical blockage clearing with a few changes.

■ Put your hand on your forehead. (SEMB)

- You see in your mind the negative pattern being released as a darkness or heaviness being lifted right out of head. You then visualize the light, love, joy, and peace of God filling the void the mind pattern left after it came out. Some people envision a brilliant white light filling the dark hole that negative the mind pattern left.
- Next you say, "I thank God for my life and my healing."
- Next you breathe until there is a release in the flow of the exhale. This can be described as a lightness, an ease, a smooth, unrestricted, relaxed exhale. Sometimes it is accompanied by deep relaxation or other sign of release in the physical body.
- As you breathe you might start to tone or sound. This is a release in the energy blockage of the area. This is not done consciously but released via the unconscious mind. Continue to breathe until there is a smooth unrestricted exhale, deep relaxation or other release is felt in your body, or the toning has either stopped or turned into a uniform constant tone.
- Next you can reprogram the conscious and unconscious mind with affirmations. Example, "I love myself because God loves me"; use whatever God puts in your heart.

Spirit Refilling

- This is used to refill the spirit within you. It also helps keep the blockages of the heart (negative mind/emotion patterns) from trying to come back and coating your heart (hardening, or making cold).
- You do this type of breathing like the physical blockage clearing with a few changes.
- Put your hand on your heart. (SEMB)
- You then visualize the light, love, joy, and peace of God filling your heart and overflowing to every part of your being. Some people envision a brilliant white light of God's love filling their heart and flowing into their mind and every part of their body.
- Next you say, "I thank God for my life and my healing." Let everything that has breath praise the LORD. (NIV)
- Next you breathe until there is a release in the flow of the exhale. This can be described as a lightness, an ease, a smooth unrestricted exhale. Sometimes accompanied by deep relaxation or other sign of release in the physical body.
- As you breathe you might start to tone or sound. This is a release in the energy blockage of the area. This is not done consciously but released via the unconscious mind. Continue to breathe until there is a smooth unrestricted exhale, deep relaxation or other release is felt in your body, or the toning has either stopped or turned into a uniform constant tone.

Spirit of God Infilling/Outpouring
Praying in the Breath

■ This is used to commune with God at a deeper more intimate level. It is used to intercede for yourself or another by receiving from God and flowing into yourself or another His love, His power and His wisdom. Once you know God, have entered into a covenant relationship with Him, in essence have become married to Him, you receive His Spirit who now lives in you. This is the Spirit of power, of love and of all knowing, of all Truth. One of the ways we access the Spirit of God is through praying in the Spirit, or praying in the breath.

■ You do this type of breathing like the physical blockage clearing with these changes.

■ Put your hands wherever you are led to in your heart. They are usually lifted up in praise and worship.

■ You then clear your mind so God can fill your supremeconscious mind with whatever or whomever He wants you to intercede for. This may be your own or another's mind, emotion, organ, gland or body part. This is intercession led by the Spirit of God. This is praying in the breath of God.

■ Next you breathe until there is a release in the flow of the exhale. This can be described as a lightness, an ease, a smooth, unrestricted, relaxed exhale, sometimes accompanied by deep relaxation or other sign of release in the physical body.

■ As you breathe you might start to tone or sound. This is the Spirit of God flowing through you. This is not done consciously but released via the Spirit of God. Continue to breathe until there is a smooth unrestricted exhale, deep relaxation or other release is felt in your body, or the toning has either stopped or you feel a release in your heart (your spirit) that what you have interceded for has received the breath of the Spirit, the breath of God.

Your Breath is God's Breath

■ When you breathe from a free flowing, unblocked spirit (which comes from a balanced, unblocked physical body, which leads to balanced, unblocked emotions, which in turn lead to a balanced, unblocked mind), *your breath is God's breath*. This is the highest energy form, the most powerful physical act to heal yourself and others. With every breath you refill from Him and pour out to yourself and the world around you.

Deep diaphragmatic breathing is the most important physical step to bring balance, health, healing and the flow of life energy to the spirit, the mind, the emotions and the physical body. This is because it so powerfully rebalances all three parts of our being at the same time.

Whatever obstacles or mountains come into the path of our life, let us breathe the breath of Life, the breath of God into them. This is the breath of Truth, of health and of healing. With our breath we can change the frequencies of the world and entrain the world to the highest frequency that is love, that is God.

Let us make each breath we take a praise, a thanksgiving, a worship, a blessing, a prayer.

_____
_____
_____
_____
_____
_____
_____
_____
_____
_____
_____
_____
_____
_____
_____
_____
_____
_____
_____

Go Deeper

1. How does the food you eat inversely effect the oxygen content in the body, and how does that promotes the growth of cancer cells, bacteria, viruses, parasites, and fungi like candida?
2. How do high protein diets increase cancer risk?
3. Why are green sprouts the highest oxygen content food?
4. What are the five greatest physical benefits to deep diaphragm breathing?
5. What are the two greatest mental/emotional benefits to deep diaphragm breathing?
6. What are the physical, mental, emotional, and spiritual stresses and how do they block the flow of energy and life along the fascial highway?
7. What is entrainment?
8. How does positive entrainment help you heal in body, mind, and spirit?
9. How does negative entrainment prevent you from healing in body, mind, and spirit?
10. Have you ever experienced people entrainment when you were in a group of negative people?
11. If everything is made of energy, and all energy has a vibrational rate called frequency, and it is this frequency that can entrain us either positively or negatively, what are the highest frequencies to entrain us into total health of body, mind, and spirit?
12. What are the lowest frequencies to entrain us into symptoms, conditions, and dis-eases of the body and mind?
13. What are the 5 prerequisites to retrace to remove the root of your imbalances or dis-eases?
14. If each breath-filling area corresponds to a body, mind, emotion, and spirit covenant connection, what are the physical, emotional, mental, and spiritual imbalances that can occur if you do not breathe deep enough to fill the lower abdomen?
15. Do you know how to use the 6 types of breathing to remove blockages in the flow of life to your physical body, your emotions, your mind, and to refill your spirit and pour out God's Spirit to others?
16. What do the words "inspire" and "inspiration" truly mean?
17. Once you have inspired the breath of God, what can your expiration do?

_____

_____

_____

Water

Water is the most basic chemical component of all living things.

Water Facts

- Although over two-thirds of the planet is covered with water, only 3% of it is fresh water.
- Only 0.1% of the fresh water is accessible to human beings.
- Annually 3 million die from illnesses linked to contaminated water.
- At the beginning of the 21st century, 2 billion people on the planet have no real access to clean water.
- Dehydration is one of the most common causes of hospitalization among persons over the age of 65.
- Half of these people die within one year of admission.
- Total body dehydration seems to be the hallmark of aging.

Total body dehydration seems to be the hallmark of aging.

Water Facts

- 80% of Americans are chronically dehydrated.
- In 37% of Americans the thirst mechanism is so weak it is often mistaken for hunger.
- The #1 trigger of daytime fatigue is lack of water.
- A mere 2% drop in body water can trigger loss of short-term memory.
- In a University of Washington study it was shown that just one glass of water shuts down midnight hunger pangs for almost 100% of the dieters studied.
- The National Cancer Institute reported a study that showed the drinking of chlorinated water increases one's risk of developing bladder cancer by 80%.
- Chronic dehydration is the root of many serious diseases including asthma, renal dysfunction, endocrine dysfunction, adrenal exhaustion, high blood pressure, cardiovascular dysfunction, ulcers, pancreatitis, digestive dysfunction, arthritis and back pain.
- A primary cause of Alzheimer's disease is chronic dehydration.
- The majority of asthma cases are really misdiagnosed cases of chronic dehydration.
- The mucous that lines the stomach to protect it from the HCl is 98% water.
- Drinking 5 glasses of water per day may decrease the risk of colon cancer by 45%.

- The risk of breast cancer could decrease by as much as 79%.
- Non-infectious chronic pain should always be seen as an indicator for water need.
- Research indicated that 8-10 glasses of water daily could significantly ease back and joint pain in 80% of sufferers.
- The simplest way to prevent migraine headaches is regular high intake of water.
- Dry mouth is the very last sign of dehydration.
- Dehydration causes mental/ emotional stress and mental/emotional stress causes dehydration.

Water is the most abundant substance in the body.
Water Content[9]

- Birth - 78%
- Young adult - 72%
- Elderly - 50%
- Brain - 85%
- Muscle - 75%
- Bones - 22%
- Fat - 10%

Water Content Divided[10]

For an average 150 lb. man the 72% water content amounts to 45 quarts which is divided into the following:

- 30 quarts inside the cells (intracellular).
- 15 quarts outside the cells (extracellular).

Of the 15 quarts outside the cells:

- 3 quarts in the blood plasma.
- 12 quarts made up of lymph fluid, cerebrospinal fluid, synovial fluid, respiratory secretions, intestinal secretions, vitreous humor fluid of the eye.

Daily Water Loss

Throughout the day water leaves the body. Even on a cool day without perspiring we lose 9-12 cups through:

- Perspiration
- Urine
- Feces
- Respiration exhalation
- Tears

Water balance in the body is controlled by the hypothalamus that is located in the base of the brain. The hypothalamus also controls the endocrine or hormonal system.

Thirst is Not an Accurate Indicator for Water Need[11].

Sensations of thirst are controlled by the cells in the thirst center of the hypothalamus. These cells are triggered when the concentration of certain solutes like sodium increase but are not sensitive to other solute increases like urea. Also thirst sensitivity declines with age. Thirst is also not a good indicator for water need in infants, children, and people with sickness, athletes or strenuous laborers.

Fluids of the Body that Need Proper Water Intake[12]

- Blood - carries oxygen and nutrients to all the cells and removes waste products.
- Lymph - carries pathogens and waste products away from the extracellular spaces.
- Digestive secretions - include saliva, HCl, digestive enzymes, bile, and mucous membranes.
- Urine - removes water-soluble waste products.
- Cerebrospinal fluid - oxygenates and feeds the brain and spinal cord. Also one of the highest energetically charged substances in the body.
- Fluid that transports the messages from the brain and spinal cord along the peripheral nervous system.
- Synovial fluid that lubricates all joints.
- Connective tissue fluid - muscles, fascia.
- Disk fluid that absorbs the shock along the spine.
- Mucous secretions of the nose, throat, bronchial tubes, and lungs.
- Perspiration that cools the body temperature and removes toxins.
- Fluid of the vitreous humor of the eye.

Gastro-intestinal secretions[13]

1000 ml = 1 liter = about 1 quart
- Saliva - 1500ml
- Gastric - 2000 ml
- Bile - 500ml
- Intestinal - 1200ml
- Fecal - 100ml

Signs and Symptoms of Dehydration[14]

- Fatigue and weakness
- Pain = inflammation
- Headaches
- Joint pain
- Constipation
- Dry, rough skin
- Dry nose, throat, mouth
- Nose bleeds
- Nausea
- Intestinal cramps
- Low blood pressure
- Weak, irregular pulse
- Shallow, rapid breathing
- Irritability
- Irrational behavior
- Dark, strong smelling urine in small amounts.

Sub-clinical Dehydration[15]

- Over 80% of the U.S. population
- A 3% loss in body water volume causes fatigue and organ dysfunction.
- A 10% loss can be life threatening.
- **By the time one's mouth becomes dry, the body has already begun to suffer the effects of dehydration** - Michael Lam, M.D.

Highest Water Intake Needs[16]

- People who are trying to heal from sickness, disease.
- Infants fed high protein formulas.
- People who are suffering from fever, vomiting, diarrhea, respiratory discharges.
- People taking diuretics.
- People eating high protein diets.
- People living in high atmospheric pressure or very warm climates.
- People that are very active - athletes, physical laborers.

Mind/Emotional Symptoms of Dehydration

- Loss of mental clarity - brain fog
- Loss of mental focus
- Irritability
- Irrational behavior

Toxic Water

- More than 700 chemicals have been found in our drinking water, and 129 of these chemicals have been cited by the EPA as posing serious health risks. Yet the EPA only requires water to be tested for about 80 of these chemicals.

- Some of the toxins in tap water include cancer-causing substances like arsenic, benzene, chlorine, fluoride, lead, THM's (trihalomethanes), MTBE (fuel additive), nitrates and nitrites (from fertilizers), radon, nuclear waste, and perchlorate (component of rocket fuel).

- ARSENIC - occurs naturally in ground water, from industrial run off, pesticide residue. A strong poison at high doses. At low doses is linked to cancer, diabetes, and a variety of other diseases.

- CHLORINE - additive to disinfect the water. It is a known carcinogen and produces poisonous byproducts.

- FLUORIDE - a controversial additive that also is a carcinogen. It also makes bones brittle and blocks the functioning of the life-sustaining enzyme systems.

- LEAD - source is from old plumbing pipes. It causes damage to the brain, the nervous system and the kidneys.

- NITRATES, NITRITES - from farm and city fertilizers, livestock waste. In the body these are transformed into carcinogenic nitrosamines.

- MTBE - a fuel additive designed to reduce air pollution. Causes dysfunction of the stomach, liver and nervous system. Cancer risk is very probable.

- THMs - trihalomethanes that form when chlorine reacts with organic material (anything from feces to decayed leaves). Known link to bladder cancer, increased miscarriage risk.

- PERCHLORATE - a component of solid rocket fuel, munitions, and fireworks. It interferes with the normal functioning of the thyroid gland.

- PATHOGENS - sewage discharges and farm runoff can introduce E.coli bacteria, cryptosporidium and other harmful bacteria, viruses and parasites. This causes gastrointestinal symptoms and weakened immune systems.

During a recent 2-year period, 45 million Americans were served by a water system that violated at least one federal health standard:

U.S. Water News January 1998	# of Systems in Violation	Population Affected
Chronic coliform bacteria	12,246	24.7 million
Lead	3,641	5 million
Fecal bacteria	2,726	11.9 million
Nitrates	588	471,736
Chemicals/ pesticides	325	935,203

Three Types of Health Risks from Water

- Toxins, chemical, pollutants
- Pathogens
- Inorganic minerals

Inorganic Minerals

Put a drop of water on a glass and let it dry. What you will see is a very small pile of sediment. These are inorganic minerals, and heavy metals and cannot be used in your body. Only organic minerals from plants can be utilized properly. These inorganic minerals and heavy metals (lead, cadmium, mercury, aluminum) keep building up in your body because they cannot be removed naturally.

What happens when they are built up?

They clog up the system just the same way they clog up your water pipes. What areas do they clog up?

- Heart - mineral deposits can attach to the heart or its valves causing restriction/blockage of function.
- Cholesterol - a good oil made by the liver naturally, and vital to a healthy nervous system, normal blood flow. As inorganic minerals attaches to your arterial walls the cholesterol attaches to them and clogs up your arteries that is referred to as "hardening of the arteries".

Where else do these inorganic minerals and heavy metals build up and what can they cause?

- Gall bladder - gall stones
- Kidney - kidney stones
- Intestines - constipation and colon cancer
- Lungs - emphysema
- Veins - varicose
- Nerves - radiculopathy or radiating nerve pain
- Joints - arthritis, rheumatism, gout
- Eyes - glaucoma

Studies show that you may drink over 450 pounds of inorganic minerals, heavy metals and sediment in your lifetime.

What Water is Best?

- Living water
- Raw water
- Distilled water
- Reverse osmosis water

Living Water

Living water is what is produced when you juice living plants, like sprouts, which contain bioelectricity, enzymes, bioavailable organic minerals and vitamins. The best are:

- Wheat grass, Barley grass
- Sunflower greens, Buckwheat greens
- Fenugreek greens, Broccoli sprouts, Clover sprouts
- Mung bean sprouts, Adzuki bean sprouts

Why is Living Water the Best?

Dr Hans Eppinger at the First Medical Clinic of the University of Vienna found that a living food diet increased the electrical potential between the tissues cells and the capillary cells. Dr. Eppinger also showed that the living food increased the absorption of nutrients and increased the release of toxins from the cells. Most important was that Eppinger found that living uncooked foods were the only kind of food that could restore the bioelectrical potential of the tissues once their electrical potential was weakened and cellular degeneration had begun. Living food and living water are the only forms of the two that have the ability to "jump start" the sick cells back to health.[17]

Raw Water

Raw water is what is produced when you juice raw organic green vegetables rich in enzymes, bio-available organic minerals and vitamins. The best are:

■ Kale
■ Collards
■ Dandelion
■ Broccoli
■ Spinach

Distilled Water

Very pure water that has no chemicals, toxins, inorganic minerals, heavy metals or sediment. This water is excellent for not only its purity but also for its ability to draw out excessive inorganic minerals, salts, toxins and chemicals.

Dr. Alexander Graham Bell, inventor of the telephone and one of America's greatest minds, wrote of the benefits of distilled water and how it prolonged his life. *"I have found that distilled water is a sovereign remedy for rheumatism—at least as far as my own case is concerned. Some years ago doctors could not find anything to relieve me. The attack came just as I was investigating certain subjects relating to the deposits of salts. One was about the deposits of salts in the human body. A well-known scientist had written a book in which he said that old age came from such deposits, and that the ills of advanced years were due to lack of their elimination. This man thought that when such deposits went to the joints, it caused rheumatism. When they went to the kidneys, he had kidney trouble and stones in the urinary organs, and when they lodged in the arteries, they produced what is called hardening of the arteries. In the same way when such deposits coated the nerves, they produce sciatica. At the time, I had been studying about the Dead Sea, the Great Salt Lake and other bodies of water that have no outlets. The Dead Sea is one fourth salt and the Great Salt Lake is loaded with salt. It occurred to me that my body was much like the Dead Sea and that it needed plenty of ways to get salt out. I knew that distilled water was pure. I thought that if I drank plenty of it, I might get rid of some of the salts that were covering my sciatic nerves. I tried drinking it, and it worked like a charm. Within a short time my sciatica left me and I have been free from rheumatism from that day to this. I have kept up my drinking of distilled water and I attribute my almost perfect health largely to it."*

Reverse Osmosis Water

This is water that has been ultra-filtered to remove chemicals, toxins, and heavy metals. Inorganic minerals are retained which make it less desirable than distilled water.

Conditions Proven to Improve with High Water Consumption[18]:

- Peptic ulcers
- Arthritis
- Hypertension
- Low back pain
- Intermittent claudication
- Migraine headaches
- Colitis
- Constipation
- Obesity
- Edema
- Asthma
- Allergies

How Much Water Per Day?

- 32 ounces per 50 pounds of body weight.
- 48 ounces per 50 pounds of body weight when in a health challenge.

What can you do about your tap water?

Up to 2 pounds of water can be absorbed through your skin in a long hot shower. So even if you aren't drinking your toxic tap water you are still taking it in through your shower or bath. Remedy:

- Shower filter for chlorine and some other toxins.
- Complete house system to filter toxins, chemicals.
- If you cook with water make sure it is distilled.

Covenant:
An agreement between two parties; each binding themselves to specific obligations, a legal contract.

Covenant:
A compact made by the passing between pieces of flesh - cutting a covenant.

Covenant

- Two parties enter an agreement to strengthen their weakness. This agreement lasts at least 8 generations.
- A bond for life or death.
- Always accompanied by the shedding of blood.
- Taking of oaths.
- If covenant is broken one party MUST kill the other party as payment for the breaking of the covenant, there is no choice in this, it must be done or the covenant has no power. The covenant's power is that the two have become one and will give everything they have to meet the need of the covenant partner, even to the giving of one's life for the other.
- **MORE** - Covenant is the most powerful relationship two people or two groups can ever have. Covenants were created by God to bind two together so they became an inseparable one. Covenant means love in the strongest and highest degree. It is "I will live to lift you up, even if it costs me everything - even my life." Covenant is love, is commitment, it is perseverance, it is obedience, it is never ever quitting or giving up on your covenant partner. First and foremost is our covenant with the Living God; it binds us to Him and Him to us, inseparable for life, for death and into eternal life. Next is the covenant with our self, our spirit covenanted to our mind and our body. The three inseparable, all-willing to die for each other, all committed to take care of the other with all their strength. Next is the covenant with our spouse, our partner for life, our other half that completes us. In this covenant of love we look out for their best interest, we lift them up, we give all we have to help them be all they can be. The last covenant is our covenant with each other, all seen as "all are one." In this covenant we receive from God to pour out to the world around us - as directed by the Truth He speaks to our heart.

What is a covenant made of?

- Promises
- Shedding of blood
- Seal

Marriage: a Covenant Relationship

- Exchange of marriage vows - terms of the covenant: for richer or poorer, in sickness and in health until death do us part.
- Ring - the visible sign of the covenant.
- Woman takes on the husband's name.
- The two become one, each eagerly waits to rush and meet the other's needs, while praying and planning to give to the other.

Marriage-Two Becoming One

If you are looking for someone to complete you, do you look for someone who is just like you or someone who is the opposite of you? You look for your opposite so that your weaknesses are her/his strengths and her/his weaknesses are your strengths.

The two become a greater more complete one rather than each other by themselves.

This covenant works only if the two are one with God, otherwise, instead of looking to help the other's weakness, you just see weakness, and burden.

Covenant - Marriage

How would a woman feel, and what would she say if her husband sat on the couch watching TV and said:

■ Honey, change the channel for me.
■ Honey, get me my glass of water on the counter.
■ Honey, pick up my coat on the floor.

She would say, "I can do those things for you but why can't you do them yourself?"

Now if her husband is on the couch lying there sick, she rushes to do those things and meet all his needs because where he is weak, she is strong, where he cannot do for himself, she does for him. This is love; this is the covenant.

Covenant with God

How do you think God feels and what would He say if His covenant partner sat passively asking:

■ God, heal my body.
■ God, take away all these problems.
■ God, heal my marriage.
■ God, make me prosper.

He would say I can do for you and give to you all that I AM once you have given all that you have and all that you are.

Now if you are listening to His voice of peace spoken into your heart and are in faith obediently taking the action steps He has shown you at 100% of your ability, that is when He meets you with the rest, with all that He IS. This is the place of miracles, the place of healing. This is love. This is the covenant.

The Covenant of Life

■ Covenant with God
■ Covenant with one's self
■ Covenant with one's spouse
■ Covenant with others

'Love the Lord your God with all your heart and with all your soul and with all your mind and with all your strength.' The second is this: 'Love your neighbor as yourself.' There is no commandment greater than these. (NIV)

Covenant with One's Self

- This is loving yourself.
- This is the body-mind-spirit covenant.
- Covenant means all members are willing to give everything to the other in need, even if it means dying.
- Your body will die for your mind or your spirit (heart).
- Will your mind be allowed to be put to death for your spirit (heart)?
- Will your mind be allowed to be put to death for your body?
- **MORE** -your body will do whatever you tell it to. It is a true covenant partner. Your spirit is the strongest covenant partner because it receives the Truth, the Way, and the Life. Your mind is the covenant breaker, not willing to look out for the other two, not willing to die for the other two.

You Must Die

In the body/mind/spirit covenant of loving yourself you must die to:

- Your flesh (negative mind/emotion/body energy).
- Your ego-self filled mind.
- The world system of knowledge.

If we do not die, we cannot live.

A seed must die for it to bring forth a tree.

A key in life is to die (to the old lie-filled mind) before you die (physically).

Covenant with One's Self

Modern research shows that body and soul cannot be observed separate from one another. Body and soul do not form two separate substances. Instead, they comprise the one individual human in an inseparable union. The body is one aspect of the whole individual existence.

- Keep your whole being - spirit, soul, and body - free from every fault (imbalance/blockage) at the coming of our Lord. (TEV)
- Do you not know that your body is a temple of the Holy Spirit, who is in you, whom you have received from God? You are not your own; you were bought at a price (covenant). Therefore honor God with your body. (NIV)
- It is not the spiritual that comes first, but the physical, and then the spiritual. (TEV)

- **MORE** - God made Adam from the dust of the earth (physical minerals). He then breathed the breath of life into him. God made man physical first and then He breathed His breath of life into us and it became our spirit, our breath of life.

- What a strange thing a body would be if it had only one part! So he has made many parts, but still there is only one body. The eye can never say to the hand, "I don't need you." The head can't say to the feet, "I don't need you." And some of the parts that seem weakest and least important are really the most necessary. …. So God has put the body together in such a way that extra honor and care are given to those parts that might otherwise seem less important. This makes for happiness among the parts, so that the parts have the same care for each other that they do for themselves. If one part suffers, all parts suffer with it, and if one part is honored, all the parts are glad. (TLB)

- Offer your bodies as living sacrifices, holy (whole in body, mind and spirit) and pleasing to God (following your heart, not your head/old mind) - this is your spiritual act of worship. Do not conform any longer to the pattern of this world (world, ego, flesh, lie-filled old mind), but be transformed by the renewing of your mind (from the Truth-filled heart). Then you will be able to test and approve what God's will (His will is revealed in your heart so His will and your will are one) is - his good, pleasing and perfect will. (NIV)

How to Heal Your Body/Mind/Spirit

- Enter covenant with the Living God.
- Enter covenant with yourself - your body, your mind and your spirit.
- Do all you have been shown in your heart and never stopping no matter how long it takes, and the rest will be done for you (healing is not your responsibility, it is God's. Your responsibility is to be faithful and obedient to what He has shown you in your heart).
- Start the race strong and finish it strong.
- Only thing that stops the power of God and His flow of healing and blessing is you:
    - Quitting
    - Stopping
    - Giving up
    - Not believing in the Truth that your heart has shown you.

How is health and healing accessed?

Two ways.

First

- From the Spirit of God filling the spirit (heart) of the person with Truth. This Truth then flows into his/her supremeconscious mind (mind of God). This Truth also begins to set him/her free from both conscious (thinking) and unconscious (stored memory) negative mind patterns and emotional toxins. This supremeconscious mind then leads the person into specific action steps to restore his/her physical health.

Second

- From doing the easiest things to change first - breathing properly to increase oxygen intake, proper daily water intake, proper diet, proper daily amount and onset of sleep, proper daily exercise, learning how to say no to what negative mental, emotional and physical activities are slowly killing you (fasting), learning how to hear the voice of God spoken into your heart and mind (the Truth, the Way, the Life).

- From taking these action steps you can then begin to use energy that was being used to keep you alive in survival mode, for deeper inner healing (letting go) of stored negative mind patterns and emotional toxins from your past and those that were generationally passed to you. As you become freer in mind and emotions you begin to open spiritually to the love of God and seek to intimately know Him in your heart.

Health / Healing flow from;

Spirit of God - the Truth, the Way, the Life;

into

Spirit of Man - knowing God, being filled with His Spirit, and partaking of the tree of life,

into

Mind - **Supremeconscious** - filled with all Truth;

      Conscious - willfully choosing Truth and reprogramming with Truth;

      Unconscious - releasing stored lies, reprogramming with Truth;

into

Emotions - replaced with spiritual states of being: love, joy, peace, hope;

into

Body - bringing health and healing.

Why Should I Work on My Body First?

- God formed the man from the dust of the ground and breathed into his nostrils the breath of life, and the man became a living being. (NIV)

- It is not the spiritual that comes first, but the physical, and then spiritual. (TEV)

- **MORE** - It takes less energy to remove physical blockages (-1X), than mental/emotional blockages (-10X), than spiritual blockages (-100X). Most people are so blocked or imbalanced in body, mind and spirit, that they won't allow the Truth into their heart. It has been hardened, and coated by the old mind. So if we have no access through the front door (the mind) we come in the back door (the physical body) because it is not as heavily guarded. As the physical body starts to balance (with the 7 basic steps to total health), the life energy turns inward to release the stored negative emotional toxins; this then leads to a releasing of or "letting go of" the negative mind patterns, the lie-filled old mind. This then leads to a softening, and warming of the hard/cold blocked heart so it can receive the Truth, the Truth that will set them free and heal them in body, mind and spirit.

Health / Healing is accessed from

Body - 7 basic steps to total health,
which when balanced starts to balance
Emotions - releasing stored emotional toxins from organs, glands, tissues and body parts,
which when balanced open the mind up to Truth.
Mind - Supremeconscious -Truth flowing from the heart,
    Conscious - willfully choosing Truth, and reprogramming the
    old mind with Truth,
    Unconscious - releasing stored lies, reprogramming with Truth.
    Which when reprogrammed and renewed with Truth allow the
Spirit of Man - knowing God in your heart, partaking of the tree of life,
to be filled with the
Spirit of God - the Truth, the Way, the Life,
and flow God's Spirit unhindered to bring the kingdom of God, the Spirit of God into the hearts and minds of men, women and children.
This is the new heaven (Spirit) and new earth (body/physical), God's creations living as He created them to.
Body, Mind, Emotions and Spirit as One
Once you balance the physical body, the energy for healing is directed inward to the stored emotional toxins (blockages); as these release, the negative mind patterns start to release from the unconscious (stored) mind, if we choose to change our conscious (thinking) perceptions (I can heal, I will not die, I have not fulfilled my call). Once the stored negative mind patterns are released, the stored negative emotional toxins have been released, the body is balanced with the 7 steps, then the spirit can flow unhindered to heal and maintain health of the whole being.

Water –The Beginning of Everything

Greek philosophers believed water to be the original substance and that all things were made from it. In the story of the creation water plays an elemental part.

- In the beginning God created the heavens and the earth. Now the earth was formless and empty, darkness was over the surface of the deep, and the Spirit of God was hovering over the waters. (NIV)
- And God said, "Let there be an expanse between the waters to separate water from water." So God made the expanse and separated the water under the expanse from the water above it. And it was so. God called the expanse "sky." And there was evening, and there was morning - the second day. (NIV)

What is Water?

- The most basic element of the planet.
- A medium to carry - a carrier.
  - To carry life - blood.
  - To carry oxygen, nutrients to every cell - blood.
  - To carry waste products chemicals and toxins out of every cell, in essence to clean or purify the cells of the body - blood and lymph.
- Spiritually symbolic of purification, the washing or carrying away of sin (separation from God).

What else can Water Carry?

- High Frequencies
- Low Frequencies
- Blessings

Transferring of High Frequencies

- When handkerchiefs or cloths that had touched his skin were placed on sick people, they were healed of their diseases, and any evil spirits within them came out. (NLT)
- Millions annually visit religious shrines, such as the one at Lourdes in France, with the hope of being miraculously healed (faith + obedience + action = healing).
- Special water that has been blessed and is used to bless churches, homes, and articles of devotion. Other water was blessed for the use of warding off the unclean spirit and as a safeguard against sickness and disease.
- SEMB - carrier of frequencies to positively entrain the body, mind, and emotions.

Water and Words[19]

■ Studies in Japan showed that written or spoken words actually changed the crystalline structure of water.

■ The study showed that words are vibrations of our natural world. Beautiful words create higher frequency vibrations that produce a beautiful natural world as seen by the beautiful crystalline structure of water. The study also showed that negative words produced lower frequency vibrations that produce irregular and broken crystal formation.

■ The study also showed that prayer for water changed its crystal structure from irregular broken to beautiful crystalline geometric shapes.

The Hundredfold Return/Loss

1. If the physical act has negative frequencies it is counted as a one fold loss. (-1X)

2. If the physical act has positive frequencies it is counted as a one fold return. (1X)

3. If the physical act has positive frequencies both physically and mentally it is counted as tenfold return. (10X)

4. If the physical act has positive frequencies physically, mentally and spiritually it is counted as hundredfold return. (100X)

The Hundredfold Return/Loss Example

1. Someone dreads cleaning the house - negative energy. (-1X)

2. Someone cleans the house doing it to the best of his/her physical ability. (1X)

3. Someone cleans the house to the best of his/her physical ability while listening to a teaching tape on how to improve his/her total health, renewing and reprogramming his/her mind with the Truth; he/she actually looks forward to this time. (10X)

4. Someone cleans the house to the best of his/her ability while listening to the tape, and begin to give thanks and praise to God for his/her life, for the moment, for the ability to clean the house. He/She makes cleaning the house worship to God. (100X)

*So whether you eat or drink or whatever you do,
do it all for the glory of God.* (NIV)

Let everything that has breath praise the LORD. (NIV)

Entrainment Frequencies

Highest Frequencies to positively entrain to higher states of health and healing are:

■ Spirit states of being - love, joy, peace, hope.

■ The breath of God = the breath of man = spirit

■ Supremeconscious mind - this flows from an unblocked heart/spirit. It is the mind of God in man.

■ Living water, living food especially when connected to the spiritual state of praise, and thanksgiving. (100X)

■ Exercise when it is combined with praise, thanksgiving and prayer. (100X)

■ SEMB

Lowest Frequencies to negatively entrain to lower states of health and dis-ease are:

■ Negative Mind Patterns - based in lies instead of Truth, the world system (knowledge vs. knowing), ego (self), flesh (negative mind/emotion/body complex), religion, time, and space bound old mind.

■ Negative Emotions - fear, anxiety, worry, frustration, self-criticism, boredom, resentment, bitterness, loneliness, hopelessness, guilt, grief, anger, and hate.

■ Lack of breathing.

■ Toxic water; dead, deficient, toxic, preserved or processed food.

■ Lack of sleep.

■ Lack of exercise.

Water and the Mind

■ **Baptize** - means to dip or immerse. Let the water we take into our body remind us that we are to be immersed in the Truth and not in the lie, in the knowing of God, not the knowledge of men or the world.

■ **Repent** - means to change your mind, to go in a 180-degree opposite direction. To go with your Truth-filled heart instead of your world/ego/self/lie-filled mind. Renewing or reprogramming your mind with Truth. Thinking about what (in your Truth-filled heart not, in your old lie-filled mind) is true, lovely, right, pure, of good report, excellent or praiseworthy. As he thinks in his heart (not his mind) so is he. (NKJV)

Blessing[20]
Bless

make holy: to bestow holiness on somebody or something in a religious ceremony.

protect: to watch over somebody or something protectively.

thank: to express heartfelt thanks to somebody.

Old English *blētsian*, from a Germanic base that also produced English *bleed* and *blood*; the original sense seems to have been "**to mark with blood**".

- **MORE** -the word "bless" is a covenant word. When we are blessed by God it is to say we are His covenant partner and whatever we need He rushes in to give to us, to bless us, once we have done and given all we are able, all that He has shown us in our heart and supremeconscious mind.

Holy[21]

sacred: relating to, belonging to, or coming from a divine being or power.

saintly: devoted to the service of God.

pure: morally and spiritually perfect and of a devoutly religious character.

consecrated: dedicated or set apart for religious purposes - holy water.

awe-inspiring: of a unique character, evoking reverence. Old English *hālig*, from a Germanic word that is the ancestor of English *whole*, the underlying idea being "**unimpaired,**" or unblocked.

BLESS, BLESSING[22]

- The act of declaring God's favor and goodness upon others. The blessing is not only the good effect of words; it also has the power to bring them to pass. The patriarchs pronounced benefits upon their children, often near their own deaths, even if spoken by mistake; once a blessing was given it could not be taken back.

- Leaders often blessed people, especially when getting ready to leave them.

- One can also bless God, showing love to Him in doing what He has put in one's heart (faith with action and obedience), also with thanksgiving and songs of praise.

- God also blesses people by giving life, riches, fruitfulness, or plenty. His greatest blessing is His Spirit living in our heart and forgiving our sins (separating from God).
- "Cup of blessing" meaning the cup of salvation or wholeness in body, mind and spirit.

How Do We Bless God?

- We give Him **thanks** for our life, our very breath and for all things because in all things we will have the victory that leads to freedom.
- We **praise** Him for who He IS, the creator and sustainer of all things including us, His most precious creation. To us He is our prize, our treasure because we are His prize, His treasure.
- We worship Him, we love Him, we acknowledge that He and He alone is worthy of our life, our time, our energy, our passion. To love excessively, unquestioningly.
- We bless Him by being in covenant with Him. The word "bless" means "to mark with blood." Whatever He asks of us (He speaks to our heart, not to our head), we rush to fulfill His request.

How Do We Bless Our Water?

- We thank God for this water that will heal our body and cleanse our unrenewed mind and emotions, and for His Spirit that He has placed in our heart (one of the symbols of the Spirit of God is water).
- We praise Him for who He is, the creator and sustainer of all things including us, His most precious creation. To us He is our prize, our treasure because we are His prize, His treasure.
- We worship Him, we love Him, we acknowledge that He and He alone is worthy of our life, our time, our energy, our passion. To love excessively, unquestioningly.
- As we lay our hands on the water, the spirit, mind and body frequencies are at the high level. These frequencies are imparted or transferred to the water, the carrier of these frequencies. (SEMB)
- We speak Words of Life over the water, Words of Truth.
- Physically - see the water as pure, able to bring oxygen, and nutrients to every cell in the body. Also able to remove the chemical, toxins, inorganic minerals and salts.
- Will - we see the water as an action step we have been called to by God and our will, our choice, is to be faithful and obedient to what He has spoken into our heart.
- Mind - as we take our action steps in faith we begin renewing our mind (conscious thinking, and unconscious storage) with Truth instead of lies, with the "knowing" of God spoken from our heart rather than the knowledge of man, and the world.

- Mind - thinking about what (in your Truth-filled heart, not in your old lie-filled mind) is true, lovely, right, pure, of good report, excellent or praiseworthy. As he thinks in his heart (not his mind) so is he. (NKJV)
- Emotions - we see all emotions from past and future gone and replaced with spiritual states of being: love, joy, peace, hope, and with passion and compassion in the eternal present moment.
- Words - we speak words of life (the tongue has the power of life and death), words of blessing, words of health and healing.
- Spirit - you are doing what God has put in your heart (spirit); you are doing it with thanksgiving and praise as worship to Him. You are blessing Him and in turn you are being blessed by Him. (100X)
    - Offer your bodies as living sacrifices, holy and pleasing to God-this is your spiritual act of worship. Do not conform any longer to the pattern of this world (world, ego, flesh, lie-filled old mind), but be transformed by the renewing of your mind (from the Truth-filled heart). Then you will be able to test and approve what God's will (His will is revealed in your heart so His will and your will are one) is - his good, pleasing and perfect will. (NIV)

How Do We Bless Our Family?

- Physical - see them as His body, His feet, His hands, His voice to this world.
- Mind - see their minds as His mind, renewed to the Truth, consciously thinking about only what is true, lovely, pure, right, of good report, excellent, and praiseworthy.
- Will - see their will as only to do His will spoken into their hearts.
- Emotions - see them free from all emotions of past and future, being replaced with love, joy, peace, hope, passion, and compassion.
- Words - speak only Words of Life, of blessings, of health, of prosperity over them.
    - Prosper - **flourish:** to flourish or thrive, from Latin *prosperare*, from *prosperus* "doing well." [23]

Beloved, I pray that you may prosper in all things and be in health, just as your soul (your will, your supremeconscious, and conscious mind) *prospers.* (NKJV)

May the Lord bless (covenant blessings) *and protect you; may the Lord's face radiate with joy because of you; may he be gracious* (covenant word-freely giving) *to you, show you his favor, and give you his peace.* (TLB)

"For I know the plans I have for you," declares the LORD, *"plans to prosper you and not to harm you* (my covenant partner), *plans to give you hope* (knowing) *and a future. Then you will call upon me* (your covenant partner) *and come and pray to me* (with a pure heart that I have filled with Truth), *and I will listen to you. You will seek me and find me when you seek me with all your heart* (not your mind).*"* (NIV)

- Spirit - thank God and praise God for them, offer them up as a worship to God. Let them be a blessing to Him. (100X)
- Spirit - speak any other words over them that God has put into your heart about them. Impart God's love, joy, peace, hope and passion to them. (100X)
- See them as they truly are, not as who they appear to be. See them unblocked, balanced and victorious in all areas of their life and free. See them knowing the Truth that will set them free. Free to receive and free to give, free to flow from the Spirit of God to others.

How Does God Bless Us?
- The blessing of His Spirit
- The blessing of salvation = wholeness = saved, healed, delivered, set free in spirit, mind and body.
- The blessing of healing in spirit, mind, and body.
- The blessing of miracles in spirit, mind, and body.
- The blessing of eternal life = one with Him forever (in covenant with Him).

How can you love, and bless your neighbor as yourself?
Love yourself - this is the body/mind/spirit covenant. Then you will be the True shining Light to the world in body, mind, and spirit and that Light will entrain all those around you to the highest frequency, which is Love.

_____

_____

_____

_____

_____

_____

Go Deeper

1. Do you know that water is the second most crucial physical element your body needs to take in to live, heal, and be in total health, and that 80% of Americans are chronically dehydrated, and that thirst is NOT an indicator for water need? What should this lead you to do?

2. Does water content have to drop from 78% in an adult to 50% in the elderly? Can you see that if the brain is 85% water and that in the elderly water drops to 50%, it is inevitable that they will have some neurological and mental imbalance symptoms because of this drop?

3. Do you understand that only a 3% loss in body water volume causes fatigue and organ dysfunction? What should this lead you to do?

4. Do you know the symptoms of your body telling you it needs more water?

5. What are the 3 types of health risks from water and which one is the least known?

6. Do you know the 4 best types of water? Which one is best and why?

7. How much water is required daily to be in total health?

8. What are 6 things water can carry?

9. Do you understand that if everything is energy, then the words we speak are either the Right energy or the wrong energy, and this energy can positively or negatively affect the mind, emotions and even the physical, as seen when word changed the crystalline structure of water? When you know this in your heart, what will it lead you to do?

10. Do you understand how the hundredfold principle affects every part of your life? How does the hundredfold principle apply to the water you drink?

11. How do you bless your water and what effects will that have on your total health? Why?

12. How can we bless our family?

13. How do you bless God, and how does He bless you?

14. How can we bless the world around us?

15. If the word "holy" means whole or unimpaired, how does this give new meaning to the Words, "offer your bodies as living sacrifices, holy and pleasing to God - this is your spiritual act of worship"? (NIV)

16. How can drinking water be worship to God?

_____
_____
_____
_____
_____
_____
_____

Food

Food - Types
- Living
- Raw
- Cooked vegetable products
- Cooked animal products

Living Food

Living food are sprouted seeds, grains and nuts that contain bioelectricity, enzymes, bioavailable organic minerals and vitamins. The best are:

- *Wheat Grass, Barley Grass*
- *Sunflower Greens, Buckwheat Greens*
- *Fenugreek greens, Broccoli sprouts*
- *Clover sprouts, Alfalfa Sprouts*
- *Mung Bean Sprouts, Adzuki Bean Sprouts, Lentil Sprouts*
- *Sprouted Quinoa, Amaranth, Millet, Rye*
- *Sprouted Almonds, Brazil Nuts*

Why is Living Food the Best?

Dr Hans Eppinger at the First Medical Clinic of the University of Vienna found that a living food diet increased the electrical potential between the tissues cells and the capillary cells. Dr. Eppinger also showed that the living food increased the absorption of nutrients and increased the release of toxins from the cells. Most important was that Eppinger found that living uncooked foods were the only kind of food that could restore the bioelectrical potential of the tissues once their electrical potential was weakened and cellular degeneration had begun. Living food and living water are the only forms of the two that have the ability to "jump start" the sick cells back to health.[24]

Living Food

- Every animal in nature that lives a long disease-free life eats living food filled with bioelectricity, bioenergy, enzymes, bioavailable minerals and vitamins.
- The herbivores eat living, growing grass, leaves, plants.
- The carnivores eat living animals.

The Miracle of Living Food

- Dr. P.R. Burkholder of Yale University found over a 1500% increase in B vitamin content in sprouted oats (living) as compared to cooked oats (dead).[25]

Living Sprouts vs. Raw vs. Cooked

Sprouted oats had 13 times more vitamin B2 than raw oats and 100 times more vitamin B2 than cooked oats. B vitamin content differences in oats showed an average loss of 87% in vitamin content after cooking.

The Greatest Miracle of Living Food

- **Miracle** - Act of God: an event that appears to be contrary to the laws of nature and is regarded as an act of God, from Latin *miraculum* "object of wonder," from *mirus* "wonderful."[26]
- Put a weighed and measured sprout seed in a test tube that is sealed with nothing but distilled water (no minerals). The miracle of life is demonstrated. As the sprout starts to grow, its vitamin, mineral, protein, carbohydrate and essential fatty acid content skyrocket.
- Something from nothing! This defies all natural laws. God designed this *something from nothing* miraculous "wonderful" living food for our total health of body, mind and spirit.
- **MORE** -this definitively shows that living food is God's designed food for our healing, health, and life. Why? Because His signature is upon it. With this simple illustration it can plainly be seen that living food is truly miraculous. It brings forth all that is needed for life from within itself. How else can one explain vitamin, mineral, protein, carbohydrate and essential fatty acid content increasing exponentially with nothing added but non-mineral-containing distilled water?

Life brings forth life.
Living food makes living, healthy people.
Dead food makes dying, dis-eased people.

Raw Food

- Raw food is food that has never been cooked. It is rich in enzymes, bioavailable organic minerals and vitamins.

Cooked Vegetable Food

- Devoid of bioelectricity, enzymes, an average loss of 87% vitamin and minerals.
- Calories to sustain life for a period, but nothing to restore or regenerate life.

Cooked Animal Food

- Toxic because chemicals store in the fat cells of animals as you eat up the food chain. Includes heavy metals.
- Hormones, antibiotics, bacteria, parasites, and cholesterol.
- Most difficult food to digest.
- Devoid of bioelectricity, enzymes, an average loss of 87% vitamin and minerals.
- Calories to sustain life for a period, but nothing to restore or regenerate life.

Plant vs. Animal Food Diet[27]

- A vegan diet is a vegetarian diet with no animal products at all included. No dairy, no butter, no cheese, no yogurt, no eggs, nothing from animals.
- 50% of Americans presently die from cardiovascular disease. This drops to less than 4% with a vegan diet.
- German Cancer Research Center showed that immune system strength is twice as strong in a vegan as compared to an animal product consumer.
- Nine out of 10 Americans will die from either cardiovascular disease or cancer and of these 90% between 60-90% could be prevented with diet (vegan) and lifestyle changes.
- The China Project was co-sponsored by Oxford, Cornell, and the China Department of Health, and proved that the greatest causes of disease came from two diet sources: cholesterol and animal protein, not plant protein. So the lowest incidence of disease occurred when these two were excluded from the diet. This is a vegan diet.
- Dr. Foster studied 200 cancer patients that were healed without any conventional medical treatment. The highest common factor between them all was that 87% of them changed their diet to vegetarian.
- Dr. Dean Ornish's Program for Reversing Coronary Heart Disease, besides daily exercise and relaxation techniques, includes a predominately vegetarian diet to reduce coronary blockages as severe as 90% so these patients did not need bypass surgery.
- The University of Oslo in Norway found that arthritis pain was substantially reduced in patients when a vegetarian diet was eaten. No pain reduction was seen when animal products were eaten.
- The average bone loss in meat-eating women, age 65, was 35% whereas the vegetarian female, age 65, lost only 18%.

- Countries with the highest consumption of meat and animal fat have the highest rate of breast cancer. Thailand's animal fat intake is 1/10th that of the US and breast cancer is 1/20th the rate.
- Risk of dying from prostate cancer is 3.6 times higher in men who eat animal products versus those who are vegan.
- Risk of dying from ovarian cancer is three times higher in women who eat animal products versus those who are vegan.
- Lessons from the animal kingdom. The animals that live the longest (i.e. tortoises) are vegetarian. The animals that are the biggest and strongest are vegetarian (i.e. elephants). Elephants do not drink milk and do not eat meat, yet they are some of the strongest animals on the planet. They are never protein deficient or calcium-deficient with their diet of leaves and grasses. Gorillas are three times the weight of a man and 30 times as strong. Not bad for a vegetable diet. So much for the myth that you need meat to be strong.
- Length of the digestive tract in animals who eat vegan diets (plants only, non-animal) is 8-12 times the length of the torso. This allows for digestion and absorption of nutrients from the plant material. The length of digestive tract of meat-eating carnivores is three times the length of the torso so as to move the quickly putrefying meat out of their system. Man's digestive tract is the length of a plant eater, not a meat-eater.
- The saliva of meat-eating carnivores is acidic to predigest proteins. Saliva of vegetable-eating herbivores is alkaline for carbohydrate digestion. Man has alkaline saliva.

Plant vs. Animal Food Diet[28]

- In a series of experiments a diet high in cooked animal protein was fed to rats with liver cancer. Their tumors grew rapidly.
- When the diet was changed to cooked plant protein the tumors stopped growing.
- The experiments did not include living plant food, but result would most probably have been shrinking (healing) of the tumors.

Raw vs. Cooked

- In 1946 Dr. Francis Pottenger conducted a research project to see the differences in health benefits in raw food versus cooked food. In the study he took 900 cats and put half of them on a totally raw diet and the other half on the same food, except it was cooked. The cats that ate the raw diet were very healthy and produced healthy kittens each successive generation. The cats that ate the cooked food did not fare so well. They developed all the diseases common to mankind: heart disease, cancer, pneumonia, diabetes, thyroid disease, kidney disease, liver disease, arthritis, osteoporosis, diarrhea, decreased sexual interest and paralysis. The first generation of kittens from the cooked food parents, were sick and abnormal, the second generation were diseased or dead, and by the third generation the mothers were sterile[29].

Three-part experiment done on rats to access diet and health:

- **Group 1** - a group of rats was fed a raw diet consisting of vegetables, seeds, nuts and whole grains. These rats grew very healthy and never suffered from any disease, never became fat, mated regularly, were gentle, affectionate and lived in harmony with each other. After reaching an equivalent of 80 human years they were put to death, and their organs, glands and tissues were found to be in perfect condition with no signs of aging or deterioration.

- **Group 2** - the next group of rats was fed a diet of cooked food, white bread, meat, milk, salt, soft drinks, candies, cakes, vitamins, minerals and medicines for any ailment. This group, from early on in life, contracted colds, fevers, pneumonia, heart disease, cancer, arthritis, poor vision and cataracts. Most of this group died prematurely and became very antisocial, fighting, stealing each other's food, and trying to kill each other. This caused them to have to be separated to avoid total destruction of the group. Epidemics of sickness affected the group and as they died they were autopsied and found to be in advanced degeneration in all their organs, glands and tissues. Their offspring were all sick and had the same problems their parents had.

- **Group 3** - in this group the rats were fed the same diet as Group 2, the average American diet, and had all the diseases and behaviors that were exhibited in Group 2. Extreme sickness, antisocial behavior and early death were all seen. Some of this group were put to death at an equivalent human age of 40 years and were autopsied and found to have extensive degeneration of all parts of their bodies.

- In the next part of the Group 3 Experiment, the rats, after an equivalent age of 40 human years, were put on a strict fast with only water to drink for several days (after eating the American diet for 40 equivalent years). Then when food was reintroduced into their diet it was only the raw food that group 1 received. This diet was alternated with times of fasting and within one month the behavior was completely different, having become very docile, playful, living together in harmony with each other. Then once again at the age of 80 human years equivalent these rats were autopsied and found to have no signs of aging or disease just as in group 1.

■ **MORE -** this experiment shows the amazing healing power of living/raw food. Most amazing of all is that after 40 equivalent years of the SAD (standard American diet) and lifestyle, once fasting and living/raw foods were introduced, their behavior reverted back to one of balance and harmony. Their physical body reversed all imbalances, conditions, diseases, and all signs of aging. If human beings can get this revelation that even if they have abused the temple of God's Spirit - their body, it is not to late to reverse symptoms, conditions, diseases, and aging. They need only to become proactive with the 7 basic steps to total health, obeying in faith God's Truth spoken into their hearts, never quitting, stopping, or giving up. This is when one starts living life to the full, this is when one really starts living in body, mind and spirit.

The Physical Environment for Healing (See Appendix)

Hippocrates
the father of medicine said,
"Let your food be your medicine."

The doctor of the future will give no medicine but will interest his patients in the care of the human frame, in diet, and in the cause and prevention of disease.
-Thomas Edison

Biological Transmutation[30]
■ Presented by C. Louis Kervran nominated for the 1975 Nobel Prize in Physiology.
■ Hypothesis: Elements can change from one to another in biological systems.
■ This phenomenon is not chemical; it goes deep into the atom, starting at the nucleus.
■ **Nature (God)** moves particles from one nucleus to another-particles such as hydrogen, oxygen and carbon nuclei. Thus transmutation.
■ K>Ca, Mn>Fe, Na>K, Mg>Ca.
■ Chickens with no calcium source in their diet produced soft-shelled eggs; when given an inorganic natural form of potassium produced hard-shelled eggs in 20 hours.

How many mgs? What % of RDA?

- When food is eaten in the living state the mgs and percentages do not matter very much any more.
- The miracle of living food is in effect.
- The mgs, and percentages do not reflect what really is absorbed into the body…what is truly bio-available to the cells.
- **MORE -** when living food is consumed it makes all that you need, because it is alive and has all or can be transformed into all that you would ever need. Look at an elephant with its strong muscles, bones and health. All it eats all day is growing leaves and grass so this must have all the calcium, protein, fat, iron and other essential nutrients right there in that living food. So much for mgs and RDA.

Lessons from Nature

- How can an elephant have the biggest bones, strongest muscles of any land animal and eat just leaves?
- How can a gorilla eat just vegetables and be three times the weight of a man and 30 times as strong?
- Why don't animals in the wild get cancer, heart disease, diabetes, etc., and yet have high stress of survival?
- The answer is LIVING FOOD.

Foods you want to eat

- Sprouted seeds, grains, legumes and nuts
- Grasses - wheat, barley, rye
- Algaes
- Green vegetables
- Vegetables
- Root vegetables
- Sea vegetables
- Avocados

Foods you do not want to eat

- Sugar
- Salt
- Caffeine
- Dairy products
- Animal products
- Refined flour

Sugar - Death to the Immune System

■ A study on sugar intake and immune strength was conducted in which three groups of mice were injected with an aggressive malignant mammary tumor. Prior to injection the dietary blood sugar was altered to produce three levels: high blood sugar, normal blood sugar (relative), and low blood sugar. After 70 days 66% of the high blood sugar mice had died, 33% of the normal blood sugar mice had died, and only 5% of the low blood sugar mice had died.[31]

■ **MORE** -the importance of this study cannot be emphasized enough. Sugar greatly suppressed immune function. When most people hear this they think, "I don't eat sugar," but the truth is that every thing you eat that is cooked turns into sugar. This includes bread, flour, pasta, potatoes, all cooked vegetables, rice, and cooked beans. This is a major reason why animals in the wild do not get cancer, heart disease, diabetes or any other ailments common to the human race. They eat NOTHING COOKED.

Living/Raw Food vs. Cooked

■ Digestive Leukocytosis - a rise in the white blood cell (WBC) count that begins 30 minutes after a meal when cooked or processed food has been consumed.

■ This occurs because cooked, processed food has no enzymes to digest the food, so the WBCs have to use their enzymes to eat your breakfast, lunch and dinner.

■ Living/Raw organic foods produced **no increase** in the white blood cell (WBC) count.

■ Stovetop or oven cooked foods cause a **mild increase** in the WBC count.

■ Pressure-cooked or canned foods cause a **moderate increase** in the WBC count.

■ Processed foods, refined flours and sugar cause a **severe increase** in the WBC count.

■ Processed meats (deli meats), microwaved foods cause **extremely severe increase** in the WBC count equivalent to what is seen in food poisoning.[32]

■ **MORE -** the body talks and teaches us if we only listen. It is obvious from the digestive leukocytosis observation that the body is telling us what it wants, and what it does not want. It is also telling us which food is best (organic living/raw food) and which is worst (refined flours, sugars, processed deli meats, and microwaved food.

Life Force

The life force is God's sustaining energy that has been put into every living thing. It is energy from God that reverses the natural law of entropy. Entropy states that everything in the universe goes from a state of order to disorder, a state of complexity to less complexity, from birth to death, everything is breaking down, not building up. The life force energy in a biological system produces negative entropy. Simple molecules such as oxygen, water, amino acids, essential fatty acids, and simple chain sugars are turned into complex biological molecule and structures like DNA, RNA. Dead food can sustain life for a period of time, but not regenerate life. Entropy returns when the life force leaves the biological system; death and decay results. Life force is in you and should be in the food you eat - living food, if you want to maintain your life force, your health.

The greatest physical blockage to our wholeness, our total health in body, mind and spirit is FOOD.

The Covenant of Life
■ Covenant with God
■ Covenant with oneself
■ Covenant with one's spouse
■ Covenant with others

Covenant
■ Two parties enter an agreement to strengthen their weakness. This agreement lasts at least 8 generations.
■ A bond for life or death.
■ Always accompanied by the shedding of blood.
■ Taking of oaths.
■ If covenant is broken one party MUST kill the other party as payment for the breaking of the covenant, there is no choice in this, it must be done or the covenant has no power. The covenant's power is that the two have become one and will give everything they have to meet the need of the covenant partner, even to the giving of one's life for the other.

What is a covenant made of?
■ Promises of blessing and cursing.
■ Shedding of blood representing giving ones life for the covenant partner.
■ Seal is the visible sign of the covenant.

Covenant Words
- **Love** - you will die for your covenant partner.
- **Grace** - freely you receive from your covenant partner, freely you give.
- **Friend** - name for covenant partner.
- **Remember** - the blessings of the covenant.

Marriage: a Covenant Relationship
- Exchange of marriage vows - terms of the covenant: for richer or poorer, in sickness and in health until death do us part.
- Ring - the visible sign of the covenant.
- Woman takes on the husband's name.
- The two become one, each eagerly waits to rush and meet the others needs, while praying and planning to give to the other.

Covenant - Marriage
How would a woman feel and what would she say if her husband sat on the couch watching TV and said:
- Honey, change the channel for me.
- Honey, get me my glass of water on the counter.
- Honey, pick up my coat on the floor.

She would say I can do those things for you but why can't you do them yourself?

Now if her husband is on the couch lying there sick she rushes to do those things and meet all his needs, because where he is weak she is strong, where he cannot do for himself she does for him. This is love; this is the covenant.

Partners in Covenant
- Partner **A** desires to purchase a piece of property valued at $100,000. Partner **A** asks partner **B** for the $100, 000 when he has $50,000 in the bank.
- This is an abomination to the covenant - asking for something from your covenant partner that you yourself have.
- You must get to the end of yourself before your covenant partner gives from himself.
- Abomination - Most of the Hebrew words translated "abomination" have the meaning of "impure," "filthy," and "unclean" - that which is foul - smelling and objectionable to a holy God... All of us have been sinful (separated from God by following our world/ego/flesh/religion/lie-filled old mind instead of our Truth-filled heart); even our best actions (if done from our mind, not our Truth-filled heart) are filthy through and through. (TEV)

Covenant with God

How do you think God feels and what would He say if His covenant partner sat passively asking:

- God, heal my body.
- God, take away all these problems.
- God, heal my marriage.
- God, make me prosper.

He would say I can do for you and give to you all that I AM once you have given all that you have and all that you are. Now if you are listening to His voice of peace spoken into your heart and are in faith obediently taking the action steps He has shown you at 100% of your ability, that's when He meets you with the rest, with all that He IS. This is the place of miracles, the place of healing. This is love. This is the covenant.

> ***'Love the Lord your God with all your heart and with all your soul and with all your mind and with all your strength.'* The second is this: *'Love your neighbor as yourself.'* There is no commandment greater than these." (NIV)**

Covenant with One's Self

- This is loving yourself.
- This is the body-mind-spirit covenant.
- Covenant means all members are willing to give everything to the other in need, even if it means dying.
- Your body will die for your mind or your spirit (heart).
- Will your mind be allowed to be put to death for your spirit (heart)?
- Will your mind be allowed to be put to death for your body?

Modern research shows that body and soul cannot be observed separate from one another. Body and soul do not form two separate substances. Instead, they comprise the one individual human in an inseparable union. The body is one aspect of the whole individual existence.

- Keep your whole being-spirit, soul, and body-free from every fault (imbalance) at the coming of our Lord. (TEV)
- Do you not know that your body is a temple of the Holy Spirit, who is in you, whom you have received from God? You are not your own; you were bought at a price (covenant), therefore honor God with your body. (NIV)
- It is not the spiritual that comes first, but the physical, and then the spiritual. (TEV)

■ What a strange thing a body would be if it had only one part! So he has made many parts, but still there is only one body. The eye can never say to the hand, "I don't need you." The head cannot say to the feet, "I don't need you." And some of the parts that seem weakest and least important are really the most necessary. ...So God has put the body together in such a way that extra honor and care are given to those parts that might otherwise seem less important. This makes for happiness among the parts, so that the parts have the same care for each other that they do for themselves. If one part suffers, all parts suffer with it, and if one part is honored, all the parts are glad. (TLB)

■ Offer your bodies as living sacrifices, holy and pleasing to God - this is your spiritual act of worship. Do not conform any longer to the pattern of this world (world, ego, flesh, lie-filled old mind), but be transformed by the renewing of your mind (from the Truth-filled heart). Then you will be able to test and approve what God's will (His will is revealed in your heart so His will and your will are one) is - his good, pleasing and perfect will. (NIV)

Does the food you eat balance the Body/Mind/Spirit Covenant? Does it balance the covenant with yourself?

■ Most spiritual nutrient – air.
■ Second most spiritual nutrient – water.
■ Third most spiritual nutrient – food.
■ Does the food you eat feed your body, feed your mind and feed your spirit? Or does it feed your flesh?

Three Aspects of the Flesh

■ Conscious (negative mind patterns - lies, thinking - lies, attitudes - the old lie-filled mind), Unconscious (negative stored mind patterns - lies, thinking - lies, attitudes - the old lie-filled mind, or negative stored mind patterns - lies, thinking, attitudes - the old lie-filled mind passed to you from prior generations) and Supremeconscious mind (the mind of God in you is blocked/bound).

■ Emotions (negative energy charged events that originate from the old, lie-filled mind).

■ Physical Body (negative energy stored in the tissues, organs, glands).

How to Know You are Bound by the Flesh

■ Cannot stop the activity for any length of time.
■ Feel you have lost control, your body, mind and emotions run you, they tell you what to do instead of the reverse.
■ You do what you do not want to and you do not do what you truly desire.

Flesh - Any Bondage that has taken Physical Form

- Food
- Smoking
- Drinking
- Drugs
- Power
- Money
- Sex
- Entertainment
- TV

Truth about the Bondages

- *Food* - You can live 30 days without food and be healthier.
- *Smoking* - A toxin, carcinogen, and drug addiction-nicotine.
- *Alcohol* - A toxin, carcinogen, and drug-like addiction.
- *Drugs* - Toxins, and addiction forming.
- *Power* - You are complete in yourself, you need no recognition, no status, nobody, only being filled with the Truth/God your source for life.
- *Money* - God will supply all your needs, not too much, not too little.
- *Sex* - Love vs. physical act, addiction, lack of true love.
- *Entertainment* - None needed when you are living your purpose.

The Greatest Bondage of the Flesh is FOOD

Who wants Sugar?

- Your cells do not want sugar.
- Your brain does not want sugar.
- Your organs do not want sugar.
- Your glands do not want sugar.
- Your tissues do not want sugar.
- Only your Flesh (negative body/mind/emotions) wants sugar.

Your flesh, is it a bear on a leash that drags you, or is it a toy poodle that you totally control?

Anatomy of the Flesh

- Physical act caused by a negative emotion.
- Negative emotion caused by a false belief (lie).
- False belief/Negative mental pattern (lie) causing blockages of the heart, which all lead to feeding the old mind (lie-filled instead of

121

Truth-filled mind), which manifests in the following aspects of that old, unrenewed with Truth, mind:

- World
- 5 Senses
- Ego/Self mind
- Personality mask
- Past/Present Belief Systems
- Religion
- Time
- Space/Physical

Why Do We Feed the Flesh?

- We do not know who we are.
- We do not know what our purpose is.
- We do not feel loved.
- We do not feel joy.
- We do not feel peace.
- We do not feel hope.
- We seek pleasure outside of God.

Whatever You Feed Grows

Feed the flesh and the flesh grows.

Feed the tumor and it grows.

Feed the negative emotions and they grow.

Feed the world-filled knowledge mind and it grows.

Feed the spirit-filled heart the Truth and it grows.

Whatever You Starve Dies

Starve the flesh and it dies.

Starve the tumor and it dies.

Starve the negative emotions and they die.

Starve the world knowledge-craving mind and it dies.

Starve the spirit-filled heart of the Truth and it dies.

Flesh Trigger

- Doing, seeing, hearing, tasting, smelling or touching anything that evokes the old negative mind/emotion/body response.
- Example - Not only will eating the wrong food trigger the flesh response but also when you eat healthy food that you have prepared to taste like the wrong food. Even though its physical benefits are much better the negative mind/emotion pattern is turned on and the flesh is still fed.

Have you ever been tempted by air? No.
- Have you ever been tempted by water? No
- Have you ever been tempted by food? YES!
- Why only food?
- The air that God made has been unchanged by mankind.
- The water that has been made by God has been unchanged by mankind.

Why are you tempted by food?
- Food has been changed by fallen mankind to feed the flesh instead of the body, mind, and spirit.
- Do you crave sprouted seeds, nuts, grains and greens? No, because they are still in the living/raw uncooked, unprocessed state that God created them in.
- The reason you crave cooked, processed, man-made food is because it feeds the flesh.
- Animals in the wild do not crave the leaves and grass they eat, they just know they are supposed to eat it.

What does your food represent?
- Love - memories of baking cookies with mom.
- Family - family dinner, family holiday gatherings, time of fellowship.
- Social - the world's entire social structure revolves around food, but what food? Is it God made food that feeds the body, mind and spirit or is it cooked, processed food that feeds the flesh?

What are you doing when you eat food?
- You are taking into your body something that becomes you. The food you eat becomes you; it becomes your cells.
- The food that you eat becomes your cells, your organs, your glands, your tissues, your thoughts, your emotions, and your behavior.
- Since the food and you become one, in essence you are entering a covenant with the food.

What have you brought into yourself and become one with?

Don't you know that he who unites himself with a prostitute is one with her in body? For it is said, "The two will become one flesh." But he who unites himself with the Lord is one with him in spirit. Don't you know that your body is a temple of the Holy Spirit, who is in you, whom you have received from God? You are not your own; you were bought at a price (covenant). Therefore honor God with your body. (NIV)

Who Opens the Door to the Flesh?
You do!

If someone does not bring the truth, do not invite, accept or admit him into your house (body) or encourage him in any way. Anyone who **encourages** him becomes a partner (covenant partner) in his lie. (NLT/AMP)

Encourage defined - *to feed the feeling or thought: to assist something to occur or increase.*

You have the free will to open the door or close it to the lies, the world, the negative mindsets and negative emotions around you, to your flesh, to your ego, to past or future thinking. The choice is up to you.

- **MORE** - your free will gives you the ability to open or close the door to the old mind, the world system, the ego, the flesh, and the lies. Once you have opened the door to the old mind, the flesh, you have given it authority over your heart/spirit and your body. How far do you have to open the door to the old mind, the flesh to have it come into your house in full force? Just one little crack. Just one little bite. And once the door is open it will take every ounce of your will, and your heart to close the door.

Hundredfold Principle

- One fold is the physical. (1X)
- Tenfold is the mental/emotional. (10X)
- Hundredfold is the spiritual. (100X)
- Everything in your life is connected to this principle.
- When we do things, think things, say things, know things, there is the hundredfold principle always being demonstrated.

Hundredfold Decrease

- 1 Fold Decrease (-1X) - if the food has no life in it, then it will in time decrease the life of the body (life produces life, death produces death) (physical).
- 10 Fold Decrease (-10X) - if the food represents a lack of love, a reward for something done right or a pleasure to make you feel better about things that have not turned out they way you wanted them to (mental/emotional).
- 100 Fold Decrease (-100X) - if the food feeds the flesh (the negative mind, emotion, body energy) the flow of the Spirit is blocked. If the flesh increases the Spirit flow decreases (spiritual).

Hundredfold Increase

- 1 Fold Increase (1X) - if the food has life in it, then it will bring life, health and strength to the body (life produces life) (physical).
- 10 Fold Increase (10X) - if the food brings balance to our mind, keeping it pure, if it reminds us (brings back into our memory) of our covenant with God, our covenant with our self, keeps us thinking on whatever is true, whatever is right, whatever is pure, whatever is lovely, whatever is excellent or praiseworthy (mental/emotional).
- 100 Fold Increase (100X) - if the food is received with thanksgiving, and praise is given to God, for the food, seen as a gift from God to restore your total health. If you treat the eating of the food as a worship, offering our body up to Him to be used for His purpose- receiving to give. This brings healing and health of body, mind and spirit (spiritual).

Consecrated[33]

- from Latin *consecrare*, literally "to make sacred."
- **To be holy (whole) or set apart.**
- **Declare holy:** to declare or set apart a building, area of ground, or specific spot as holy or sacred (consecrate your food).
- **Bless** (Old English *blētsian*, "to mark with blood") to remember the covenant (bless your food - to make it a covenant meal).

Everything we take into our body, into our mind, into our spirit - air, water, and food - should be consecrated (set apart, holy, and blessed) and all should have the 100 fold increase in our being.

What is the Temple?

- It is the place of worship.
- It is the house of God.
- It is where the Spirit dwells.
- It is our body.
- Are we defiling the temple - not keeping it holy (whole, complete, not lacking anything in body mind and spirit)?
- Don't you know that you yourselves are God's temple and that God's Spirit lives in you? If anyone destroys God's temple, God will destroy him, for God's temple is sacred, and you are that temple. (NIV)

How much is too much?

- How much of the wrong food is too much? Is it one piece of bread, one slice of cake, one bite of a sweet roll, one taste of a cookie?
- Adam and Eve only took one bite of the forbidden fruit to break the covenant with God. One bite that we are all paying for even now.
- A bite, a taste represents a break in the body/mind/spirit covenant you have with yourself which causes a 100 fold decrease in your total health of body, mind and spirit. (-100X)

Just one time with another woman/man

- If someone has an extramarital relation with another woman/man, he/she has defiled the temple. He/She has opened the door of his/her temple to negative body/mind/spirit energy. He/She will reap the 100fold (-100X) decrease in his/her total health, in his/her life, in his/her being. The price for defilement is very high: the breaking of the covenant of life - the covenant with God, the covenant with yourself, the covenant with your spouse and the covenant with your neighbor.

Just one bite of the wrong food does the same.

- It breaks the covenant of life: the covenant with yourself (your covenant between your body, your mind, and your spirit), and when that covenant is broken it negatively affects the covenant with your spouse, the covenant with God, and the covenant with your neighbor.
- How with yourself? 'Love your neighbor as **yourself** ' (This is the body mind and spirit covenant with yourself. Only once you are in covenant with yourself, once you are balanced in all areas, can you be the True, whole Light of the world, can you love your neighbor - entrain them to the frequency of total health in body, mind and spirit). There is no commandment (Word of Truth) greater than these." (NIV) Keep your whole being-spirit, soul, and body-free from every fault (imbalance) at the coming of our Lord. (TEV) If one part suffers, all parts suffer with it, and if one part is honored, all the parts are glad. (TLB)
- How with God? - Offer your bodies as living sacrifices, holy and pleasing to God - this is your spiritual act of worship...and everything that does not come from **faith** (believing, trusting and relying upon Truth that has been spoken into your heart) is sin (separation from God instead of consecration - set apart, holy for God). (NIV)
- How with your spouse? What you do to one covenant partner you do to both covenant partners. If one part suffers, all parts suffer with it, and if one part is honored, all the parts are glad. (TLB)

■ How with your neighbor? If you cannot keep the body/mind/spirit covenant by loving yourself how can you be the shining covenant light in body, mind, and spirit to the world around you? You become a 100 fold decrease (-100X) to those around you. You become a negative entrainment energy.

Would you let a robber into your house? How about a murder? NO!

Yet with every bite of the wrong food, you let the thief come in the front door to steal your 100 fold blessing and you let the murderer in to put you to slow death, blocking the 100 fold blessing!

What happens when health challenged people committed to the heart-led journey of total health take just one bite of the wrong food?

■ When you have entered into the body/mind/spirit covenant, the covenant with yourself, every part of your being (your spirit/heart, your supremeconscious mind, your will, and every cell in your body) wants you to become balanced, whole, healed.

■ When you break this covenant with just one bite of the wrong food, your body/mind/spirit being revolts with a great increase of symptoms. Why?

■ You have said with your heart, and your will that, you want to be whole as God created you. **You** (your spirit/heart and body) will hold **you** (your mind) to that covenant agreement.

■ This is awesome; this is God working in you.

Can you now see how one seemingly innocent bite can negatively affect your whole life? Your covenant of life?

■ Like a cancer, the negative energy you let in through the front door of your house will begin to grow and spread throughout all parts of your house until it has negatively affected every part of the whole, every part of your body, mind and spirit.

How do you separate from the blessing of the Covenant of Life? By Disobeying.

- You do not, in faith, obey His word spoken into your heart.
- You do not take the actions steps and keep taking the action steps He has called you to take for as long as He has called you to take them.
- You do nothing when He has put something into your heart.
- His blessings come when you do all that you can; this is when He does all that He IS. *This is the place of miracles, the place of life.*
- He replied, "Blessed rather are those who hear the word of God (the Truth spoken into their heart) and obey it." (NIV)
- "If you love me, you will obey (do and never stop doing) what I command." (NIV)
- "If anyone loves Me, he will keep My word (that was spoken into your heart); and My Father will love him (fulfill His part of the covenant), and We will come to him and make Our home with him. He who does not love Me does not keep My words (does not listen to and obey the Word of Truth that God has placed in his heart, instead he willfully chooses to listen to and obey the lies that have been placed in the mind); and the word which you hear is not Mine but the Father's who sent Me." (NKJV)
- "If you obey my commands (Truth I have placed in your heart), you will remain in my love (my covenant), just as I have obeyed my Father's commands (His Truth placed in my heart) and remain in His love. I have told you this so that my joy may be in you and that your joy may be complete. My command is this: Love each other (every part of your being - your body, your mind and your spirit) as I have loved you. Greater love has no one than this, that he lay down his life for his friends (covenant partners)." (NIV)

"So whether you eat or drink or whatever you do, do it all for the glory of God." (NIV)
Glory means praise and thanksgiving offered as an act of worship to God.

How do you stay Holy, Pure and Consecrated before God?

How do you live the covenant of life to the full?
- Make everything in your life a 100 fold blessing (100X).
- Listen to His voice spoken into your heart every moment of your life.

- In faith (believing, trusting and relying upon the Truth He has spoken into your heart), obediently take the action steps He has shown you.
- Never stop, quit, give up or shrink back, no matter what. This pleases Him.
- Offer your body (mind and spirit) as a living sacrifice - a burnt (Spirit of God consumed) offering, holy (whole in body, mind, and spirit) and pleasing to God. This is your spiritual act of worship.
- Speak only words of life, these are His words spoken into your heart. The Right Word (His word) spoken at the Right time brings forth life, health, healing, victory, freedom - He sent forth his word and healed them. The tongue has the power of life (when it speaks from a Truth-filled heart) and death (when it speaks from a world/ego/flesh/religion lie-filled mind). (NIV)
- Thank Him, praise Him, and worship Him for your healing, for your wholeness, for your total health.
- Enter his gates with thanksgiving and his courts with praise; give thanks to him and praise his name. For the LORD is good and his **love** (covenant with you, His covenant partner) endures forever, his faithfulness continues through all generations. (NIV)
- Who may ascend the hill of the LORD? Who may stand in his holy place? He who has clean hands (doing from being, not just doing to do) and a pure heart, who does not lift up his soul to an idol (the old world, ego, flesh, lie-filled mind) or swear by what is false. He will receive blessing from the LORD. (NIV)
- Idol defined - any object of worship other than the one true God. Offering our body (mind, and spirit) as worship.
- Their destiny is destruction, their god is their stomach, and their glory is in their shame. Their mind is on earthly things. (NIV)

How do you stay Holy, Pure and Consecrated before God?

- Fast - denying anything access into your house that is not holy and pleasing to God. Anything that will not give the 100 fold blessing.
- Fast from anything you think you need to, anything you think you have to have.
- Fasting feeds the spirit, the supremeconscious mind (mind of God in us), and balances the body. Fasting starves the flesh (old mind filled with negative thought patterns, negative emotions, negative energy and lies).
- Practice multiple fasts at once - Food and TV.
- Every day of your life should include some form of fasting - this is the food for the spirit, soul and body.

- Fast in time periods you can handle and build upon them - 1 meal, 1 day, 1 week, 1 month, 1 year - always being led in the heart by God, not in the mind by doing a religious act.

I Need My Food!

- If you need it you are not free from it and when you are free from it you can have it, or not have it, it makes no difference.
- If you need the tumor to go, it will not; once you know that you are healed in your spirit, and you know you are healed in your mind and will, and you know you are healed in your body, then you are truly healed. When you do not need the tumor to leave anymore, you are free from the tumor. That is when the tumor now can leave. The apostle Paul said, "I can live or die, have everything or nothing."

What is Food?

- Food is the same thing that everything else is.
- 99.9% energy, less than .1% physical.
- What kind of energy is the food you are eating? Is it the 100 fold increase bringing wholeness (holiness) to body, mind and spirit? Or is it the 100 fold decrease bringing sin (separation from God) and death (separation from life)?
- The free will choice is always yours - choose blessing or cursing, life or death.
- Know that once you make the choice of life and never stop, quit or give up, your covenant partner will be there, His power is made perfect in your weakness (when you reach the end of your ability, He gives all His, all that He IS).

What would you say to God if He gave you the choice to eat or never have to eat again? Which one would you choose?

How much will you push through?

- I will not eat that piece of cake, bread.
- My flesh rises up and says, "You have to have that piece."
- Your conscious and unconscious mind is filled with "why you need the piece"- pleasure, reward, need some happiness.
- Reprogram your mind with Truth - no cell, tissue, gland, organ, body part, nor supremeconscious mind nor spirit needs it. Only your flesh needs it.
- Could you say no if there was a gun to your head!
- Could you say no if God appeared to you and said no!
- You can fast for 30 day on water alone and be healthier.

■ **MORE** - if you can say "no" to the food when a gun is at your head, or when God physically appears to you and tells you, it means you have the ability, the free will choice to say "no". So why don't you? You choose to follow your old mind, your flesh mind instead of your heart/spirit. Do you have to get a diagnosis of terminal disease before you decide to say "no"?

Addiction

■ Anything that binds you, keeps you in chains, prevents you from being free.

■ Desires that if not fulfilled trigger negative mind patterns and negative emotions because either you cannot have what you desire or you are denying yourself what you desire.

■ Any desire that makes you unhappy or upset if not satisfied.

■ A mental/emotional programming that triggers negative emotional responses, and arouses the conscious/world/ego/self/flesh-filled mind because the situation does not fit the programmed pattern in your mind.

Addiction vs. Preference

Addiction

■ Causes you unhappiness sooner or later.

■ Desires that have a demand, attachment or **expectation** connected to them and if not fulfilled produce a negative mental pattern and negative emotion.

Preference

■ Never causes you unhappiness.

■ Desires that have no demand, attachment or expectation connected with them so they do not produce negative mind patterns or negative emotion.

Pleasure vs. Pleasing

■ **Pleasure**[34]

■ 1. Happiness or satisfaction: a feeling of happiness, delight, or satisfaction

■ 2. Sensual gratification: gratification of the senses.

■ **Pleasing** to be all that God created us to be and to do all that God has called us to do. To be in the covenant of life in faith, obediently taking the action steps He has put in your heart. And to never quit, stop, give up or shrink back.

Pleasing to God

■ So do not throw away your confidence (your knowing in the heart); it will be richly rewarded. You need to persevere so that when you have done the will of God (what He has put in your heart), you will receive what he has promised (covenant blessings).... But my righteous (one who follows the Truth revealed in his heart rather than the lies in his head/mind) one will live by faith. And if he shrinks back (turns to follow the old flesh, ego, world, lie-filled mind), I will not be pleased with him. But we are not of those who shrink back and are destroyed, but of those who believe and are saved (healed, delivered, set free and made whole in body, mind and spirit). (NIV)

- So then, those who are in the flesh (in the old mind) cannot please God. (NKJV)
- Those who live only to satisfy their own sinful (separating from God-old mind driven) desires will harvest the consequences of decay and death. But those who live to please the Spirit (following their Truth-filled heart) will harvest everlasting life from the Spirit. So do not get tired of doing what is good (following the Truth spoken into your heart). Do not get discouraged and give up, for we will reap a harvest of blessing (covenant promise) at the appropriate time. (NLT)
- And without faith (believing, trusting and relying upon the Truth that has been revealed to your heart and obediently taking the action steps that Truth has revealed) it is impossible to please God. (NIV)
- Offer your bodies as living sacrifices, holy and pleasing to God - this is your spiritual act of worship. Do not conform any longer to the pattern of this world (old mind), but be transformed by the renewing of your mind (with Truth). Then you will be able to test and approve what God's will is (you will know His will, it is what He placed in your heart and confirmed with His love, joy, peace, and hope) - his good, pleasing and perfect will. (NIV)

Let all your food be a covenant meal

- With every bite remember the blessings of the covenant of life:
    - Covenant with God
    - Covenant with yourself
    - Covenant with your spouse
    - Covenant with your neighbor.
- Remember the 100 fold increase of blessing.
- Remember who you are, remember who He IS, remember that your purpose is to be whole, healed, delivered, set free from all things.
- You prepare a table before me (covenant meal-remembering your covenant partner will always meet you with all He is when you have done all that you can) in the presence of my enemies (your greatest is your old lie-filled, unbelieving mind). (NIV)

Mind Tests

In mastering the mind there will always be tests along the way.

■ To see how far you have come.
■ To strengthen you in your journey.
■ To separate you from the .1% physical and operate in the 99.9% spiritual.
■ To break the mind barrier.
■ Test failed = temptation fallen back into the world system of lies.
■ Test passed = more Truth has filled your being: mind/ emotions/body.

Tests - Types and Forms

■ Things from the past that resurface to pull you back into the "old" you. The you that was controlled by the:

> World system of lies/ego/self/5 senses
> Flesh (negative mind/emotion/body)

■ Pain or symptoms returning when they were gone.
■ Loss of family, friends, relationships, money, home, job.

How to Pass the Test

■ *Stay in the present moment.*
■ *Watch the situation* (negative mindset, negative emotion) *but do not become it* (watching the movie but not going into it - no emotions elicited, watching your crying child in the store but not giving him what he wants).
■ *See it as it is*! A test to grow you, not as a temptation to destroy you.
■ *Keep the physical balanced.* This is accomplished by doing the 7 basic steps to total health daily; this is critical to deep inner healing.
■ *As the negative mental pattern or emotion arises remember that was from the "old/lie" filled you.* Thank God that it is leaving because it can never again enter the "new/Truth" filled you.

People Who Have Passed the Test

■ Abraham - loss of son
■ Job - loss of prosperity, family and health
■ Jesus
    ■ Tested with food.
    ■ Tested with testing God.
    ■ Tested with power.

Testing is to mature us, to help us in our journey to discover our completeness, our wholeness, our lack of nothing. To set us free.

Lessons from the Greatest Tests

■ Food is the greatest temptation, it is also the path to passing the greatest test>greatest victory>freedom.

- Tests are meant for us to grow spiritually, mentally and physically. We do not test God; we do not question God's infinite wisdom. His ways are not man's ways.
- God's Word spoken into our heart is the Right Word at the Right time.
- We are to only worship God, and this worship is to be with our body, our mind and our spirit.
- When we know Him we can have the hope (knowing in the heart) that produces the faith (believing, trusting and relying upon the Truth that has been revealed to your heart and obediently taking the action steps that Truth has revealed) that can move mountains, or raise a son from the dead.

The Wilderness and the Promised Land

- The Wilderness is NOW. It is the tests, the mountains that have been put in your path.
- The purpose of the wilderness is to come to know the covenant of life in all its aspects. To know how to love God, know how to love yourself, to know how to love your spouse, and to know how to love your neighbor.
- The Wilderness is as good as it gets because it is you and God, the two living as one.
- The Promised Land is yours when you have passed all the tests in the wilderness. The Promised Land is yours when you do not need it, you already have all that you need. You have victory in all things, which has made you free.

Knowing

- Knowing is God speaking to our heart, our mind and our body with His love, His joy, His peace.
- When God's knowing is in your spirit/heart it is called love.
- When God's knowing is in your heart that begins to fill your mind and will, it is called hope, patience and confidence.
- When God's knowing is in your heart and it manifests into physical form it is called faith, action, obedience and perseverance.
- The greatest desire of mankind is to know God, know His voice and know His will (direction or path) for their lives, to know they are making the right decisions.
- This knowing comes with a deep sense of inner peace, the calm in the midst of the storm.
- To hear His voice of peace spoken into your heart, you must be still - still the mind, still the emotions and still the body. Still - to bring into balance and harmony the body, mind and spirit. To hear His peace in your heart you must first balance the physical, then the mind and

emotions will be renewed and released, then the spirit can flow unhindered bringing peace to your heart, mind, and body.

How to Heal Your Body/Mind/Spirit

- Enter covenant with the Living God.
- Enter covenant with yourself - your body, your mind and your spirit.
- Doing all you have been shown in your heart and never stopping no matter how long it takes and the rest will be done for you (healing is not your responsibility, it's God's, your responsibility is to be faithful and obedient to what He has shown you).
- Starting the race strong and finishing it strong.
- Only thing that stops the power of God and His flow of healing and blessing is **you**:
    - Quitting
    - Stopping
    - Giving up
    - Not believing in the Truth.

Battle vs. War

- We might lose the battle but we will not lose the war.
- Make a new battle plan each day.
- For the battle is the LORD's (when we do all that He has placed in our heart to all of our ability, He does the rest). (NIV)

How to Win the War?

- Get to the end of yourself.
- You must die to the flesh, to the world, to the self - the old you.
- Never ever give up or quit or stop.
- Fast from anything that you think you need (except the Living God).

Why are you climbing the mountain of total health?

- To kill your self - ego mind.
- To kill your flesh filled mind.
- To kill your world mind.
- To get to the end of your self, which is the beginning of Him.
- If we do not die we cannot live.

What is at the top? Victory and Freedom

Being brings forth Doing

- You must first crawl
- Then you can walk
- Then you can run
- Then you can climb
- Then you can fly
- Then you can be, and out of the being will come the doing of God's will, His good, pleasing, perfect will.

Go Deeper

1. Do you understand the miracle of living food, how something can come from *no-thing*, and that living food makes living, healthy people, and that dead, cooked food makes dying, dis-eased people?

2. What else comes from *no-thing*?

3. Do you understand how detrimental cooked animal protein and cholesterol are to your total health?

4. In the Pottenger cat study, and the three - group rat study, what miracle of God is demonstrated?

5. Why do animals in the wild rarely get sick while domesticated dogs and cats get the same diseases that people do? Why are elephants not calcium or protein deficient when all they eat is grass and leaves?

6. Do you now understand how hazardous to your health sugar is in all forms, including bread, pasta, even cooked vegetables, grains, and legumes like potatoes, rice, and beans?

7. What part of your body/mind/spirit covenant wants sugar, and why?

8. Why does cooked food cause a rise in the white blood count? Why is microwaved food so detrimental to your health? What does this tell you about its effect on your total health?

9. Do you understand the "whatever you feed grows, and whatever you starve dies" principle and how it affects your total health of body, mind, and spirit?

10. Why is food tempting but air and water are not?

11. Do you understand why food can be so detrimental to your total health of body, mind, and spirit when love and family are attached to it?

12. Do you understand that, when you eat food, it becomes a part of your cells, in essence it becomes you, and you become it?

13. How do you consecrate your food and what does that do to it?

14. Why does just one bite of the wrong food negatively affect your total health?

15. What is you really expressing when you say, "I need my food?"

16. Do you fully understand the difference between: Addiction vs. preference, pleasure vs. pleasing?

17. What are four of the mind tests, and what happens when we pass or fail them? How do you pass them?

18. Do you understand the difference between knowing and knowledge?

19. How do you get to the promised land of total health?

Sleep

After breathing oxygen, sleep is the second most important step in your physical health.

How Important?
- You can only go 3 minutes without oxygen.
- You can only go 2 days without sleep.
- You can go 5 days without water.
- You can go 30+ days without food.

Sleep Facts
- The average number of hours of sleep we were created to have in a day was 12 (4380 hours per year).
- The minimum number of hours of sleep to heal, repair and to stay in total health is 9.5 (3468 hours per year).
- The average number of hours of sleep now is 6.95, which is 2537 hours per year.
- The loss from 12 hours to 9.5 is 912 hours per year or 76 days.
- The loss from 12 hours to 6.95 is 1843 hours per year or 153 days.
- In 1910 average American night sleep was 9.5 hours. In 1975 it had dropped to 7.5 hours. Now it has dropped to 6 hours and 54 minutes.
- 67% of Americans have sleep disorders, a 33% increase in the last 5 years.
- 70 million Americans suffer from insomnia.
- Over 100 million Americans fail to get a good night's sleep.
- Over 95% of the American population does not sleep the 9.5 hours of sleep the body needs to heal, repair and maintain total health.
- Sleep Disorders-Insomnia, Sleep apnea, Restless-leg syndrome, Narcolepsy affect over 112 million Americans.
- Insomnia - 70 million.
- Sleep apnea - trachea closes while sleeping blocking the air flow, causing the sleeper to break deep sleep up to hundreds of times a night - 30 million.
- Restless-leg syndrome - sensations of pain, tingling, needles, causing the legs to twitch or move, leading to sleeplessness - 12 million.
- Narcolepsy - uncontrollable episodes of falling asleep during the day- 250,000.
- 56% of adults report daytime drowsiness as a definite problem.
- 37% report it interferes with daily activities.
- 30% report a drop in job performance.
- 50% report a drop in performance of family duties.

Sleep breakdown by age and day[35]

Age Group	Hours of Sleep-work days	Hours of sleep-weekends	% Adults who skip sleep to get more work done
18-29	6.8	7.8	53
30-64	6.9	7.5	44
65+	7.2	7.3	32

Fallacies about Sleep

■ I do not need that much, I do fine with just 6 hours of sleep.
■ I will catch up on the weekends.
■ I have never slept more than 7 hours since I was 18 and have been doing fine. I have lots of energy and never get tired.
■ If anyone sleeps more than 8 hours they must be sick.
■ There is not enough time to sleep more than 8 hours in a day.

What does lack of sleep cause?[36]

■ Overweight.
■ Increases all craving/addictions to food.
■ Increases chances of diabetes.
■ Decreases fertility and makes one impotent.
■ Raises blood pressure.
■ Increases chances of heart disease.
■ Throws your immune system completely off track increasing your chances of developing cancer, infections, autoimmune disease and allergies.

Lack of sleep (less than 9.5 hours) greatly increases your risk of all diseases along with greatly hindering the process of healing that occurs at night while you are in deep sleep.

When were you designed by God to go to sleep?
When the sun goes down.

When were you designed by God to wake up?
When the sun comes up.
How many hours is that per night?
An average of 12 hours.

What is the minimum amount you can sleep and still heal, repair and maintain total health in body, mind and spirit?
9.5 hours, and of this at least 3 hours must be before midnight.

Sleep Connections[37]

■ Sleeping controls hormone production.
■ Hormone production controls stress and appetite.
■ Stress and appetite control reproduction.
■ Reproduction controls aging.

Sleep and Hormones

Loss of sleep not only affects at least 11 different hormones in the body, it also affects neurotransmitter production especially dopamine and serotonin. This directly affects mental/emotional health.

Hormones

■ Melatonin and prolactin - these talk back and forth with your immune system and metabolism (to keep the fire burning so all enzymes and metabolic pathway perform to perfection) - this is all controlled by light and dark cycles.
■ Insulin and prolactin control brain chemistry and dopamine and seratonin levels that in turn affect your behavior and mood.[38]
■ When one goes out of balance they all go out of balance.
■ Melatonin affects the pituitary gland function.
■ Pituitary gland makes part or all of most of your hormones. When it is thrown out of balance it will affect your:

- **Thyroid** - metabolism, energy.
- **Thymus** - immune function.
- **Pancreas** - blood sugar, appetite, immune function.
- **Adrenals** - stress management, pain control, immune function.
- **Ovaries/testes** - reproduction, anti-aging.
- All these will go out of balance with less than 9.5 hours of sleep.

Light-Dark Cycle

- This cycle turns hormone production on and off.
- Turns the immune system on and off.
- Produces the proper neurotransmitter production on the right timing, each day and each season.[39]

All of life flows in a never-ending rhythm of cycles. These cycles are governed by the rotation of the earth on its axis (24 hour periods of light and dark - Circadian rhythm) and on the rotation of the earth around the sun (365 days of varying lengths of the light-dark cycle-seasons). The most crucial cycle to ALL LIFE is the light-dark cycle. If this cycle is interrupted unnaturally it is one of the greatest factors that leads to imbalance, disharmony, symptoms, conditions and dis-eases of the body-mind complex of human beings and animals alike.

Biorhythms-Cycles of Mental/Emotional/Physical

- All organs and glands not only cycle through a daily 24-hour cycle, they also cycle through the monthly and seasonal cycles. The monthly cycle (lunar) is of extreme importance because mind, emotion and physical states all follow these cycles or rhythms.
- Physical cycle - about 23 days.
- Emotional cycle - about 28 days.
- Mental cycle - about 33 days.
- Hormones cycle especially in women, following the lunar cycle.[40]

Chronobiology

- The biology of time and the how the cycles and rhythms affect our health and life.
- Founder Dr. Franz Halberg of the University of Minnesota.
- Studies showed that women who underwent breast cancer surgery the week before and around the time of their menstrual period were 4 times more likely to suffer a recurrence of the cancer than those who had surgery between day 7 and 20 of their monthly cycle. This was because during the menstrual period the immune system is suppressed.[41]

24-Hour Organ/Gland Cycle

- 11PM-1AM Gall Bladder
- 1AM-3AM Liver
- 3AM-5AM Lung
- 5AM-7AM Large Intestine
- 7AM-9AM Stomach
- 9AM-11AM Spleen/Pancreas
- 11AM-1PM Heart
- 1PM-3PM Small Intestine
- 3PM-5PM Bladder
- 5PM-7PM Kidney
- 7PM-9PM Sex Organs
- 9PM-11PM Thyroid/Adrenals
- **MORE** - these are the times that each organ and gland is rejuvenating, and recharging for another day. So if you go to bed at 10PM you upset the self-balancing, healing mechanism of the thyroid gland and the adrenal glands. This affects your metabolism, your immune system, and your energy. If you go to bed at 11PM you not only throw the thyroid and adrenals out of balance (cumulative effect) but you also make your body toxic because the gall bladder and liver (they are connected so if one goes out of balance so does the other) cannot rebalance. This cycle is also affected in the opposite way. If you eat toxic food, it will throw your liver out of balance, which will cause it to need more energy to recharge/rebalance, so you start waking up at 3AM every night because of the imbalance in the organ, causing an imbalance in the 24-hour organ/gland cycle.

Light and Dark Cycle

Studies done on the light-dark cycle

- University of Chicago study proved that shining a light from a fiber optic tube behind the knee of a subject who was completely covered (in the dark) still stopped melatonin production. This shows that skin cells can record light and send this information to your pineal gland that produces or stops producing melatonin. When melatonin production is stopped (in the light), immune function is altered.[42]
- Study published in the *Journal of Laboratory Animal Science* on enhanced neoplastic growth and metabolism in animals maintained in a constant light environment. The study proved how minimal light 0.2 lux (less than that of a candle) disrupted the normal circadian production of melatonin. The results showed that only 0.2 lux

inhibited melatonin production and increased the rate of tumor growth and metabolism.[43]

Light-Dark Cycle and Night Work

■ Studies done on night shift workers show that their bodies never adjust to the reversal of the waking and sleeping cycle.

■ Night workers suffer a higher incidence of colds and depression than day workers and tend to have chronically imbalanced immune systems predisposing them to recurrent infections, cancer, autoimmune disease and allergies.[44]

The worst invention for your physical health was? The light bulb.

Why?

Because it forever upset the light-dark cycle that regulates our health and our life.

Sleep and the Immune System

■ Study done at Johns Hopkins University on the effects of chemical carcinogens and sleep patterns in mice.[45]

  ■ The mice were injected with man-made poisons like Windex, plastics, and components of antiperspirants.

  ■ The short-sleep mice started developing tumors at such a rapid rate they could not tell which substances were the cause.

  ■ The long-sleep, mice no matter what toxin was given, did not develop tumors at all. They were immune to all the carcinogens.

  ■ Also noted was that the short-sleep mice became withdrawn and paranoid.

■ **MORE** - this is an amazing study that shows that when we get enough sleep, our body works just the way God created it to. It is immune to the carcinogenic effects from the toxins. When we sleep the 9.5 hours we were created to, keeping in rhythm with the light-dark cycle, our body can do all the things it needs to do to keep us in total health.

- National Institute of Health research found that 6 hour of prolactin production in the dark is the minimum necessary to maintain immune function, including T cell and natural killer cell production. But to get 6 hours of prolactin production you need at least 3.5 hours of melatonin production first before any prolactin is produced.[46]

- Melatonin is one of the most potent antioxidants known. The less melatonin the more free radicals, the more aging. **This means without 9.5 hours of sleep per night you will age and degenerate 4 times faster.**[47]

- That is easy enough, then all you have to do is take melatonin supplements and all the problems are solved, right?

- Wrong. When you take melatonin it decreases your natural production of the hormone. This can have disastrous effects on your immune system and your hormonal system.

- God's ways are not man's ways.

- God's food is not man's food.

- God's hormones are not man's hormones.

- 80% of your immune systems strength is located in the intestinal tract because most toxins will enter through the mouth.

- The friendly bacteria in your intestinal tract coexist with you to produce beneficial vitamins and aid in digestion.

- These bacteria also produce an endotoxin - LPS. When the levels of LPS (over the course of the day) rise high enough in the blood it causes us to go to sleep and triggers an immune response. This immune response not only brings the bacterial count down in the gut, it stimulates the entire immune system of the body to clear all bacteria, viruses, parasites, fungi, and cancer cells.[48]

- Sleep is the most potent immune balancer, bringing a low immune response (causing bacterial, viral, parasitic, fungal infections and cancer) up, and an over-active immune response (autoimmune disease and allergies) down.

- Sleep produces melatonin (a strong antioxidant) and prolactin which balances the immunity while you sleep. Without enough sleep (9.5 hours of darkness) you block the flow of life in the immune system which results in **both**
  - Hypoimmune (underactive) function which leads to pathogen growth, and cancer; and
  - Hyperimmune (overactive) function that leads to autoimmune disease and allergies.

Hormones of the Dark

Short hours of dark sleep reduce:

- **Melatonin** secretion - this decreases white blood cell immune function.
- Decreased **prolactin** at night causes a decrease in T cell and NK cell production; also this means too much prolactin during the day which causes autoimmune disease and carbohydrate cravings.[49]
- Increased **insulin** levels - they remain high when they should drop to zero at night - this causes over production and eventual exhaustion - diabetes or excessive sugar in the blood to feed the pathogens.
- Increased **cortisol** levels at night cause decreased levels for the next day - this means less stress resistance, less pain tolerance.
- **Dopamine** (a neurotransmitter that controls thought processes and emotional response) is cortisol dependent. Without cortisol your dopamine is low so you can experience brain fog, memory loss and cognitive dysfunction and motor function loss.
- Remember melatonin is not secreted when any lights are on; this means ANY light, even as dim as a candle.
- When melatonin is not secreted due to not enough sleep (9.5 hours in the DARK), this throws off all the other hormonal glands. It is a chain reaction. A blockage in one causes a blockage in all. Melatonin is secreted by the **pineal gland**. With this gland thrown out of balance because of not enough dark it in turn throws the pituitary or master hormone producer out of balance.
- **Pituitary** makes most of the hormones or precursors of most of the hormones in the body. Pituitary imbalance causes thyroid imbalance or dysfunction.
- **Thyroid gland** - when the lack of dark sleep causes this hormone to decrease, it causes the metabolism to slow and the body temperature will start to decrease. All enzymes for all cellular function that maintain your life are dependent on the 98.6 degrees F. As this decreases you decrease your immune system response, you decrease function of all other organs and glands, you gain weight, your bowels slow down, your thoughts become foggy, scattered, your memory fails.
- **Thymus gland** - this is next in the endocrine connection. Decreased melatonin will affect a decrease in the immune function of the thymus causing either hyper (overactive) or hypo (underactive) immunity.
- **Pancreas** - regulates digestion and blood sugar. When you do not get the dark sleep required it throws the digestion tract off with bloating, gas, constipation or diarrhea. Also Leaky Gut Syndrome occurs,

which causes every meal you eat to be consumed by your white blood cells, which causes further immune stress. Also toxic by-products of mal-digestion start to store in any gland, organ or tissue causing them to become dysfunctional or dis-eased.

- **Adrenal glands** - secrete adrenaline to prepare you for action, to give you energy and to boost your immune system. Less dark sleep = sick and tired, dysfunctional and drained, dis-ease in the making.
- **Female/male reproductive glands - ovaries/testes -** when less than 9.5 hours of dark sleep occurs, this causes dysfunction and potential dis-ease of the female and male reproductive system. Infertility and impotency are common along with an acceleration of the aging process.
- Lack of the 9.5 hours of dark sleep first negatively affects the entire hormonal system, which then negatively affects every organ, every tissue and every cell in the entire body. This is not to mention the mental functions along with emotional responses.

Sleep and Fat

- As the days get longer in the summer months all mammals and **MAN,** physiologically prepare for a winter of food scarcity; carbohydrate cravings go up to eat more so as to store more fat in preparation for the winter.
- Insulin and cortisol levels stay elevated to mobilize the blood sugar. As the light is longer and the dark is shorter, food turns to fat very quickly and cholesterol is produced to protect the cell from cold.[50]
- This means if you do not get the 9.5 hours of dark sleep your body thinks it is the end of summer, so it turns everything you eat into fat and starts producing cholesterol. Also your sugar cravings skyrocket. These cravings are from lack of dark sleep, not lack of food.
- Since every carbohydrate you eat turns to fat and cholesterol, you in time start coating your arteries and increase your chances of heart disease, stroke and hypertension.
- Another sign of heart disease coming is depression because the dopamine/serotonin/insulin ratio is thrown out of balance. The long artificial days and short dark nights increase cooked carbohydrate cravings which produces depression and also increased cholesterol and fat in the body, even in a thin person.

Sleep and Sugar

- The pre-hibernatory physiology seen in mammals is: hyperlipidemia (high cholesterol), high blood pressure, and insulin resistance (so all carbohydrates turn into fat).[51]

- God intended mammals to have all the above, then either go to sleep for the winter or fast during the winter.
- For animals to survive the winter (short days and long dark nights) they had to become insulin resistant during the long days and short nights of summer so that all the carbohydrates they would eat would be sent into fat cell storage or cholesterol production.
- The fat stored would be energy for the fast and the cholesterol would protect the cell membranes from freezing.
- The carbohydrates eaten in the long days would turn into insulation and stored energy.
- When we do not get the necessary 9.5 hours of dark sleep because we stay up past the sunset with artificial light, we simulate a never-ending late summer day, which triggers all carbohydrates consumed to turn into fat and cholesterol. This increases chances of dying from the #1 killer in America - heart disease.
- This also makes us insulin resistant and develops into the #3 cause of death in America - diabetes.

Sleep and the Mind

- National Institutes of Mental Health state that the primary cause of depression, manic depression, bipolar disorder and schizophrenia is being out of rhythm in the light-dark cycle.[52]
- Cortisol, the hormone that helps you deal with stress and pain, is high during the day and drops during the night. High cortisol and high insulin is meant to be short term in longer days, but if the days are never-ending (with artificial light) this puts the mind in a state of panic.
- When the insulin/cortisol cycle is off due to short dark nights, true maniac depression and schizophrenia can occur.[53]
- Too little dopamine due to short dark nights can lead schizophrenia, manic depression, and bipolar disorder.
- Too much serotonin due to overeating refined carbohydrates (due to long artificial light days) and insulin resistance (serotonin and insulin work together; if one goes up, so does the other) cause you to feel paralyzed like you cannot do anything, paranoid, withdrawn and defensive.[54]
- Depressed, tired people have low dopamine and high serotonin levels.
- Dopamine controls memory and learning and motor function.
- High serotonin levels cause rigidity of behavior that can be repetitive as in obsessive-compulsive disorder.

■ High serotonin gives signs of tight stomach, pounding heart, high blood pressure, cold clammy hands, and a dry mouth.[55]

■ **The answer is found in 9.5 hours of dark sleep and elimination of all cooked, processed carbohydrates, including man-made fruit.**

Albert Einstein needed 10 hours of sleep to merely function and another two hours to do physics.

The Stages of Sleep

■ **Stage 1** - Light Sleep: muscles relax and body temperature drops as you drift in and out of the waking state.

■ **Stage 2** - Transition: heart rate, breathing, and electrical activity of the brain slow down.

■ **Stage 3,4** - Deep Sleep: the body shuts down to all stimuli, it is harder to awaken. Large, slow brain waves (delta waves) are seen; organs and tissues are repaired.

■ **Stage 5 - REM Sleep**: Eyes move, heartbeat and blood pressure rise, body is paralyzed. Brain activity greatly increases and vivid dreams occur. REM sleep occurs 70-90 minutes after you fall asleep and lasts about 30 minutes. Then the cycle begins again every 70-90 minutes.[56]

■ REM sleep is when the brain renews its energy stores, clears short-term memory and most importantly releases any built up negative energy from the day, or from the past. **In essence REM sleep is when you mentally/emotionally detoxify your self.**

■ The more hours you sleep in the dark night, the longer and longer the REM sleep intervals become, causing more renewing, more releasing of these stored mental/emotional toxins.

■ Remember that healing flows from spirit to mind/emotions to body. The longer the dark sleep the greater the healing in spirit/mind/emotion/body.

Sunlight

Just as the dark is critically important so is the light.

Without sunlight there would be no life on this planet. The base of all energy for all life, all cellular function, comes from the production of ATP (cell fuel) from the breakdown of sugars (grown from the sunlight) combined with oxygen. This highest energy and oxygen source is in chlorophyll-containing green plants.

Health benefits of Sunlight[57]

- Increases immune system response.
- Increases energy, endurance and muscular strength.
- Increases stress tolerance.
- Increases female/male hormone production.
- Decreases aging process.
- Decreases blood sugar.
- Decreases cholesterol.
- Decreases blood pressure and resting heart rate.
- Decreases depression, anxiety, and emotional highs/lows.
- Causes the production of vitamin D.

What Causes Poor Sleep?

- Low oxygen.
- Dehydration.
- Poor diet - refined, processed sugars, starches, poorly digested toxic animal products, caffeine, and salt.
- Lack of exercise.
- Present mental/emotional stress; future/past thinking.
- Stored mental/emotional toxins - past/generational.
- Any blockage in the flow of energy of life, causing excesses and deficiencies (floods and droughts).
- Organ/gland imbalances – 24-hour cycle.

What can you do?

- Go to bed as soon as you can after the sun goes down.
- Make sure you sleep 9.5 hours from that time in complete darkness - no light whatsoever.
- Wake up at dawn every morning.
- Take the TV out of your bedroom.
- Your bedroom should be the healthiest room in your house so remove carpet, drapes, and all electrical appliances.
- Get a Gauss meter and check EMF levels; some people cannot sleep unless the bedroom is 0.5mG or below.
- Unplug everything in the bedroom - keeps EMFs low.
- Purchase an all-wood bed frame and a mattress that is made out of natural materials. Metal conducts electricity, which over-stimulates the body.
- Sleep on your back with pillows or a sofa cushion under your knees or on your side with a pillow pinched between your knees to avoid nerve stress.
- Mattresses last 10 years tops. Replace with all natural.

- If there is outside lights where you live you must get light-proof blinds or drapes.
- Never take naps during the day unless it is absolutely necessary.
- If you are sound sensitive put a fan outside your door so it drowns out other noises.
- Exercise everyday - this will help you sleep better.
- Ground yourself to the earth by walking barefoot (grass/sand).
- Don't drink liquids within 3 hours of bedtime. Waking up at night to go to the bathroom breaks up the sleep cycle.
- All sugars and caffeine should be eliminated from the diet immediately.
- Don't eat anything stimulating before sleep, even health promoting items - this includes pepper, garlic, and onions.
- Get 30 minutes of sunlight per day in non-peak times - not between 10AM and 2PM.
- Remember when it is time to rest, rest, and when it is time to work, then work.
- **The American lifestyle predisposes us to dis-ease because we do not live by the light-dark cycles, we do not honor the 24-hour organ/gland cycle, we push when we should rest and we rest when we should push.**

Take a Lesson from the Animal Kingdom

Animals in the wild do not get cancer, heart disease, diabetes or any of the other dis-eases that mankind does. Why?

- They eat living food.
- They live in the moment.
- They live by the light-dark cycle.

The further we deviate from this schedule, the more we open ourselves up to imbalances, conditions and dis-eases of the body/mind complex.

How does the body rest?

- When the spirit (heart) is filled with peace.
- When the mind is filled with Truth.
- When the emotions (present, past, future, generational) have been replaced with love, joy, peace, hope, passion and compassion.
- This is when the body rests, this is when the body sleeps; this is when the body *heals*.

Rest in Him, cease striving, stop working (and doing from yourself), start being (one with Him), be in the moment, and know. Be still and know that I AM... (NIV)

Then comes His peace, then comes His doing; in and through you.

What is Good?

- Good is God, and doing what the Spirit of God living in your heart leads you to do.
- Jesus healed only those that the Spirit of God told Him to.
- After God finished creating He said, "it was Good," this was to say that it was perfect, complete and nothing ever need be added.
- Good (God) is not good (man's works and deeds).
- Good deeds can turn into bad deeds, good emotions can swing to bad emotions (happy-sad cycle), life-is-good can in a moment be turned into life-is-bad (good-bad cycle). These are all a product of our unrenewed old, ego, flesh, world, lie-filled mind.
- Good deeds of man are just eating from the fruit of the tree of knowledge of good and evil, the tree of good and bad.
- This good leads to expecting good in return and, if it is not returned, then the ego/world/flesh/religion filled old mind is fed.

Good is God.
Where there is Good there is the Way, the Truth, the Life, the Spirit.
Where there is Good there is no other way, no lie, no death, no flesh.

Doing good deeds

- I am going to help that person because it seems like the right thing to do (in my mind) - not realizing you might be interfering with their life journey - actually prolonging their pain and suffering.
- I am going to help that person because the Spirit of God has given me an overwhelming desire (in my heart) to do so - this is God doing His work through you - miraculous results are always seen - a life is changed, healed, released from bondage.

This is your part of the Covenant of Life, your part in the "love your neighbor as yourself"- joyfully rushing in to be used by God **when led by the Spirit of God living in you.**

A key in life is to be still, wait on God, do *no-thing* until He leads you, and when He does, get your mind out of the way and let the Spirit of God flow from your heart.

Do not try to do, just let go and let the Spirit of God lead you every step of your journey. Do what and only what He has called you to do, any more is in your own power and ability and this is like filthy rags to God.

The Spiritual Law of Opposites

- God's ways are not man's ways.
- There is a way that seems right (good) to a man but in the end it leads to death (separation from God). (NIV)
- God speaks through His Spirit who lives in your heart (the knowing), He does not speak through your mind (the knowledge).
- The doctor, the tests say you are sick but in your heart you know you are healing, your disease can become your blessing because to overcome it you must grow.
- Many times if you do the opposite that the world, the ego, the 5 senses, the flesh, the religion filled mind says, you are doing what God has put in your heart.

God has no opposite, needs no help

- The tree of life is where we enter the everlasting covenant relationship with God, where we become one with Him, where we receive the Spirit of God, where we receive eternal life, where we receive all knowing, all Truth. It is the place where God works and flows through us.
- The tree of the knowledge of good and evil is the place of man's knowledge, opinions, and thoughts. It is the place of man's abilities in himself, it is the place where man tries to do good (like God) in himself, where man tries to be like God without having the Spirit of God living in him, where his good is really bad because the True Good, God, is not in it.

The Spiritual Law of Opposites

- Life (eternally one with God in body, mind, and spirit) and death.
- Blessing (all that is His is yours, His covenant partner) and cursing.
- Truth (God's Word spoken in your heart) and lie.
- Good (God) and bad.
- Light (see the Truth, as things truly are) and darkness.
- Awake (aware of the Truth in the heart) and asleep (led by the old lie-filled mind).
- I have set before you life (the Truth revealed in your heart) and death (lie-filled old mind), blessings (walking in the Light, receiving from God your covenant partner) and curses (walking in the darkness, not receiving from God because you are not in covenant with Him). Now choose life. (NIV)
- They exchanged the truth of God for a lie, and worshiped and served created things rather than the Creator - who is forever praised. (NIV)
- God said, "The man has now become like one of us, knowing good and evil." (NIV) (After Adam and Eve broke the covenant with God by eating from the tree of knowledge of good and evil, their minds fell from grace and were filled with the lie. This elicited the first negative emotion of fear.)
- Even the darkness will not be dark to you; the night will shine like the day, for darkness is as light to you (the light of God is always shining above the clouds of your life situations and as you stay in His eternal present moment, the I AM never-ending Light shines, there is no more darkness). (NIV)
- So then, let us not be like others, who are asleep, but let us be alert (awake and watchful) and self-controlled. …But since we belong to the day, let us be self-controlled (flows from the Spirit), putting on faith (believing in the Truth which was spoken into our heart, and taking the physical action steps revealed to us) and love (covenant) as a breastplate, and the hope (knowing) of salvation (we are healed, set free, delivered, and made whole in body, mind, and spirit) as a helmet. (NIV)
- Life, Blessing, Truth, Good, Light, Awake
  These all represent products of the heart, the Spirit, a union or oneness with God.
- Death, cursing, lie, bad, darkness, asleep
  These all represent the products of the old mind - the world, ego, flesh, religious, past and future, physical, lie-bound mind, a separation from God.
- When we have experienced the darkness, how much brighter is the light?

152

- Once we have experienced dis-ease, how much more we value health.
- In marriage our covenant partner is our opposite. The two have become a complete ONE.

The Way of Peace

- I will praise the LORD, who counsels me; even at night my heart instructs me. I have set the LORD always before me. Because he is at my right hand, I will not be shaken (because He is my covenant partner). Therefore my heart is glad and my tongue rejoices; **my body also will rest secure**, because you will not abandon me (your covenant partner). …You have made known to me the path of life; you will fill me (my heart) with joy in your presence, with eternal pleasures at your right hand. (NIV)
- Great **peace** have they who love your law (the Truth spoken into our heart), and nothing can make them stumble. I wait for your salvation (wholeness in body, mind, and spirit), O LORD, and I follow your **commands** (the Truth spoken into our heart). I **obey** (listen to my heart and I do what it tells me to) your statutes, for I love them greatly. I **obey** your precepts and your statutes, for all my ways are known to you. (NIV)
- "Though the mountains be shaken and the hills be removed, yet my unfailing love (covenant) for you will not be shaken nor **my covenant of peace** be removed," says the LORD, who has compassion (covenant word) on you. (NIV)
- A heart at peace gives life to the body, but envy rots the bones. (When you follow your heart filled with Truth, peace flows to every part of your being; when you follow the self, ego, flesh, world, lie-filled old mind patterns, this produces emotional toxins which destroy organs, glands and tissues of the body.) (NIV)

The Covenant of Life

- Covenant with God
- Covenant with one's self
- Covenant with one's spouse
- Covenant with others

Covenant

- Two parties enter an agreement to strengthen their weakness, the two becoming one. This agreement lasts at least 8 generations.
- A bond for life or death.
- Always accompanied by the shedding of blood.
- Taking of oaths.

- If covenant is broken one party MUST kill the other party as payment for the breaking of the covenant, there is no choice in this, it must be done or the covenant has no power. The covenant's power is that the two have become one and will give everything they have to meet the need of the covenant partner, even to the giving of one's life for the other.

What is a covenant made of?

- Promises of blessing and cursing.
- Shedding of blood representing giving ones life for the covenant partner.
- Seal is the visible sign of the covenant.

Marriage: a Covenant Relationship

- Exchange of marriage vows - terms of the covenant: for richer or poorer, in sickness and in health until death do us part.
- Ring-the visible sign of the covenant.
- Woman takes on the husband's name.
- The two become one, each eagerly awaits to rush and meet the others needs, while praying and planning to give to the other.

Covenant -Marriage

How would a woman feel and what would she say if her husband sat on the couch watching TV and said:

- Honey, change the channel for me
- Honey, get me my glass of water on the counter
- Honey, pick up my coat on the floor

She would say I can do those things for you but why can't you do them yourself?

Now if her husband is on the couch, lying there sick she rushes to do those things and meet all his needs because where he is weak, she is strong, where he cannot do for himself, she does for him. This is love; this is the covenant.

Partners in Covenant

- Partner **A** desires to purchase a piece of property valued at $100,000. Partner **A** asks partner **B** for the $100,000 when he has $50,000 in the bank.
- This is an abomination to the covenant - asking for something from your covenant partner that you yourself have.
- You must get to the end of yourself before your covenant partner gives from himself.
- Abomination - Most of the Hebrew words translated "abomination" have the meaning of "impure," "filthy," and "unclean" - that which is foul-smelling and objectionable to a holy God....

All of us have been sinful (separated from God because we have followed our old lie-filled mind instead of our Truth-filled heart); even our best actions are filthy through and through (if done from our old, unrenewed, lie-filled mind instead of our Truth-filled heart). (TEV)

Covenant with God

How do you think God feels and what would He say if His covenant partner sat passively asking:

- God, heal my body.
- God, take away all these problems.
- God, heal my marriage.
- God, make me prosper.

He would say, "I can do for you and give to you all that I AM once you have given all that you have and all that you are."

Now if you are listening to His voice of peace spoken into your heart and are in faith obediently taking the action steps He has shown you at 100% of your ability, that's when He meets you with the rest, with all that He IS. This is the place of miracles, the place of healing. This is love. This is the covenant.

> **'Love the Lord your God with all your heart and with all your soul and with all your mind and with all your strength.' The second is this: 'Love your neighbor as yourself.' There is no commandment greater than these. (NIV)**

Covenant with One's Self

- This is loving yourself.
- This is the body-mind-spirit covenant.
- Covenant means all members are willing to give everything to the other in need, even if it means dying.
- Your body will die for your mind or your spirit (heart).
- Will your mind be allowed to be put to death for your spirit (heart)?
- Will your mind be allowed to be put to death for your body?

Modern research shows that body and soul cannot be observed separate from one another. Body and soul do not form two separate substances. Instead, they comprise the one individual human in an inseparable union. The body is one aspect of the whole individual existence.

- Keep your whole being-spirit, soul, and body-free from every **fault** (imbalance) at the coming of our Lord. (TEV)

■ Don't you know that your body is a temple of the Holy Spirit, who is in you, whom you have received from God? You are not your own; you were bought at a price (covenant). Therefore honor God with your body. (NIV)

■ It is not the spiritual that comes first, but the physical, and then the spiritual. (TEV)

■ What a strange thing a body would be if it had only one part! So he has made many parts, but still there is only one body. The eye can never say to the hand, "I don't need you." The head cannot say to the feet, "I don't need you." And some of the parts that seem weakest and least important are really the most necessary. ... So God has put the body together in such a way that extra honor and care are given to those parts that might otherwise seem less important. This makes for happiness among the parts, so that the parts have the same care for each other that they do for themselves. If one part suffers, all parts suffer with it, and if one part is honored, all the parts are glad. (TLB)

■ Offer your bodies as living sacrifices, holy (whole in body, mind and spirit) and pleasing to God (following the Truth-filled heart) - this is your spiritual act of worship. Do not conform any longer to the pattern of this world (world, ego, flesh, lie-filled old mind), but be transformed by the renewing of your mind (from the Truth-filled heart). Then you will be able to test and approve what God's will (His will is revealed in your heart so His will and your will are one) is - his good, pleasing and perfect will. (NIV)

Hundredfold Principle

■ One fold is the physical. (1X)
■ Tenfold is the mental/emotional. (10X)
■ Hundredfold is the spiritual. (100X)
■ Everything in your life is connected to this principle.
■ When we do things, think things, say things, and know things there is the hundredfold principle always being demonstrated.

Hundredfold Decrease

■ 1 Fold Decrease (-1X) - if you do not get the 9.5 hours of dark sleep, then it will in time decrease the life of the body (physical).

■ 10 Fold Decrease (-10X) - if the decrease sleep is for your own gain, feeding your ego, filling your mind with world filled TV, movies (mental/emotional).

■ 100 Fold Decrease (-100X) - if the lack of sleep causes you to feed the flesh (the negative mind, emotion, body energy) by either eating dead, cooked, pleasurable food, or being addicted to the TV/computer, the flow of the Spirit is blocked. If the flesh increases, the Spirit flow decreases (spiritual).

Hundredfold Increase

- 1 Fold Increase (1X) - if you get to bed when the sun goes down, and get up when the sun comes up getting 9.5 hours of dark sleep, it will bring life, health and strength to the body (physical).
- 10 Fold Increase (10X) - if the sleep reminds us (brings back into our memory) of our covenant with God, our covenant with our selves, keeps us thinking on whatever is true, whatever is right, whatever is pure, whatever is lovely, whatever is...excellent or praiseworthy.... And the God of peace will be with you (mental/emotional). (NIV)
- 100 Fold Increase (100X) - if the sleep is offered as a worship to God: offer your bodies as living sacrifices, holy and pleasing to God-this is your spiritual act of worship (spiritual). (NIV)

The Mind of Peace

- You will keep in **perfect peace** him whose mind is **steadfast** (still), because he trusts in you (His covenant partner). (NIV)
- What does a man get for all the toil and anxious striving with which he labors under the sun? All his days his work is pain and grief; even at night his mind does not rest. (NIV)
- Do not be anxious (old lie-filled mind) about anything, but in everything, by prayer (listening to the Truth revealed in your heart) and petition, with thanksgiving, present your requests to God. And the **peace** of God, which transcends all understanding (of the mind), will guard your hearts and your minds (supremeconscious, conscious and unconscious)... (NIV)
- For the mind set on the flesh (lie-filled old mind) is death, but the mind (supremeconscious mind - the mind of God in us, and the conscious mind renewed with Truth and willfully listening to the heart) set on the Spirit is life and peace, because the mind set on the flesh is hostile toward God; for it does not subject itself to the law of God (Truth in the heart), for it is not even able to do so, and those who are in the flesh cannot please God (because they do not listen to the Truth-filled heart). (NASU)
- Their destiny is destruction, their god is their stomach, and their glory is in their shame. Their mind is on earthly (world/ego/flesh) things. But our citizenship is in heaven (whose home is the Truth-filled heart). (NIV) Where is heaven? "The kingdom of God (heaven) is within you." It is in your heart.
- Therefore I tell you, do not worry (old lie-filled mind byproduct) about your life, what you will eat; or about your body, what you will wear. Life is more than food, and the body more than clothes.

Consider the ravens: They do not sow or reap; they have no storeroom or barn; yet God feeds them. And how much more valuable you are than birds! Who of you by worrying can add a single hour to his life? Since you cannot do this very little thing, why do you worry about the rest? Consider how the lilies grow. They do not labor or spin. Yet I tell you, not even Solomon in all his splendor was dressed like one of these. If that is how God clothes the grass of the field, which is here today, and tomorrow is thrown into the fire, how much more will he clothe you, O you of little faith (not believing in the Truth that has been revealed to your heart and taking the actions steps that Truth calls for)! And do not set your heart on what you will eat or drink; do not worry about it. For the pagan world runs after all such things, and your Father knows that you need them. *But seek his kingdom, and these things will be given to you as well.* (NIV) (Follow the Truth He speaks into your heart rather than the lies the world, flesh and ego speak to your mind.)

The Kingdom of Peace

- For the kingdom of God is not a matter of eating and drinking, but of righteousness (right with God = covenant with God, following your heart of Truth), peace and joy in the Holy Spirit. (NIV)
- But the fruit of the Spirit is love, joy, peace, patience, kindness, goodness, faithfulness, gentleness and self-control. Against such things there is no law (nothing of the mind). (NIV)
- The kingdom of God does not come with your careful observation, nor will people say, 'Here it is,' or 'There it is,' because the kingdom of God is within you. (NIV)

Knowing

- Knowing is God speaking to our heart, our mind and our body with His love, His joy, His peace.
- When God's knowing is in your spirit/heart it is called love.
- When God's knowing is in your heart, which begins to fill your mind and will, it is called hope, patience and confidence.
- When God's knowing is in your heart and it manifests into physical form, it is called faith, action, obedience and perseverance.
- The greatest desire of mankind is to know God, know His voice and know His will (direction or path) for their lives, to know they are making the right decisions.
- This knowing comes with a deep sense of inner peace, the calm in the midst of the storm.
- To hear His voice of peace spoken into your heart, you must be still - still the mind, still the emotions and still the body. Still - to bring into balance and harmony the body, mind and spirit.

■ To hear His peace in your heart you must first balance the physical, then the mind and emotions. Then the Spirit can flow unhindered bringing peace to your heart, mind and body.

How to Heal Your Body/Mind/Spirit

■ Enter covenant with the Living God.

■ Enter covenant with yourself - your body, your mind and your spirit.

■ Doing all you have been shown in your heart and never stopping no matter how long it takes and the rest will be done for you (healing is not your responsibility, it's God's; your responsibility is to be faithful and obedient to what He has shown you).

■ Starting the race strong and finishing it strong.

■ Only thing that stops the power of God and His flow of healing and blessing is **YOU**:
  ■ Quitting
  ■ Stopping
  ■ Giving up
  ■ Not believing in the Truth.

Sabbath Rest

■ There remains, then, a Sabbath-rest for the people of God; for anyone who enters God's rest (His covenant partnership) also rests from his own work (product of the old lie-filled mind instead of the Truth-filled heart).... Let us, therefore, make every effort to enter that rest, so that no one will fall by following their example of disobedience. (NIV)

■ Disobedience is **not listening** to your heart and **not taking** the actions steps your heart shows you, but instead listening to your head, your old, unrenewed, lie-filled mind and doing what it tells you.

■ Disobedience is also doing anything (even good works) apart from what God puts in your heart.

■ Everything that does not come from faith (believing the Truth He has spoken into your heart and taking the physical action steps you have been shown) is sin (separation from God). (NIV)

What is God's name?
His name is "I Am," not "I was" or "I will be".
God is only in the present moment,
not future and not the past.

How to Know You are *Not* in the Present Moment

■ You are thinking, analyzing, remembering and planning.

■ You are bored, stressed, uneasy, tense, frustrated, anxious, and worried.

■ You have negative emotions - fear, dread, resentment, bitterness, unforgiveness, guilt, regret, sadness, and grief.

How to Know You are in the Present Moment

■ You experience an incredible sense of love, joy, peace and hope.

■ You feel God's love so strong that nothing else matters but this moment. You are in love. When you fell in love each moment lasted for days, even weeks. You were present in the moment and stayed present. When you added time, everything changed; you took your eyes off the moment and went into the future with job/career, family/responsibility, and yourself.

■ You see God in everything and everyone.

■ You are never bored, not thinking, not remembering, not emotional, just "being" who you were created to be.

How to "Be" in the Present Moment

■ See the love of God in everything and everyone; see them as spirit beings with blockages and imbalances.

■ See the big picture in life as God sees it; always remember you are 99.9% spirit being and .1% physical.

■ Live every moment as if you had no more moments but this one.

■ Practice silence. This stills the mind (absent in the mind, present in the moment).

■ Object focus - flowing water, fire.

■ Body awareness - focus on breathing, on feeling the energy of life flow into each part of your body.

Nobody can steal your joy, your present moment unless you let them by going back into the old you, the world/ego/self/flesh/lie-filled mind that lives in the past and the future.

You are like the ocean, there may be storms, waves, hurricanes, or calm at the surface but deep down under it is always calm.
This is timeless.
This is deathless.

There are no problems in life, only situations, conditions and tests to help us grow in our ultimate purpose
to be free in spirit,
to be free in mind,
to be free in body.

Being brings forth Doing
- You must first crawl
- Then you can walk
- Then you can run
- Then you can climb
- Then you can fly
- Then you can be
- And out of the being will come the doing of God's will, His good, pleasing, perfect will.

To be in the presence of God you MUST be in the present moment. The more totally present you are in the moment the more Peace of God you will experience.

How do we grow closer to God?
- First principle - It is not the spiritual that comes first, but the physical, and then the spiritual. (TEV)
- Stay balanced with the 7 basic steps to total health: air, water, food, sleep, exercise, fasting and prayer.
- Next the body/mind/spirit covenant will direct the energy of healing to release old mind patterns and negative stored emotional responses from your present, future, past and generations.
- Next you will be presented with tests, everything in life is a test. Pass the test and you grow. Fail the test and you will take it again. When you fail, just have a new battle plan for the next moment and keep the 7 basic steps balanced.
- As you pass your tests you become free. The freer you become the more the Spirit of God can flow **in you** to bring total health to your body, mind and spirit and **through you** to touch the world around you.

■ Then you will live life to the full, being one with God and keeping His commandments of 'Love the Lord your God with all your heart and with all your soul and with all your mind and with all your strength.' The second is this: 'Love your neighbor as yourself.' There is no commandment greater than these. (NIV)

■ Then you will be, and out of that being you will do all the Good (God) works that He has created you for.

■ You will know the Truth and the Truth will set you free. (NIV)

When you lie down, you will not be afraid;
when you lie down, your sleep will be sweet.
I will lie down and sleep in peace,
for you alone, O LORD,
make me dwell in safety. **(NIV)**

_____
_____
_____
_____
_____
_____
_____
_____
_____
_____
_____
_____
_____
_____
_____
_____
_____
_____
_____
_____
_____
_____

Go Deeper

1. What are 7 things that lack of sleep causes and what does this mean to your total health of body, mind, and spirit?
2. What does nature teach us about sleep?
3. Why is the Light – Dark cycle so critical for health and healing?
4. What happens to your body when you go to sleep past 9PM, according to the 24-hour organ/gland cycle?
5. What time should you go to sleep to maintain total health of body, mind, and spirit and why is the time that you go to sleep more important that just how many hours you sleep?
6. Since we live in a very toxic environment, why are the effects of chemical carcinogens and sleep patterns in mice so important to us?
7. How much faster does your body degenerate and age when you do not get the right number of hours of sleep, getting to bed at the right time, and why does this occur?
8. How does lack of 9.5 hours of dark sleep cause you to increase your cholesterol and increase your heart disease risk (the #1 cause of death in America)?
9. How does lack of 9.5 hours of dark sleep cause you to become insulin resistant, increasing your diabetes risk (#3 cause of death in America)?
10. How does lack of 9.5 hours of dark sleep increase your risk of all diseases and disorders of the mind, especially anxiety, depression, manic depression, bipolar disorder, obsessive – compulsive disorder, and schizophrenia?
11. Is sunlight good or bad for you, does it help you heal or increase your cancer risk, and how does, oxygen, water, food, and sleep affect this?
12. Why does the American lifestyle predispose us to disease?
13. What are the 3 critical lessons we can learn from the wild animals?
14. When is doing good deeds not good?
15. Why is the spiritual law of opposites so vital to your total health of body, mind, and spirit?
16. What does the "Sabbath Rest" really mean and how does it affect our physical health, our mental/emotional health and our spiritual health?
17. Why is it so vital to stay in the present moment?
18. How does the hundredfold principle apply to your sleep?
19. How can sleep be turned into a powerful worship to God?

Exercise

Exercise Facts

- 9 out of 10 Americans get little or no exercise on a daily basis.
- 40% of Americans are completely sedentary (much higher in the elderly).
- Only 20% of Americans are said to be active in any reasonable amount.
- Only 5% of Americans get the amount of exercise needed to maintain health.
- In 1900 human labor accounted for 80% of the total calories expended to work the land, even though tractors and combines were in widespread use.
- Today human labor accounts for only 1% of calories expended because of automation.

Entropy is the natural process of breaking down. Work is the orderly application of energy. Entropy is slowed by work, without work energy just dissipates. One of the best ways to slow entropy is give the body and mind something to do.

Reversing Previous effects of Entropy

Tufts University researchers showed 10 markers for age that are considered reversible with exercise:[58]

- Lean body (muscle) mass, strength, body fat
- Basal metabolic rate, aerobic capacity
- Blood pressure, blood sugar imbalance
- Cholesterol/HDL ratio
- Bone density
- Body temperature regulation
    - Muscle mass - the average American loses 6.6 pounds of muscle every 10 years after young adulthood - answer is exercise.
    - Strength - between the ages of 30 and 70 the average person loses 20 % of the motor units (muscles and motor nerves) in the muscle groups everywhere in the body – answer is exercise.

- Basal metabolic rate (how many calories needed to sustain itself) decreases 2% every 10 years after the age of 20 - improved with sleep and exercise.
- Body fat - between age 20 and 65, the average person doubles their ratio of fat to muscle. This increases even higher if a person overeats and has a sedentary lifestyle - answer is living/raw diet, sleep and exercise.
- Aerobic capacity - by age 65 the body's ability to use oxygen efficiently decreases by 40% - breathing technique, exercise and diet improve.
- Blood sugar - as an average person ages the blood sugar stability decreases, increasing the chances of diabetes - answer is living/raw diet and exercise.
- Cholesterol/HDL - this ratio gets higher as normal Americans age, diet and exercise are big factors - answer living/raw diet, sleep, exercise.
- Bone density - calcium is lost from bones as average Americans age, increasing the risk of osteoporosis, but why? High protein diets and lack of exercise - the answer is living/raw food and exercise.
- Body temperature regulation - the steady 98.6 degrees F decreases with age, making people more vulnerable to cold weather. Answer - sleep and exercise.

Researchers from Tufts University have proven that building muscle mass and strength late in life after age 45 can significantly rejuvenate your WHOLE physiology.

The more you use the body the better it gets, the more the muscles strengthen, the denser the bones become. Age is not a factor.

Weight Training and the Elderly

- Tufts University study selected the frailest nursing home residents and put them on a weight-training program. The age group was 87 to 96.[59]
- Within eight weeks wasted muscles came back by 300%.

- Coordination and balance improved, activities of daily living, which were given up now returned.
- Residents who were unable to walk unassisted could now get up and walk to the bathroom in the middle of the night by themselves.
- What was thought to be injurious to them actually caused them to thrive. They now believed they could do things that fear had taken away (break mind barrier).

Weight Training and Ages 60-72

- Tufts research took men between ages 60-72 and put them on supervised weight training sessions 3 times per week for three months.[60]
- The men were to train at 80% of their maximum they could lift one time.
- After three months the strength had greatly increased, the size of their quadriceps had more than doubled, the size of their hamstrings had more than tripled; these men could lift heavier boxes than the 25 year-olds working in the training lab.
- The men in this study felt much younger and much better about themselves than they had in years.

A person who is confined to complete bed rest for two weeks will have the same bone and muscle loss as someone who has aged ten years.

Disuse Syndrome

- When the body is not being used it begins to shut down in **ALL systems.**
- Stanford's Dr. Bortz found when a person gives up physical exercise the following appear[61]:
  - Heart, arteries and the cardiovascular system become at risk.
  - Muscles and bones become more fragile.
  - Obesity becomes a high risk.
  - Depression begins.
  - The body begins to biologically age much faster than its calendar years.

Depression and Exercise

- Russian cosmonauts when subjected to the inactivity of space flight started to become depressed, but as soon as they were put on an exercise program in space the depression stopped.[62]
- Neurochemicals called catecholamines are very low in depressed people. These are raised to normal levels with regular exercise.

Aerobic capacity, Gravity and Aging

- Swedish physiologist Bengt Saltin tested the effects of complete bed rest on the human body.[63]
- Tested men ranged from extremely fit to sedentary. They were to remain lying in bed 24 hours a day for 3 weeks.
- All the subjects, no matter what their previous physical condition was, suffered an aerobic capacity decrease equivalent to 20 years of aging.
- When the subjects were allowed to stand 5 minutes a day without moving the loss was almost completely prevented - this is the positive effect of gravity on our bodies.

Bone Density in Runners vs. Non-runners

- Tufts Aging Center showed an increase in leg bone density in runners even though their body weight was 20% lighter.[64]
- An amazing result of the research was that the bones in the forearm also become denser even though they were not bearing any weight load.
- The whole body started to respond to the exercise, not just some parts.
- **MORE** - what you do to one part you do to the whole. God made our body so miraculous that when one area is stressed, the message is sent out through out all the cells to prepare for the stress so they ALL respond. This is the body, mind, spirit covenant in action, all looking out for the other - "all are one."

Use it or lose it.
When you use it, your whole being benefits.

Exercise and Death Rate

- Study done among Harvard alumni tracked 16,936 graduates found that those who burned 2,000 or more calories a week in exercise had a 28% lower death rate.[65]

Walking vs. Sedentary Life

■ Study at Brown University on 4,500 people between the ages of 40-85 showed that those who remained only moderately active by walking regularly gained a 25-year advantage in performance over those who retired to a sedentary life.[66]

Walking vs. Running

■ Study done at the Institute of Aerobics Research led by Dr. Blair showed the importance of moderate exercise. 10,224 men and 3,120 women who appeared to be in good health were tested. They participated in a treadmill test. Based on their level of fitness they were divided into 5 groups. Group 1 - the least fit. Group 5 - the most fit. The test was conducted over 8 years.

■ Results were that the least fit (group 1) had a death rate more than 3 times higher than the most fit (group 5).

■ The most important finding was that the most benefit from the exercise was found between group 1 and group 2. **Walking 30 minutes per day (the activity of group 2) reduced premature death almost as much as running 30 to 40 miles per week (activity level of group 5).**[67]

■ Further found was that in groups 2 through 5 deaths were lower from all causes, when compared to the sedentary group 1.

The God designed exercise is walking.

Types of Exercise

■ Cellular - increased lymphatic flow, increased gravity effect on cells.
■ Cardiovascular - increased heart rate.
■ Strengthening - increased muscle strength and mass.
■ Stretching - lengthening connective tissue, muscles, fascia, tendons.

Cellular Exercise

■ Cellular exercise is one that utilizes the forces of acceleration, deceleration and gravity as it strengthens every single cell in the body at the same time. Cellular exercise or rebounding is the ultimate exercise for the immune system causing the circulating white blood cell count to triple. This threefold increase in WBC's literally means your immune system can consume cancer cells, bacteria, viruses, parasites and fungi three times as fast.

- Cellular exercise
  - Strengthens veins and arteries
  - Strengthens internal organs, glands
  - Strengthens muscles, tendons, bones, tissues
  - Strengthens eyes, ears, and skin
  - Increases lymphatic circulation
  - Increases strength
  - Increases endurance
  - Increases cardiovascular fitness
  - Increases weight loss
  - Increases balance, coordination, rhythm and timing
  - **Exercises and strengthening all cells**. According to Albert Carter, rebounding authority, "*Your cells depend upon the diffusion of water through their semi-permeable cell membranes to carry oxygen, nutrients, hormones and enzymes into the cell and flush out metabolic trash. The rate of diffusion of water into and out of the cells under normal conditions is 100 times the volume of fluid inside each cell each second. The oscillation of the cells between an increase G force and no G force 200 times a minute (with rebounding) increased the diffusion of water, into each cell at least threefold.*"[68] Also the strength of the cell is determined by the strength of its cell membrane. Sickly or weak cells rupture and die easily while healthy cells resist rupturing. Exercising at a higher G force causes the cells to naturally strengthen their membranes, thus producing stronger and healthier cells.
  - **Increased lymphatic circulation**. This is probably one of the greatest benefits of all. Cellular exercise can increase lymph flow by up to 30 times. The lymphatic channels are made up of one-way valves that open when the pressure below them is greater than above them and close when the reverse occurs. The up and down motion that occurs while rebounding activates the one-way valves to their maximum and this happens two hundred times a minute.[69] The lymphatic system is the heart of the immune system and lymphatic circulation is vital to the movement of the white blood cells to destroy bacteria, viruses, parasites, fungi and cancer cells. If the lymph fluid moves slowly the white blood cells cannot get to and fight the invaders or abnormal cancer cells quickly enough, so disease develops.

It is also vitally important to know that the circulating white blood cell count triples after just one minute of rebounding and stays that way for 1 hour. This means more white blood cells to eat cancer cells, bacteria, viruses, parasites and fungi. The lymphatic system is a major route for the body to detoxify itself. The more lymphatic movement, the more detoxification and cleansing (at least tripled).

- **Increases strength and endurance** by exercising in a higher gravitational force atmosphere. Jumping on a rebounder can increase G forces up to 3.5, which means that your muscles adjust to an increased G force by becoming stronger.[70]

- **Increased cardiovascular fitness** - NASA report stated that rebounding is up to 68 percent more efficient than running. This rebounding developed more biomechanical work with less energy expended, thus less oxygen used and less demand placed on the heart. Also the ratio of oxygen consumption compared to biomechanical conditioning is more than twice as efficient as treadmill running.

- **Increase weight loss.** The NASA study showed that rebounding was 68% more efficient than treadmill running, so it hits the 90% fat burning stage in less than half the time of regular aerobic type exercises.

- With regular cardiovascular aerobic exercises like jogging, bike riding, aerobics, etc., the following time is allowed before we start burning fat:

- First 10 minutes burns   90% glucose, 10% fat
  20-30 minutes burns   70% glucose, 30% fat
  After 30 minutes burns   10% glucose, 90% fat

- **Because rebounding is 68% more efficient than the other cardiovascular aerobic exercises it hits the 90% fat burn stage in approximately 12 minutes instead of 30 minutes. This means it takes less time to burn more fat.**

- Increases Neurological Organization.

- Dr Akselsen of the Texas Association of Children with Learning Disabilities found, in over 40 years of working with learning disabled children, three common denominators in all of them: extremely poor coordination, balance and rhythm.

- According to Dr. Akselsen, *"Rebounding should start in nursery school. I see mind/body improvement occur throughout the growth period of the human organism. When I work with a child who has all kind of coordination problems culminating in learning disabilities, it means he or she has not worked with the gross and fine motor nerve/muscle coordinates. When you are rebounding you are moving and exercising every brain cell as you are each of the other body cells. Toxic heavy metals are leached out of these brain cells to free up neurons to work more effectively. Better nourishment has a chance to penetrate the cell walls too. Furthermore, rebounding has you work from the outside, from the nerve endings toward the brain.*"[71]

- Neurological Reorganization
  Mrs. Franet, teacher of aphasic students (loss of the ability to speak or comprehend words), shares the progress of one of her students once rebounding was introduced. "At the beginning of the school year Frances could not coordinate her small motor development enough to draw a circle or copy a single letter. Her hand eye coordination was nil. Her speech was unintelligible.
    - After one month of rebounding she was bouncing with two feet by herself. In four months, Fran was running and dancing on it.
    - In four months she could read her name when she wrote it. She could draw circles. In six months she could trace the letters of her last name. In eight months she could copy her last name. In nine months she could write her name by herself…Frances's verbal expression developed along with her written and motor expression. She was using simple sentences, gradually extending them into whole paragraphs by the end of these nine months. Her receptive language improved also."[72]

What you do to one part of your being, you do to it all. When you develop your body, it in turn develops your mind, and when you free your mind from the world's knowledge, the lies, the flesh, the ego, time and physicality, your body heals.

Cardiovascular Exercise

- Any exercise that causes a sustained increase in the heart rate has the beneficial effects of:
    - Increasing the movement of oxygen, nutrients into the cells and increasing the movement of waste products out of the cells.
    - Increasing the strength of the heart muscle itself, which makes it pump more efficiently, less beats per minute with more blood being pumped.
- Examples of cardiovascular exercise include walking, bike riding, swimming, running and, the best, rebounding cellular exercise.

Benefits of Cardiovascular Exercise

- Lowers the death rate from all diseases.
- Reduces cancer risk.
- Reduces heart disease risk.
- Lowers blood pressure.
- Reduces stress.
- Increases mental abilities.
- Acts as an antidepressant.
- Increases the immune system response.
- Reduces body fat.
- Reduces constipation.

Strengthening Exercise

- Defined as any exercise that causes the muscle fibers to break down so they can rebuild larger, causing a greater ability to contract against gravity or weight = strength.
- Examples include weight training, body training (push-ups, pull-ups, sit-ups), isometric training, and strength bounce rebounding.

Benefits of Strengthening Exercise

- Building muscle mass and strength can significantly regenerate ones whole physiology.
- By keeping the spinal support muscles (back and front) strong you keep the nervous system in balance, which in turn keeps the organ/gland function at optimal levels.
- Blood pressure decreases.
- Blood sugar stabilizes.
- Metabolism increases.
- Bone density increases.

Strengthening and stretching exercises are done to reverse the negative affects of gravity and poor posture.

Muscles that are weak become overstretched; they must be strengthened. Muscles that are over tightened must be stretched. Strengthening and stretching should be done to the entire body especially emphasizing ideal anterior to posterior (front to back) posture.

Stretching Exercises

- Defined as an elongation or lengthening of the connective tissue of the body. This includes muscles, tendons, and fascia.
- Slow sustained lengthening of the connective tissue allows more maximal contraction of the muscle fibers.
- Lengthening of the connective tissue allows for a release in any stored tension, toxin or emotions stored in the fascia.

Stretching

- When one goose swims into another goose's space there is a short-term conflict, then the geese flap their wings and continue to swim gracefully in opposite directions as if nothing ever occurred.
- The flapping of the wings is a stretching to release any negative energy that would try to store in the system after the conflict.
- Cats always stretch when they get up before they walk, run or jump. Stretching prepares for motion.

Benefits of Stretching

- Increases strength by lengthening the muscles so they can contract more fully, more powerfully.
- Increases flexibility and movement, life is motion.
- Releases tension, stress (similar to REM sleep) both physical and mental/emotional that tries to store in the tissue.
- Improves posture/structure and structure dictates function. The nervous system is controlled by the structure and posture of the spine. The nervous system controls organ/gland function.
- Improves organ/gland function via the embryonic nerve levels and the energetic pathways, i.e.: The liver is embryonically/energetically connected to the rhomboid muscles, which are in the middle upper back especially on the right. If the liver is dysfunctional then one will have pain/tightness or weakness in the rhomboid muscles in the middle back. Conversely if the rhomboid muscles are tight/weak from poor posture or muscle weakness from disuse then the liver can become dysfunctional.
- The muscles support the spine and the spine houses the nervous system and the nervous system controls all organ and gland function.

- Since the specific muscles share embryonic/energetic pathways with specific organs and glands, what you do to one, you do to the other.
- If you tighten or weaken a muscle due to overuse, under use, injury or poor posture, you negatively affect the organ/gland associated with it. When you stretch and strengthen the muscle you positively affect its associated organ/gland.

Organ/Gland/Body Part/Muscle

Organ/Gland	Body Part	Muscles
Stomach	Neck, Shoulder, Elbow, Wrist	Pectoralis clavicular Brachioradialis Neck flexor
Spleen	TMJ, Shoulder	Mid trapezius Low trapezius
Pancreas	Mid back(L), Shoulder, Low back, Wrist, thumb	Latissimus dorsi Opponens pollicis
Large Intestine	Low back, Pelvis, Knee	Tensor fascia lata Hamstring, Quadratus lumborum
Lung	Shoulder, Ribs	Deltoids,Diaphragm, Anterior serratus, Coracobrachialis
Bladder	Entire spine, Sacrum, Pelvis, Ankle,Foot	Ant.tibial, Peroneus longus,brevis Sacrospinalis, Iliacus

Kidney	Lumbar spine, Shoulder, hip	Psoas, Up. trapezius, Iliacus
Liver	Mid back (R), Shoulders	Pectoralis sternal Rhomboids
Gall Bladder	Knee, Lower neck, Hip	Popliteus, Iliacus
Small Intestine	Pelvis, Knee, Pubic bone	Quadriceps, Transverse, rectus abdominus
Heart	Shoulder(L), Scapula (L) Ribs	Subscapularis
Thyroid	Shoulder, Elbow, Wrist	Teres minor
Adrenals	Pelvis, Knee	Gracilis, Sartorius Gastrocnemius Soleus
Male/Female	Pelvis,Hip,Neck,Elbow, Thumb	Piriformis, Gluteus med/max

The Best Exercise for the Cell

■ Rebounding cellular exercise done as the:
   ■ **Health bounce** - feet stay on the rebounder and a vibrational up and down rhythm is achieved (approximately 200 times per minute) to exchange fluids in and out of the cell.
   ■ **Strength bounce** - one jumps up so feet leave the rebounder. This greatly increases the G forces on all cells of the body strengthening every cell. It increases the longevity of the cells by strengthening their membranes.

The Best Exercise for Lymphatic Movement

■ Rebounding cellular exercise done as the:
   ■ **Health bounce**-feet stay on the rebounder and a vibrational up and down rhythm is achieved (approximately 200 times per minute) to exchange fluids in and out of the cell. This is done along with deep diaphragm breathing exercises of maximum inhalation and release while doing the health bounce. **Just 1-3 minutes of these combined, cause a more than tripling of the lymphatic flow for 1 hour. This means 3 times more white blood cells to eat bacteria, viruses, parasites, fungi and cancer cells. This also means a tripled rate of the removal of toxins out of the system.**

The Best Exercise for Cardiovascular Fitness

■ Rebounding cellular exercise done as the:
   ■ **Aerobic bounce**- walking, jogging or running on the rebounder. Starting at 1 minute per day and progressing up to 30 minutes per day.
   ■ **Walking** outside on a softer surface at same schedule.

The Best Exercise for Strengthening

■ Rebounding cellular exercise done as the:
   ■ **Strength bounce** - one jumps up so feet leave the rebounder. This greatly increases the G forces on all cells of the body strengthening every cell. Increasing the muscle tone and strength. Regular strength bouncing on the rebounder greatly increases the strength of all the muscles of the body.
   ■ **Health bounce** - this is done moving the arms and legs, torso in different positions to stress muscle groups. Can be done with weights to increase the muscle stress.
   ■ **Machine or free weight training**

The Best Exercise for Stretching

- Rebounding cellular exercise done as the:
  - **Health bounce** - this is done moving the arms, shoulders, hips, legs, neck and torso in different positions to stretch various muscle groups. When stretching is done as you do the vibratory rhythmic health bounce, it not only stretches the muscle groups but also strengthens them at the same time. Include deep diaphragm breathing in the exercise and you have an ideal stretch to the area.
  - **Static stretching** done standing, sitting or lying on the floor.
- All stretching should be to reverse gravity/postural strain, especially in the front to back plane.

Goal Oriented vs. Heart's Desire

Goal Oriented

- Exercise to bring down cholesterol number.
- Exercise at 70% maximum aerobic capacity.
- Exercise because the research shows the benefits.
- Exercise because you should or because you have to.

Heart's Desire

- Exercise because you KNOW it is in your heart.
- Exercise because you are one in body, mind and spirit. You love yourself.
- Exercise because God has called you to take care of His temple.
- Exercise because it brings glory to God, it becomes a worship to God. (100X)

The African tribal messenger runs up to 50 miles barefoot on hot sand in scorching sun and when he reaches his destination he does not hyperventilate, he does not have heart palpitations, he does not perspire, he is not dehydrated, he does not tear muscles or pull ligaments. Why not?
The African tribal messenger runs as one in spirit, in mind and in body. He runs one with nature and one with God. His running (doing) comes out of his being (one with God, one with nature).

The American jogger runs to lose weight, decrease his cholesterol, to get in shape, to meet his fitness goals, to reduce his stress, to feel better about himself. He runs as if he is running for his life. He injures his back, knees ankles and feet. What is the difference? The American jogger runs to achieve a goal, to improve himself in some way.

He runs for the physical benefits shown him in his mind. He doesn't run to be one with God, one with nature. He runs for the running (doing) alone instead of the running (doing) coming from the heart (being one with God).[73]

How do we grow a strong muscle?
Stress the muscle until it breaks down, then it will rebuild larger and stronger.
How do we grow strong spiritually?
Stress (suffering) the old (world/self/flesh/religion/time/physical bound) mind until it breaks down (dies), then the Spirit of God will flow into your heart (spirit) and supremeconscious mind unhindered.

Most Important Areas to Exercise
- Not your body
- Not your mind
- Your spirit
- Your free will
- Your faith

Physical exercise has some value, but spiritual exercise is valuable in every way, because it promises life both for the present and for the future. This is a true saying, to be completely accepted and believed.
(TEV)

Surely you know that many runners take part in a race, but only one of them wins the prize. Run, then, in such a way as to win the prize. Every athlete in training submits to strict discipline, in order to be _crowned with a wreath_ that will not last; but we do it for one that will last forever (victory that leads to freedom when we persevere with what is in our heart). That is why I run straight for the finish line; that is why I am like a boxer who does not waste his punches. I harden my body with _blows_ (suffering) and bring it under _complete control_ (by following my heart not my mind - breaking the mind barrier), to keep myself from being disqualified. (TEV)

Physical vs. Spiritual Training
Physical
- To win a medal.
- To be someone.
- To be better than everyone else.
- To be self disciplined.
- To be in control.

Spiritual Training
- To have victory/freedom.
- To be "one with God."
- To be "one with each other"- love your neighbor as yourself.
- To have self control.

To let Gods Spirit control and guide you.
- Do we run this race we call life for physical rewards or spiritual ones?
- Be careful not to do your 'acts of righteousness' before men, to be seen by them. If you do, you will have no reward from your Father in heaven (doing from a religious mind instead of a Truth-filled heart). (NIV)
- But love your enemies, do good to them, lend to them without expecting to get anything back. Then your reward will be great (when following what God speaks to your heart, not what religion/ego speaks to your mind). (NIV)

■ His work will be shown for what it is… It will be revealed with fire, and the fire will test the quality of each man's work. If what he has built survives, he will receive his reward. (The fire is God's Spirit and His Spirit does not consume what was done from your Truth-filled heart, but will totally burn up and destroy that which was done from a ego, religion, world-filled old mind.) (NIV)

Self Discipline vs. Self Control

■ Self discipline is a product of the mind
■ Self discipline will always fail if it is put to a strong enough test, a great amount of suffering. Why? Because it is of the conscious mind and the mind has limitations.
■ Self Control is of the Spirit
■ Self Control will never fail no matter what the test or how great the suffering because it is God working in and through you. Why? Because once you put your old mind (world/lie/self/ego/flesh/religious/time/physical mind) to death, the spirit (heart) and supremeconscious mind (the mind of God in you) flow with the self control that never ends, because it comes from the infinite and eternal God.

To grow spiritually there must be some stress applied (suffering)

Types of suffering include:
■ Sickness and dis-ease.
■ Broken relationships - marriage, family, friends.
■ Foundation shaken - built on sinking sand of the worlds' knowledge (lies).
■ Financial crisis, job loss.

Suffering: Good vs. Not Good
Good

■ Good = God
■ Brings you to the end of yourself, your ego, your world of knowledge = lies, your flesh, your religion, your past and future, your physical world.
■ Brings you to the point where you finally let go of (die to) the ego, the world, the lies, the flesh, religion, time, and the physical.

Not Good

- Not good = yourself
- Trying to hold on to your ego, your world of knowledge, your flesh, your religion, your future and past, your physical world.
- Not willing to let go (to put to death) your ego, your knowledge, your flesh, your religion, your past and future, and your physical world.

We also rejoice in our _sufferings_, because we know that _suffering_ produces _perseverance_; _perseverance_, _character_; and _character_, _hope_. And _hope_ does not disappoint us, because God has poured out his _love_ into our hearts by the Holy Spirit, whom he has given us. (NIV)

Suffering

- Literal meaning is "pressure."
- It is the pressure applied that makes us grow spiritually, it is what causes us to let go of the old mind filled with the world, knowledge of man, the ego, the flesh, religion, past and future, and our physical existence as we know it.
- Out of the most severe trial, their overflowing joy and their extreme poverty welled up in rich generosity. For I testify that they gave as much as they were able, and even **beyond their ability.** (NIV) (When they let go of their mind, and followed their heart, they flowed supernaturally and gave beyond their physical ability.)

Perseverance

- Meanings are: endurance, patience, patient waiting, steadfast.
- The concept of never giving up, never stopping, never quitting, and not shrinking or falling back all are implied, to keep choosing the Truth each moment.
- Consider it pure joy…whenever you face trials of many kinds, because you know that the testing of your faith develops perseverance. Perseverance must finish its work so that you may be mature and complete, not lacking anything (not lacking anything spiritually, mentally, or physically - this is being balanced in body, mind and spirit, this is wholeness, this is total health). (NIV)

Character

- Meanings are: *a proving trial, tried character, a specimen of proof, experience.*
- Character means you have been tried and tested and have stood strong, having gained the experience from the test, you have grown and proved yourself as one who overcomes all things that are put in your path of life.
- This service that you perform is not only supplying the needs of God's people but is also overflowing in many expressions of thanks to God. Because of the service by which you have **proved** yourselves (by following your Truth-filled heart instead of your lie-filled mind), men will praise God for the obedience that accompanies your confession of the gospel (the Truth). (NIV)

Hope

- Meanings are: *knowing, patience, wholeness, and joyful and confident expectation.*
- Hope is the knowing in the heart that comes from God, it is the knowing that you are whole, complete, not lacking anything in spirit, mind or body. It is knowing that you are healed, delivered from bondage and set free first in the spirit, then in the mind and finally in the body. Patience is the waiting and living in the moment knowing that what God has spoken into your heart will occur.
- Hope is the knowing that your faith is built on.
- Now faith is the substance (the physical manifestation, the action steps walked out) of things hoped (known in the heart, not in the head) for, the evidence of things not seen. (NKJV)
- Against all hope (knowledge in the mind), Abraham in hope (knowing and following the Truth revealed to his heart) believed and so became the father of many nations, just as it had been said to him, "So shall your offspring be." Without weakening in his faith, he faced the fact that his body was as good as dead - since he was about a hundred years old - and that Sarah's womb was also dead. Yet he did not waver through unbelief (which comes from the mind) regarding the promise of God, but was strengthened in his faith and gave glory to God, being fully persuaded that God had power to do what he had promised. This is why "it was credited to him as righteousness." (NIV)
- Hope (knowing the Truth in the heart) is the anchor of your soul (mind, will, emotions).
- We have this hope (knowing the Truth in the heart) as an anchor for the soul, firm and secure. (NIV)
- Hope is the knowing, first in the spirit, and then in the mind, that eventually turns into the physical manifestation.

- **But hope that is seen** (having to see the physical manifestation) **is no hope** (knowing in the heart) **at all**. Who hopes for what he already has? But if we hope for what we do not yet have, we wait for it patiently (knowing in your heart that God will always provide). (NIV)

- And now these three remain: faith, hope and love. But the greatest of these is love.

- **MORE - Faith** is to believe, trust and rely upon the Truth spoken to your heart and to take the physical action steps that your heart tells you, never quitting, stopping or giving up. **Hope** is to know the Truth in the heart and follow this Truth no matter how much the ego, world, flesh, religion, lie-filled mind screams. Hope cannot always be explained, but it is always known, just like falling in love cannot be explained but is definitely known. **Love** is God. Love is our covenant with Him, our covenant of life - which includes our covenant with our self, the body/mind/spirit covenant, the covenant with our spouse, and the covenant with all humanity. Love is our giving everything we have to our covenant partner, and He in return gives us all He has, when we reach the end of ourselves.

Faith

- *To believe, trust and rely upon the Truth.*

- Faith is the physical form that hope becomes as it manifests.

- Now faith (being in the present moment, listening to your Truth-filled heart and taking the action steps your heart tells you) is the substance of things hoped for (known in the heart), the evidence of things not seen. (NKJV)

- Faith must have action steps or it is not faith.

- In the same way, faith by itself, if it is not accompanied by action, is dead. (NIV)

- Faith without action/obedience/perseverance is dead.

- Faith comes from the knowing in the heart - the hope; it does not come from the 5 senses or from the mind.

- We live by faith (our Truth-filled heart that guides our actions and steps), not by sight (not by the 5 senses that feed our old world, ego, flesh, lie-filled old mind). (NIV)

- We are called to live by faith; anything else separates us from God and does not please Him.

- But my righteous one (the one who is in covenant with me and who follows his Truth-filled heart) will live by faith (taking the action steps your heart has shown you no matter what your mind says). And if he shrinks back (quits, stops, gives up on his heart and goes back into the old lie-filled mind and follows it), I will not be pleased with him. (NIV)

- And without faith (knowing the Truth, and taking the action steps He has placed in your heart) it is impossible to please God. (NIV)
- Everything that does not come from faith (if you are following your mind it is separating you from God, if you are following your heart you are being one with Him) is sin. (NIV)
- Faith flows from hope (knowing in the heart), which comes from love (covenant with God).
- And now these three remain: faith, hope and love. But the greatest of these is love. (NIV)
- If I have a faith that can move mountains, but have not love (am not a covenant partner with God), I am nothing. If I give all I possess to the poor and surrender my body to the flames (doing good deeds from a religious, ego-filled old mind), but have not love, I gain nothing. (NIV)
- The only thing that counts is faith expressing itself through love (covenant of life). (NIV)
- Faith is how we have victory in overcoming the world, the flesh, the ego, religion, the time and space bound, lie-filled old mind.
- This is the victory that has overcome the world, even our faith. (NIV)

Love

- Love is covenant.
- Love is God.
- Love is the greatest of all.
- Love heals, delivers, sets free, makes whole.
- Love is what hope and faith flow from.
- There is no fear in love (when one is in covenant with the Living God) but perfect love drives out fear. (NIV)
- Covenant of life is loving
    - God (being His covenant partner)
    - Yourself (body/mind/spirit covenant)
    - Your neighbor (being the total light to the world in body, mind and spirit, once you have loved, balanced yourself first)
- 'Love the Lord your God with all your heart and with all your soul and with all your mind.' This is the first and greatest commandment. And the second is like it: 'Love your neighbor as yourself.' (NIV)
- Greater love has no one than this, that he lay down his life for his friends (friend means covenant partner). (NIV)

The Covenant of Life

- Covenant with God.
- Covenant with One's Self.
- Covenant with One's spouse.
- Covenant with Others.

Covenant

- Two parties enter an agreement to strengthen their weakness. This agreement lasts at least 8 generations.
- A bond for life or death.
- Always accompanied by the shedding of blood.
- Taking of oaths.
- If covenant is broken one party MUST kill the other party as payment for the breaking of the covenant, there is no choice in this, it must be done or the covenant has no power. The covenant's power is that the two have become one and will give everything they have to meet the need of the covenant partner, even to the giving of one's life for the other.

Covenant - Marriage

How would a woman feel and what would she say if her husband sat on the couch watching TV and said:

- Honey, change the channel for me.
- Honey, get me my glass of water on the counter.
- Honey, pick up my coat on the floor.

She would say, "I can do those things for you but why can't you do them yourself?"

Now if her husband is on the couch lying there sick she rushes to do those things and meet all his needs because where he is weak she is strong, where he cannot do for himself, she does for him. This is love; this is the covenant.

Partners in Covenant

- Partner **A** desires to purchase a piece of property valued at $100,000. Partner **A** asks partner **B** for the $100,000 when he has $50,000 in the bank.
- This is an abomination to the covenant - asking for something from your covenant partner that you yourself have.
- You must get to the end of yourself before your covenant partner gives from himself.
- Abomination - Most of the Hebrew words translated "abomination" have the meaning of "impure," "filthy," and "unclean", that which is foul smelling and objectionable to a holy God…. All of us have been sinful; even our best actions are filthy through and through. (TEV)

Covenant with God

How do you think God feels and what would He say if His covenant partner sat passively asking:

- God, heal my body.
- God, take away all these problems.

- God, heal my marriage.
- God, make me prosper.

He would say, "I can do for you and give to you all that I AM once you have given all that you have and all that you are."

Now if you are listening to His voice of peace spoken into your heart and are in faith obediently taking the action steps He has shown you at 100% of your ability, that's when He meets you with the rest, with all that He IS. *This is the place of miracles, the place of healing.* This is love. This is the covenant.

Covenant with One's Self

- This is loving yourself.
- This is the body-mind-spirit covenant.
- Covenant means all members are willing to give everything to the other in need, even if it means dying.
- Your body will die for your mind or your spirit (heart).
- Will your mind be allowed to be put to death for your spirit (heart)?
- Will your mind be allowed to be put to death for your body?

Love

- Love is obeying what God has put in your heart no matter what your mind says.
- If you love me, you will obey what I command (the Truth I have spoken into your heart). (NIV)
- If you obey my commands (the Truth I have spoken into your heart), you will remain in my love (my covenant of love). (NIV)
- This is love for God: to obey his commands (the Truth He has spoken to your heart). And his commands are not burdensome, for everyone born of God overcomes the world (system of lies). This is the victory that has overcome the world, even our faith (by taking the action steps that our Truth-filled heart has revealed to us). (NIV)
- And this is love: that we walk in obedience to his commands (the Truth He has spoken into our heart). (NIV)
- Love resides in the heart not the mind.
- Knowledge (the mind) puffs up, but love (the knowing in the Truth and obeying that Truth in the heart) builds up. The man who thinks he knows something does not yet know as he ought to know. But the man who loves (who is covenanted to) God is known by God (is God's covenant partner). (NIV)
- Now the purpose of the commandment is love from a pure heart, from a good conscience (God consciousness), and from sincere faith. (NIV)
- Love is patient, love is kind (these are from the heart, from the spirit). It does not envy, it does not boast, it is not proud. It is not rude, it is not self-seeking, it is not easily angered, it keeps no record of wrongs

Faith-Obedience-Action-Perseverance-Miracles

Faith - believe the Truth in your heart, walk it out

plus

Obedience - to listen to the Truth and walk out that Truth in faith

plus

Action - comes from faith and obeying

plus

Perseverance - never stopping, quitting, giving up, to keep choosing the Truth each moment

produces

Miracles - when you do all you can, God meets you with the rest, all that HE IS.

Words of the Heart vs. of the Mind

- Good (God) vs. good (man) vs. bad (Good is God, all else is of the old mind, good today bad tomorrow, happy today sad tomorrow).
- Faith vs. Fear (faith is trusting in the Truth spoken into your heart, fear is trusting the lie spoken into your mind).
- Hope vs. Hoping (knowing in the heart as opposed to wishing in the mind).
- Love (God) vs. Love (man) vs. Hate (God's love is covenant, the two have become one and are inseparable. It is unconditional. Man's love is conditional and can easily turn to hate).

Steps to Access Spiritual Strengthening

- **Fasting** - letting go of food, TV, shopping or anything else you can't go at least 6 months without (be led by your heart in prayer).
- **Giving** (not to get) - letting go of your possessions, your time, your money (it's all His).
- **Sowing** (not to get) - letting go of the present life (putting it to death), dying to live, taking what you have and putting it to death to have new life arise from it.
- **Silence** - being in an environment with no sound at all for periods of time. This causes the world, knowledge, lie, ego, flesh, past and future, physical mind to scream but when you push through this, then you get to the place of hearing no-thing, the place where God speaks.
- **Looking for suffering** of the ego, world mind, the flesh, past and future mind, physical or 5 senses. Being led by God into suffering.

In life if you are not growing (more one with God) then you are dying (separating from God).

190

Go Deeper

1. What does "you do to one part, you do to the whole" really mean to your body, your mind, and your spirit health?
2. What did the exercise study on the nursing home residents, ages 87-96, mean to you?
3. When one gives up physical exercise what 5 things appear, and what does this mean to you?
4. Do you now know the deeper meaning of "use it or lose it?"
5. Which is better for your total health, walking or running, why?
6. Of the four types of exercises which one is most important?
7. Why are increased lymphatic circulation and strengthening of all cells such important benefits of rebounding cellular exercise?
8. Why is rebounding exercise so important for mental function, and neurological organization?
9. How does strengthening and stretching muscles affect organ/gland function?
10. How does organ/gland function affect the strength and tension of a muscle?
11. How does strengthening and stretching muscles affect the entire nervous system, and its ability to control organ/gland function?
12. How can a left shoulder blade, shoulder, and arm pain be caused by the pancreas? How can a stomach problem cause neck pain?
13. How can stressed adrenal glands cause lower back, leg, knee pain?
14. How can liver imbalance cause mid back and right shoulder pain? How can lack of digestion cause neck, mid back, lower back, leg, and knee pain?
15. What is the single best exercise for the cells, lymphatic movement, cardiovascular fitness, and stretching, and why?
16. Why is goal-oriented exercise potentially detrimental to your total health of body, mind, and spirit?
17. Why is the African tribal messenger able to accomplish amazing feats of physical endurance, with no physical side affects?
18. What do muscle growth and spiritual growth have in common?
19. Why is physical training potentially harmful to your total health?
20. Why is self-discipline potentially harmful to your total health?
21. What is the stress applied to grow spiritually, and when is it good, and not good?
22. Which is the most powerful part of you, your mind, your will or your emotions, and why?
23. How do words of the mind negatively affect our total health?
24. Give examples of the hundredfold increase and decrease for exercise.
25. What is the most important step in exercising your faith and why?

Fasting

Fast
■ Old English word *faestan* meaning to hold fast or abstain.[74]
■ To food fast means to abstain from food.
■ To fast means to abstain from something.

What do we Fast?
■ The body
■ The conscious mind
■ The unconscious mind
■ The old mind
■ The emotions

Physical Benefits of Fasting
■ Dr. Herbert Shelton - the most renowned practitioner in the field of therapeutic fasting who had supervised over 40,000 fasts states: *"Fasting is the best way to maintain good health, eliminate pain and disease, reduce and control weight, and ultimately prolong life."*[75]

Do you starve a fever, and feed a cold, or feed a fever, and starve a cold?

YOU STARVE EVERYTHING - THIS IS FASTING
■ Animals fast when they are sick and they don't stay sick long.
■ When you are sick you lose your appetite, this is your body telling you how to heal - FAST.
■ Remember fasting, with water only, ranges from 10 to 365 days.

Ancient Fasts for Mind and Body
■ Among the ancients it was recognized as a sovereign method of attaining and maintaining marked mental and physical efficiency. Socrates and Plato, two of the greatest of the Greek philosophers and teachers, fasted regularly for a period of ten days at a time. Pythagoras, another of the great Greek philosophers, was also a regular faster, and, before he took an examination at the University of Alexandria, fasted for forty days. He required his pupils to fast for forty days before they could enter his class.
Major W.C. Gotshall, M.S.[76]

Hippocrates on Fasting

- *"The more you nourish* (feed) *a diseased body, the worse you make it."*- Hippocrates, the father of medicine.
- Hippocrates prescribed total abstinence from food while a disease was on the increase, and especially at the critical period, and a spare diet on other occasions.[77]
- Hippocrates prescribed fasting for numerous conditions. The Hippocratic Oath that every physician takes before entering practice is *"First do no harm,"* understanding the power of the body to heal itself with the basics of health including the power of fasting.
- *"Let your food be your medicine."* This is the spare diet of no excess in times of health and fast in times of symptoms, conditions and diseases.

Resting from Food

- "The moment the last morsel of food is digested and the stomach is emptied, a reconstruction process begins. New cells replace the broken down cells. The replacement of cells means replacement of tissue. The common custom of eating three to six times a day doesn't give the burdened stomach a chance to empty itself so that the repairing of the worn and wasted cells can begin. During a fast, the good cells increase in size. This rejuvenating process begins only after the stomach is emptied."[78]
  Dr. Hereward Carrington, member of the American Institute for Scientific Research at the turn of the last century.
- *"This amazing replacement of cells means replacement of tissue; replacement of tissue means a new stomach has been constructed - a new stomach in every sense of the word, as new in every anatomical sense as in the filling-in of wounds, or between the fractured ends of bones."*[79] Dr Carrington

A Whole New You

- Every cell in our entire body is replaced within one year. This means you are a whole new you in one year. The problem is if we keep doing what we have always done, we will get what we have always had. A physical as well as mental/emotional toxic, out of balance, blocking the flow of life, body.
- Doctors Carlson and Knude, of the Department of Physiology at the University of Chicago, placed a forty-year old man on a fourteen-day fast. At the end of the fast, they examined his tissues and declared that

they were of the same physiological condition as those of a seventeen-year old youth. Dr. Knude stated: "*It is evident that where the initial weight was reduced by 45%, and then subsequently restored by normal diet, approximately one-half of the restored body is made up of new protoplasm. In this, there is* **rejuvenescence**."[80]

- As you fast you lose not only all the toxins, chemicals, and drugs stored in the tissues,

- Not only do you lose all the non-vital tissue, the cysts, tumors, edematous fluid,

- You also lose the bacteria, viruses, parasites, fungi and any other pathogens because your white blood cells consume them or they die because they are no longer being fed.

- You lose ALL the OLD you, the stored mental/emotional toxins that are held in tissues.

- Once you lose ALL the OLD toxic, lie-filled you, you can rebuild the NEW, unblocked, TRUTH-filled you.

Burn it all up

- From his paper "The Fasting Cure" Dr. J.H. Kellog parallels the human body and a furnace during a fast. He says that when we stop eating the body begins to feed upon stored reserves and bodily wastes. When the body recognizes that it cannot get food, it starts burning nonessential tissue to keep going. The body draws from its stored resources and uses every particle of fat, reserve protein, vitamin and mineral excesses, morbid tissue, and superfluous fluids. It also burns all partially digested food.

- Dr. Kellog stated that uric acid, a very poisonous byproduct of protein, metabolism leaves a acid cinder or acid ash residue. All of the biochemical reactions of life in the body occur in an alkaline medium, not an acid one.

- Dr. Kellog stated that the body can only handle one and a half ounces of protein per day. Anything beyond this acidifies the body and predisposes it to acute and chronic disease.[81]

- The average American consumes 2-3 times this amount of protein.

- Fasting burns up this excessive protein in the body.

- In the completed fast, the body burns up EVERTHING that is not essential for health and life.

- When only healthy tissue remains the hunger returns, which left after the second day, the fast is finished; health has been restored by the "doctor within."

God's Design

- You were designed by God to be able to fast.
- One does not become vitamin-, mineral-, or protein-deficient, because within the body's cells are sufficient reserves of proteins, fats, enzymes, vitamins, and minerals to call upon in times of food scarcity, famine and fasting.
- Even in fasts of forty days with only water the body does NOT become deficient. It was created by God to be able to survive in times of famine.
- The longest fast recorded was 365 days with only water.

The New and Improved You

- The old is gone, the new has come.
- You need to lose all the old cells, tissues, emotions and mindsets that have stored in those cells and tissues first.
- Next the new cells and tissues are rebuilt with pure energy, pure mind and pure spirit.
- Every cell in the body is replaced within one year. Plant new seeds and you will get a new harvest.

21 Years?

- It has been said that it takes 21 years to completely renew the body, mind, and spirit.
- The first 7 years is to completely replace the physical body and remove all stored toxins from the past and the generations.
- The second 7 years is to completely replace the stored negative mind patterns and emotional toxins from your past and the generations, and reprogram your conscious and unconscious mind with Truth.
- The third 7 years is to grow and mature in the awareness of the God consciousness, intuition, communion with God and flow in spiritual gifts.

The Efficiency of Fasting

- In fasting, all non-essential cells, tissues and fluids are broken down back into their component parts of amino acids, essential fatty acids, simple chain sugars, enzymes, vitamins and minerals. This includes tumors, cysts, scars, edematous and extraneous fluids.
- Then the **miracle** of fasting reorganizes these component building blocks and reuses them to rebuild the "new" body of health and wholeness so one does not become deficient. **The body turns non-essential tissue into essential tissue.**

Deficiency from Dead/Cooked Food

■ A person becomes deficient when they eat dead/cooked food because these foods are anti-nutrients, meaning they use up your enzymes, vitamins and minerals just to digest and absorb them.

■ These dead/cooked foods are never fully digested so the white blood cells, which are high in enzyme activity, have to digest the undigested food. This causes a great imbalance in the immune system response.

■ A tremendous amount of energy is expended to try to digest and absorb this dead/cooked food, leaving the body drained of energy needed for vital functions.

■ The results: deficiency, toxicity, immune imbalance and loss of vitality of the cells, tissues, glands, and organs.

Toxemia

■ John H. Tilden, M.D. - one of the foremost natural healing physicians of the first half of the 20th century - believed the cause of all disease was a toxic build up in the tissues and fluids of the body.

■ According to Dr. Tilden, some of the causes of this toxemia were: overeating, eating wrong food, wrong food combinations, mineral/vitamin deficiencies, low nerve energy, postural tension on the nerve system, poor environment, physical excesses, sensual indulgences, killing emotions of fear, worry, rage (anger), and jealousy.[82]

The Secret to Long Life

■ The secret to long life lies in keeping the blood and bodily fluids pure and free of toxic material.

■ Dr. Alexis Carrel of the Rockefeller Institute stated, *"The cell is immortal. It is merely the fluid that it floats in that degenerates. Renew this fluid at proper intervals, and give the cell nourishment upon which to feed, and so far as we know, the pulsation of life may go on forever."*[83]

■ Dr. Carrel confirmed his idea of immortality of the cell through an experiment in which he kept a chicken heart alive for 28 years. This is quite amazing since the lifespan of a chicken is 8 to 10 years. Dr. Carrel stated that as long as the nutrients to the chicken heart were pure, and the metabolic waste was constantly removed, the heart would never have to die. The experiment was ended when an attendant in the lab forgot to change the fluids causing the heart to die.

The Physical Environment for Healing (See Appendix)

Fasting Results

■ Dr. William Esser reported after fasting 156 people who collectively complained of ulcers, tuberculosis, sinusitis, pyorrhea, Parkinson's disease, heart disease, cancer, insomnia, gallstones, epilepsy, colitis, hay fever, bronchitis, asthma and arthritis. Fast lengths were from 5 to 55 days. Some did not complete the fast.

  ■ The results were as follows: 113 completely recovered, 31 partially recovered, 12 were not helped.
  ■ 92% either improved or completely recovered.[84]

■ Dr. Paul Bragg, life extension specialist, described how chemicals and medicines can be eliminated through fasting. On a 21-day water only fast he experienced sharp pains in his bladder on day 10. When he urinated it felt like boiling water was being passed. Afterward he had the urine analyzed for chemical content. The results showed DDT which used to be used in spraying fruits and vegetables but is now banned. Other poisonous pesticide residues were also found in the urine sample.[85]

All in Time

■ Dr. Paul Bragg became such a believer in fasting that he fasted one day each week and four seasonal 7-10 day fasts. After 5 years of this systematic fasting, Dr. Bragg was enjoying a leisurely canoe ride on day 7 of a 10-day fast when he doubled over in pain from stomach cramps. He quickly paddled to shore. He evacuated his bowel and was left with a heavy, cool sensation in his rectum. A chemical analysis of his stool revealed that Bragg had passed one third of a cup of quicksilver (mercury) from the calomel medicine his mother had given him for whooping cough he had during his childhood.[86]

■ **MORE** - Our body is continually releasing stored physical, mental, and emotional toxins, as we stay balanced in the present time with the 7 basic steps to total health. The energy that was being used just to keep you existing can now be turned inward for much deeper physical, mental, emotional healing. The key to redirecting the energy for healing at deeper levels is to stay balanced in the present with the 7 basic steps.

Fasting and Chemical/Poison Elimination

■ From the *American Journal of Industrial Medicine* the article entitled "A Trial of Fasting Cure for PCB Poisoned Patients of Taiwan."

■ The study was with patients who had consumed rice oil contaminated with PCB's. After a 7 to 10 day fast the results were dramatic relief and improvement in symptoms in every one of the patients.[87]

Fasting Results

■ Dr. Herbert Shelton's Health School saw over 40,000 patients from 1928 to 1981.

■ Dr. Shelton stated that virtually every acute or chronic disease responds with astounding success to properly supervised therapeutic fasting.

■ Some of them include: common cold, multiple sclerosis, asthma, arthritis, migraines, cardiovascular disease, hay fever, colitis, obesity, eczema, psoriasis, gallstones, ulcers and tumors.[88]

Fasting and the Mind

■ Fasting has been repeatedly observed to alleviate neuroses, anxiety, and depression.

■ A Japanese clinic fasted 382 patients with psychosomatic disease with a success rate of 87%.[89]

■ Dr. Allan Cott used fasting as a treatment for schizophrenics and reported the results in *Applied Nutrition in Clinical Practice.*
  ■ Dr. Cott put 28 patients on a water-only fast. All the patients had been diagnosed as schizophrenic for at least five years and had not responded to standard treatment.
  ■ The results: success in 60% of the cases.[90]

The Power of Fasting and Living/Raw Food Diet

■ Three-part experiment done on rats to access diet and health.

■ **Group 1 -** a group of rats was fed a living/raw diet consisting of vegetables, seeds, nuts and whole grains. These rats grew very healthy and never suffered from any disease, never became fat, mated regularly, were gentle, affectionate and lived in harmony with each other. After reaching an equivalent of 80 human years they were put to death and their organs, glands and tissues were found to be in perfect condition with no signs of aging or deterioration.

■ **Group 2 -** the next group of rats was fed a diet of cooked food, white bread, meat, milk, salt, soft drinks, candies, cakes, vitamins, minerals and medicines for any ailment. This group from early on in life contracted colds, fevers, pneumonia, heart disease, cancer, arthritis, poor vision and cataracts. Most of this group died prematurely and became very antisocial, fighting, stealing each other's food, and trying to kill each other. This caused them to have to be separated to avoid total destruction of the group. Epidemics of sickness affected the group and as they died they were autopsied and found to be in advanced degeneration in all their organs, glands and tissues. Their offspring were all sick and had the same problems their parents had.

■ **Group 3** - in this group the rats were fed the same diet as group 2, the average American diet, and had all the diseases and behaviors that were exhibited in group 2. Extreme sickness, antisocial behavior and early death were all seen. Some of this group were put to death at an equivalent human age of 40 years and were autopsied and found to have extensive degeneration of all parts of their bodies

■ In the next part of the **group 3** experiment the rats after an equivalent age of 40 human years were put on a strict fast with only water to drink for several days (after eating the American diet for 40 equivalent years). Then when food was reintroduced into their diet it was only the living/raw food that group 1 received. This diet was alternated with times of fasting and within one month the behavior was completely different, now very docile, playful, living together in harmony with each other. Then at the age of 80 human years equivalent these rats were autopsied and found to have no signs of aging or disease just as in group 1.

■ **MORE** - this experiment shows the amazing healing power of living/raw food. Most amazing of all is that after 40 equivalent years of the SAD (standard American diet) and lifestyle, once fasting and living/raw foods were introduced, their behavior reverted back to one of balance and harmony. Their physical body reversed all imbalances, conditions, diseases, and all signs of aging. If human beings can get this revelation that even if they have abused the temple of God's Spirit, their bodies, it is not to late to reverse symptoms, conditions, diseases, and aging. They need only to become proactive with the 7 basic steps to total health, obeying in faith, God's Truth spoken into their hearts, never quitting, stopping, or giving up. This is when one starts living life to the full, this is when one really starts living in body, mind and spirit.

Types of Food Fasts

- **Total fast** - abstaining from all food, all drink and all water.
- **Water only fast** - abstaining from all food and drink except water.
- **Partial fast** - this can be only eating or drinking certain items and abstaining from all others, i.e. only juice.

Total Fast

- The body can only go 3-5 days without water so the longest a total fast should be is 3 days.
- *Supernatural total fast* was accomplished by Moses (80 days without food and water).

Water-Only Fast

- This is known most commonly by its misnomer - water fast.
- This is the type of fasting that has been researched the most and has the most documented results because it has no variables, one eats nothing and drinks only water for the duration of the fast (10-365 days).

Partial Fast

- This is known most commonly by its misnomers - juice fast, vegetable fast, non-pleasing-food fast, Daniel fast.
- This type of fasting is most commonly done because of its benefits along with its ability to be done while one continues his normal daily routine.

Principles of Water-Only Fasting

- After 2 days the hunger leaves.
- When the hunger reappears the fast is over (10-365 days).
- When no food is taken the body begins an overall cleaning by digesting and burning up all debris, toxic material, excessive tissue or fluid until nothing remains left but vital organs, gland and tissues.
- Signs of this cleaning house or detoxifying are bad breath, coated tongue, body odor, weakness, dizziness, lightheadedness, headaches, cramps, irritability, and emotional releases.

How the Body Eliminates Toxins and Waste Products

- 70% leave through breathing, 20% through skin, 7% through urine and 3% through the bowel.

Principles of Water-Only Fasting

- If 70% of the toxins and waste products leave from the breath, this is why a person experiences "bad breath."
- If 20% of the toxins and waste products leave from the skin, this is why a person experiences "bad body odor."

- The tongue is the tip of the 30-foot digestive/eliminative canal that ends at the anus. As the toxins are eliminated the changes affect the whole 30 feet, hence a coated tongue is seen.
- Weakness is seen because it takes a lot of energy to do this complete house cleaning of the body.
- When the fast is over hunger returns and if you do not eat, then your body will start digesting your own organs and glands. This is called starvation.
- When the hunger returns, the breath is sweet, the tongue has cleared, the skin has a fresh smell and clears.

The Length of a Water-Only (Therapeutic) Fast is determined by:

- The amount of reserves in the body (nutrients and weight).
- The amount of toxic material that has to be burned up.
- The amount of non-vital tissue that can be burned for fuel - tumors, cysts, edema fluid, scar tissue. These and all other non-essential substances will be used as fuel as the body does its therapeutic house cleaning.

How to Fast the Body

- Food – The greatest stronghold of the flesh, so the most important aspect of fasting the body.
- Water fast.
- Green Juice fast.
- Liquid living/raw plant food fast.
- Living/Raw plant food fast.
- No pleasing-to-the-flesh/taste-buds fast.
- A Living/Raw food diet should always be consumed for optimal healing and health. This could be called a permanent fast from the standard American diet (SAD).
- A Living/Raw liquid-only fast is the most powerful form in which to consume the nutrients, for greatest digestion and absorption and highest amount of nutrient extracted from the food.
- Water only fast can be done 1day per week and 3-10 days per season change (4X/year).
- Fasting type and schedule determined in prayer.

Water-only Fasting
Benefits

- The quickest way to detoxify.
- The best for deep cleaning.
- The most powerful for breaking the old mind/flesh barriers = spiritual growth.

Things to consider

- More and quicker detoxifying symptoms.
- Energy drain.
- Can become deficient if already very deficient/diseased.
- Cannot be done unsupervised by most. Time is 10-40 days.

Green Juice-only Fasting
Benefits

- The next quickest way to detoxify after water.
- The next best for deep cleaning.
- The next most powerful for breaking the old mind/flesh barriers = spiritual growth.

Things to consider

- Detoxifying is still very rapid causing detoxifying symptoms.
- Energy drain still significant.
- Less likely to become deficient but still possible depending on the time of fast.
- Can be done unsupervised by most. Time is 14-40 days.

Liquefied Sprouts/Seeds/Vegetables-Only Fast
Benefits

- Will detoxify the entire system.
- Will eventually clean all systems.
- Will break the old mind/flesh barriers = spiritual growth.
- Best for digestion and absorption of purest, health-promoting nutrients. (10% vs. 95%, chewed versus equipment liquefied)

Things to consider

- Detoxifying is still occurring but symptoms are most tolerable.
- Little to no energy drain.
- Never become deficient and will reverse all deficiencies.
- Can be done unsupervised by all. Time is indefinite.

Sprouts/Seeds/Nuts/Vegetables-Only Fast
Benefits

- Will detoxify the entire system the slowest.
- Will eventually clean all systems.
- Will break the old mind/flesh barriers = spiritual growth.

Things to consider

- Detoxifying is still occurring but slowest. Symptoms are most tolerable.
- Energy drain possible because of maldigestion/malabsorption.

- Can become deficient due to the decreased absorption (10% vs. 95%, chewed versus equipment liquefied).
- Can be done unsupervised by all. Time is indefinite.

What to expect when you food fast

First you must break down the old house, the old mind, the old you.

- **Physical detoxification signs** are bad breath, coated tongue, body odor, weakness, dizziness, lightheadedness, headaches, cramps, pain reoccurrences of old symptoms or pains.
- **Emotional detoxification signs** are emotional releases - fear, anger, sadness, resentment, bitterness, and loneliness.
- **Mental detoxification signs** are irritability, anxiety, depression, frustration, hopelessness, and self-criticism.

Secondly you must build the new temple, the new mind, the new you

- **Physical signs** are increased energy, decreased pain, symptoms and pains from past progressively leave.
- **Emotional signs** are emotions like fear, anger, sadness progressively replaced with love, joy, peace, hope and passion for living.
- **Mental signs** are increased clarity, memory, focus, perseverance, patience, and creativity. As one reprograms the conscious and unconscious mind with Truth, the mind stills, causing -
- **Increased hearing the voice of God** spoken in your heart with love, joy, hope and Truth.

How to Fast the Conscious Mind

- Still the mind - Alpha state, thought bubbles. Releasing all the thought bubbles out until there are no more, just stillness of the mind, this is the place of no-thing. (Writing down, or recording the bubbles that you need to remember or things you need to do - pick up children at 4PM, etc., so you can still the mind.)
- Stay in the present moment consciousness, awareness.
- Separate from the world/ego/self mind driven thoughts and activities like entertainment, restaurants, shopping, TV.
- Go to the place of solitude and silence - no people, no world system, no time restraints, no place to go, nothing to do.

How to Fast the Negative Emotions

- Do not deny them, do not store them, do not suppress them, just watch them as watching a movie. Do not become the movie; if you do the negative emotions are fed and they will grow. If the emotions are watched and not fed they will eventually diminish and be gone.

Action Steps to be Set Free from the Old Mind

- Fast
- Let go of the past, future, generations - consciously, and unconsciously.
- Watch all emotions as they surface - let them be but do not become them (the old you).
- Distinguish between the old you (who you thought you were) and the new you (who you truly are).
- Change your perceptions (how you see yourself and the world around you) and you change your reality (life, health).
- Still your mind (get to the place of no-thing, no thoughts just stillness, this is the place of the spirit, this is where God can speak to your heart).
- Stay away from your known flesh triggers - high stress, confrontations, ice cream shop, shopping, TV.

How to Overcome the Old Mind

- **Prayer** - Listening to the Truth spoken from your heart (spirit) into your still (supremeconscious) mind causing love, joy and peace to replace the negative emotions and finally flowing health, strength and life into the physical body.
- **Fasting** - Cutting the lifelines to the old mind in all three areas. Fasting your conscious mind, fasting your negative emotions and fasting your physical body.

**What should we fast from?
Anything we have to have, anything we need,
anything we cannot do without,
anything that binds us or enslaves us.**

"Not everything is good for you." And even though "I am allowed to do anything," I must not become a slave to anything. (NLT)

Nine Blockages of the Heart (Stronghold of the old mind)

- World
- Belief Systems
- Religion
- Ego
- Personality

205

- Flesh
- 5 Senses
- Time Past/Future
- Space/ Physicality

These 9 blockages of the heart feed the old unrenewed mind and prevent us from living in victory and freedom, keeping us in defeat and bondage.

The most powerful fasting is one that denies the body and the mind so the spirit can flow unhindered: this is food fasting.

Multiple fasting (fasting from more than one thing at the same time - food, TV, and social functions) multiples the effects of the fasting.

World vs. Spirit
World
- System of physical laws (physical observations).
- System of the 5 senses that are compiled in the mind.
- Knowledge as man perceives with his mind.
- Seeing everything from a physical point of view.
- Words of men spoken into the mind.
- System of facts and learned knowledge all based on those laws and senses.
- A learned system.

Spirit
- System of spiritual law (Truth).
- System of the 6th and 7th senses that are known in the heart.
- Truth as known in the heart.
- Seeing everything from a spiritual point of view.
- Word of God spoken into the heart.
- System of Truth and inner knowing based on the 6th and 7th senses and spiritual law.
- A known system.

How to Fast from the World
- No TV, radio, newspaper, books or anything of the world system of knowledge, facts, figures, lies.
- No association with people of the world.
- No schools or organizations that are based in the world system of lies.
- No attaining knowledge from the world system.

Where Did Our Belief Systems Come From?
- Our Family - Father, mother, siblings, grandparents, other relatives we spent time with (birth - 6 years old).
- Our Friends/Relationships (6 - 18 years old)
- The World System (birth - present)
- Our 5 Senses
- Our Ego

What Our Belief Systems Are Based On
- We assume that our family words are true.
- We assume our friend/relationships words are true.
- We assume the world system is true.
- We assume the information gathered by the 5 senses is true.
- We assume everything that is filtered through our ego is true.

Beliefs of the Past
- The world is flat.
- The sun rotates around the earth.
- We cannot fly.

Beliefs of the Present
- We are physical beings that are bound by time and space.
- We cannot defy the physical laws of the universe.
- We cannot fly.
- We cannot translocate.

How to Fast from the Belief Systems
Do not believe in anything you were ever taught that did not see "All as One," and was not based on -
- Love the Lord your God.
- Love yourself.
- Love your neighbor as yourself.
- Separate from the false belief and the person, place or thing that continues to bring the false belief (negative entrainment).

Religion

Man approaching an impersonal God with acts or good deeds to gain favor, or a higher state of being.

Religion

Any organization telling you what you have to do to gain God's favor, telling you what you must do or give, who you should help, or where you should go to be closer to God or to become more spiritual.

Religion

Jesus only rebuked one type of person, not the sinner, not the prostitute but the self-righteous, religious Pharisee.

Fasting from Religion

- Follow your heart, not the words of man or any organization spoken to your mind.
- Separate from anyone, anything that tell you what you have to do, be, give to be holy, spiritual, or closer to God. This all feeds the mind and blocks the true flow of the Spirit in your heart.

What is the Ego?

The "I", "me" or "my," the self of each person.

The Ego-Garden Connection

- Partook of the Tree of Knowledge.
- Took eyes off of God and put them on self.
- Result: The first ego act - covering themselves because they were ashamed of their nakedness.

Ego filled mind not Spirit (God) filled mind led to the first negative emotion, FEAR, and it is from fear that all other negative emotions stem.

Ego/Self Mindset

- Is like a cancer of the people of the world (all doing only for themselves).
- Division instead of unity.
- Good of self instead of good of the whole.

We are all members or parts of a whole. Can the human race survive if every part acts independently? This is the same as cancer - non or faulty communication which produces death of the whole person because of the independent-self few cells.

Ego/World
■ Trying to be somebody instead of nobody.
■ Trying to fit in the world instead of separating from it.

Two Sides of Ego
■ I am somebody- look at me!
■ I am nobody- don't look at me- but I want to be somebody- so you would look at me!

Fasting from the Ego
■ Breaking down the old mind, the old you, the "I, me, and my," you.
■ Listen and obey the heart instead of the mind - "go over to that person and say these words" says the heart. "You cannot do that, what would they think of me," says the old mind.
■ Being able to listen to your heart enough to know when you are wrong (because you listened to your old I, me, my mind) and admitting it to others and forgiving yourself (letting go).
■ Public speaking led by the heart is gift giving.
■ Letting others speak if you have always spoken.
■ Knowing that you can be right and also be wrong. Sometimes being right (in your mind) is not what God wants, but instead to be one with another.
■ Sharing truth with another because your heart leads you no matter what the outcome - your ego mind tries to talk you out of it. "I cannot do that" or "I would lose my job" or "what would they think about me?"

Personality
■ The masks we wear to hide the pain to prevent the hurt.
■ Defense mechanisms for ways we were hurt in childhood.
■ Behaviors, strategies and self-images that we have developed in order to survive in this world.
■ Collection of conditioned reactions, fears and false beliefs.
■ Type of coping mechanism that developed and became refined to adapt to our early childhood environment.

Fasting from the Personality

- You are not your personality. It is just a mask you wear. To fast from your personality is to take off the mask and be who God created you to be.
- To fast from your personality is to LET GO, you do not have to be in control, you never were in control anyway; God was, is, and always will be.
- Type A fast by resting, being still and listening to his/her heart.
- Type C fast by standing up, standing strong and speaking the Truth from his/her heart no matter what the outcome.
- Perfectionist fast by letting go and realizing that he/she was created perfect but he/she lives in an imperfect world.
- Intellectual fast by not trying to figure out everything in the mind but instead stilling the mind and learning to listen to the heart.

Three Aspects of the Flesh

- Conscious (negative thinking), and unconscious (negative information stored or passed from prior generations) old mind.
- Emotions (negative).
- Physical Body (negative mind/emotions stored in the physical gland, organs, tissues, and body parts).

The flesh is the old mind/emotion stored in the old body that wants what it wants when it wants it.

Fasting the Flesh

- Anything that you think you have to have or you need and you can't go an extended period of time without is what you should fast from.
- Food, smoking, drinking, drugs, power, money, sex, entertainment, shopping, TV, radio, and newspaper.
- Anything that feeds the flesh suppresses the flow of the Spirit, the love, joy, peace and hope in your life.

Fasting done just physically without feeding the Spirit, without being led by the heart, will temporarily tame the flesh but will not set you free from it.

Fasting removes the trigger stimulus (food, shopping) but you must renew and reprogram the conscious (thinking) mind and the unconscious (stored memory) mind with the Truth from the heart at the same time.

Starve the flesh (old mind) and feed the Spirit/Truth.

Negative Aspects of the 5 Senses
- Feeds into the negative conscious (thinking), unconscious (stored lies) mind which is filled with the
    - World system (lies, non-Truths)
    - Flesh (negative mind, emotion, body)
    - Ego (self-filled, self-concerned mind)
    - Personality (masks your true gifts)
    - False belief systems - religion
    - Time/space/physical bound thinking
- Feed the mind = suppresses the Spirit

Fasting the 5 Senses
- Close your eyes, close your ears, and open your spiritual eyes and ears to see and hear the Truth.
- Do not look at the signs and symptoms.
- Do not listen to the doctor filled with the knowledge of man.
- Do not feel the tumor; do not look at the disease.
- 5 senses feed the old world/ego/flesh/lie-filled mind.
- 6th and 7th senses feed the heart/spirit the supremeconscious mind.
- Fasting the 5 senses is passing a powerful test in your spiritual growth. Healing comes first in the spirit, then in the mind, and last it manifests in the physical body.
- "But the tumor is growing, I can see it and feel it!"
- Abraham - 100 years old, will have a son and then be told to kill him.
- Moses - parting the sea.
- See all things as God sees them.
- Hear only the voice of Truth spoken into your heart.
- See His Hand in everything, tying everything together for Good.
    - You intended to harm me, but God intended it for good to accomplish what is now being done, the saving of many lives. (NIV)

Physical Time vs. Mind/Emotion Time
Physical Time
- If you made a mistake in the past, you learn from it.
- Have a desire and take action steps (led by the heart) toward achieving it, living fully in each present moment. Not being attached to the outcome. Connecting each fully lived present moment becomes the future.

Mind/Emotion Time
- If you made a mistake in the past, you replay it over and over, living in the old mind/emotion patterns of unforgiveness, resentment, bitterness, and self-criticism. You live in the "if only I would have."
- Have a desire and need it to be accomplished for you to be fulfilled, complete, and happy. You are very attached to the outcome. The addiction has begun.

Fasting from Time
- Be and stay in the present moment.
- Live every moment as if you had no more moments but this one, living life to the full in the timeless present moment.
- Do not live for or think about the future or past.
- Fast from the "if only" and the "what ifs."
- Practice silence - This stills the mind (absent in the mind, present in the moment).
- See the love of God in everything and everyone. See them as spirit beings with blockages and imbalances.
- See the big picture in life as God sees it.

What is Your Body?
- A collection of organs, glands, tissues.
- Organs, glands and tissues are made of cells.
- Cells are made of molecules.
- Molecules are made of atoms.
- Atoms are made of proton, neutron, and electrons whirling in 99.9% empty space held together by ENERGY.
- Subatomic particles are not point-like but strings that vibrate at specific frequencies. Frequency is ENERGY.
- Your body is ENERGY.

Energy and Information
- **Everything in life consists of energy and information.**
- Energy can be negative, positive, or spirit.

- Information can be Right or wrong.
- Positive energy is energy of life, health and healing.
- Spirit energy is the energy of love, joy, peace and hope.
- Negative energy - dead, deficient, toxic food, water, air, negative thoughts and emotions.
- Information - Right or wrong, based on the knowing in the heart = Truth or based on the world system of knowledge = lie.

What Energy and Information is Your Temple built with?

- Negative energy + wrong information (the lies): eating, drinking and breathing dead, deficient, toxic food, water and air, and believing the lies.
- Positive energy + wrong information (the lies): eating, drinking and breathing living food, pure water and pure air but believing the lie.
- Negative energy + Right information (the Truth): eating, drinking and breathing dead, deficient, toxic food, water and air while knowing the Truth in the heart.
- Positive energy + Right information (the Truth): eating, drinking and breathing pure living food, water and air and knowing and following the Truth in your heart.
- Spirit energy + Right information (the Truth): transcending all natural laws by receiving and flowing in the energy from God and only knowing and following the Truth in your heart.

Fasting from Space/Physicality

- See everything as energy and information.
- See nothing as this is it, but as "all things are possible." Nothing is impossible.
- The physical is a product of the mind/emotions, which either blocks the flow of life from the spirit or freely allows the flow of life from the spirit.
- **Fast by doing things your mind says you cannot do, but your heart says you can.**
- **Look for and go into suffering (being led by the heart, not the mind). This will break the mind barrier and bring great blessing.**

Fasting Rebuilds a Whole New You

- The new you, the new tissues are built with:
  - Pure energy - living/raw food.
  - Pure thought - supremeconscious mind reprogramming the conscious and unconscious mind with Truth.

- Pure spirit - love, joy, peace and hope that flow from the heart once the 9 blockages of the heart have been removed. These blockages are from the mind. As the heart/spirit is fed and the flesh/ego/world/lie-filled old mind is starved. Wholeness and health is restored.

Who is the Master Builder?

- The heart or the mind?
- The mind was the master builder or architect of the old house called your body.
- The old house, your out-of-balance body was built with the old unrenewed ego/flesh/world/lie-filled mind. This old mind architect/builder built a body, built a foundation based on lies.
- Your old body was the physical framework the lies were attached to (stored mental/emotional toxins in the tissues).
- The unblocked, pure heart filled with Truth is the true master builder who builds the new building (new you) that is no longer a house but a temple.
- This new body will be a temple built from pureness.
- Pure energy from living food, which is the ideal building material for the Truth to attach to.
- Pure mind - the supremeconscious mind that receives the Truth from the heart. The conscious and unconscious mind that have been reprogrammed with that Truth.
- Pure spirit - love, joy, peace and hope that flow from the heart fill every cell in the body and every thought of the mind (supremeconscious).

What is the house built from?

- The old house was built from the old mind and built on lies with negative energy of death (cooked).
- The new temple is built from the heart/spirit and is built on Truth with the energy of life (living).
- We must suffer the old house (break it down) to rebuild the new, pure, holy temple and consecrate it (set it apart) for worship.
- Offer your bodies as a living sacrifice holy and pleasing to God, this is your spiritual act of WORSHIP. (NIV)

Do you not know that you yourselves are God's temple and that God's Spirit lives in you? If anyone destroys God's temple, God will destroy him, for God's temple is sacred, and you are that temple. (NIV)

Do you not know that your body is a temple of the Holy Spirit, who is in you, whom you have received from God? You are not your own; you were bought at a price. Therefore honor God with your body. (NIV)

Running the Race, Keeping the Faith

- I have fought the good fight, I have finished the race, I have kept the faith (took the action steps in following my heart). Now there is in store for me the crown of righteousness (covenant partner blessings). (NIV)
- Therefore, since we are surrounded by such a great cloud of witnesses, let us throw off everything that hinders (the old lie-filled mind, thoughts and emotions) and the sin (imbalance - separation from God) that so easily entangles, and let us run with perseverance (never quitting, stopping or giving up) the race marked out for us (our life journey). (NIV)
- You were running a good race (life journey from the heart/spirit). Who cut in on you and kept you from obeying the truth? (NIV) *Your old mind did*!
- His master said to him, 'Well done, good and faithful servant; you have been faithful over a little (followed your heart in all things), I will set you over much; enter into the joy of your master.' (RSV)

Faith

- So then, as the body without the spirit is dead, also faith (trusting the Truth in your heart and taking the action steps the Truth calls you to) without actions is dead. (TEV)
- Everything that does not come from faith (believing, trusting, and relying upon the Truth spoken into your heart and taking the action steps that Truth has revealed) is sin (imbalance - separation from God). (NIV)
- And without faith (believing, trusting, and relying upon the Truth spoken into your heart and taking the action steps that Truth has revealed) it is impossible to please God. (NIV)
- "… but my righteous one (my covenant partner) will live by faith. And if he shrinks back (goes back, listens to and follows the world, ego, flesh, lie-filled old mind), I will not be pleased with him." But we are not of those who shrink back and are destroyed, but of those who believe (in the Truth in our heart) and are saved (healed, delivered, set free, made whole in body, mind, and spirit). (NIV)

- They overcame him (father of lies, the prince of this world) by the Blood of the Lamb (the covenant with the Living God) and by the word of their testimony (speaking the Truth from their heart); they did not love their lives so much as to shrink from death. (NIV)

Faith without action steps (not following your heart) is dead and produces death, separation from God. Faith with action steps (put in your heart) is life and produces life, oneness with God.

Fasting is the physical action step that brings life, healing and wholeness to the body, mind and spirit.

The Battle

- Those who let themselves be controlled by their lower natures (old flesh, word, ego, lie-filled mind) live only to please themselves, but those who follow after the Holy Spirit find themselves doing those things that please God (following their Truth-filled heart). Following after the Holy Spirit leads to life and peace, but following after the old nature (old lie-filled mind) leads to death because the old sinful nature within us is against God (old mind vs. spirit/heart). It never did obey God's laws (the Truth revealed into the heart) and it never will. That's why those who are still under the control of their old sinful selves (old mind), bent on following their old evil desires, can never please God. (TLB)
- For those who live according to the flesh (old mind) set their minds on the things of the flesh, but those who live according to the Spirit (following the Truth revealed in their heart), the things of the Spirit. For to be carnally (5 sense) minded is death, but to be spiritually (6th, 7th sense) minded is life and peace. Because the carnal mind is enmity against God, for it is not subject to the law of God, nor indeed can be. So then, those who are in the flesh cannot please God. (NKJV)
- David said to the Philistine, "You come against me with sword and spear and javelin (physical strength), but I come against you in the name of the LORD Almighty (the covenant with God = spiritual strength), the God of the armies of Israel, whom you have defied. This day the LORD will hand you over to me…All those gathered here will know that it is not by sword or spear (physical means) that the LORD saves (heals, makes whole in body, mind and spirit); for the battle is the LORD's, and he will give all of you into our hands." (NIV)

- What causes fights and quarrels among you? Do they not come from your desires that battle within you? You want something but do not get it. You kill and covet, but you cannot have what you want. You quarrel and fight. You do not have, because you do not ask God. When you ask, you do not receive because you ask with wrong motives (from the world, ego, flesh-filled old mind instead of the Truth-filled heart), that you may spend what you get on your pleasures. (NIV)
- So I advise you to live according to your new life in the Holy Spirit. Then you will not be doing what your sinful (imbalanced - separating from God) nature craves. The **old sinful nature (the old mind)** loves to do evil, which is just opposite from what the Holy Spirit wants. And the **Spirit** gives us desires that are opposite from what the sinful nature desires. These two forces are **constantly fighting** each other, and your choices are never free from this conflict. But when you are directed by the Holy Spirit, you are no longer subject to the law (of sin and death-separation from God, and the physical laws. You can transcend them ALL). (NLT)
- So I find that this law is at work: when I want to do what is good, what is evil is the only choice I have. My inner being (heart) delights in the law of God (the Truth spoken into my heart). But I see a different law at work in my body - a law that fights against the laws that my mind (supremeconscious - mind of God in me) approves of. It makes me a prisoner to the law of sin (separation from God because I have followed the old lie-filled mind) that is at work in my body. What an unhappy man I am (when I follow my old flesh, world, ego, lie-filled mind instead of my Truth-filled heart)! Who will rescue me from this body that is taking me to death? Thanks be to God (His Spirit that lives in my heart and speaks Truth, and brings life). (TEV)
- The law of the Spirit of life (Truth in the heart) set me free from the law of sin and death(lies of the mind). (NIV)

Stand

- Use every piece of God's armor to resist the enemy (working through the old mind) in the time of evil, so that after the battle you will still be standing firm. Stand your ground, putting on the sturdy belt of truth (from the heart/spirit) and the body armor of God's righteousness (knowing what is Right in the heart and knowing your covenant partner). For shoes, put on the peace (from following the heart/spirit) that comes from the Good News (the Truth revealed into your heart), so that you will be fully prepared (for your life journey). In every battle you will need faith (to believe, trust and rely upon the Truth spoken into your heart and taking the physical action steps that Truth tells you to) as your shield to stop the fiery arrows aimed at you by Satan (the prince of this world, the father of lies whose kingdom is your old world, flesh, ego, lie-filled mind). Put on salvation (wholeness of body, mind and spirit) as your helmet, and take the sword of the Spirit, which is the word of God (the Truth spoken into your heart/spirit). Pray at all times and on every occasion in the power of the Holy Spirit (being led by the heart of Truth not the mind of lies). (NLT)

- Whoever thinks he is standing firm had better be careful that he does not fall. Every test that you have experienced is the kind that normally comes to people. But God keeps his promise, and he will not allow you to be tested beyond your power to remain firm; at the time you are put to the test, he will give you the strength to endure it, and so provide you with a way out (way up over the mountain of your challenge, causing growth and maturity in body, mind and spirit). (TEV)

The Battle

- This is the victory that has overcome the world (the old mind), even our faith (following our heart filled with Truth, taking the action steps that Truth calls for). (NIV)
- Consider it pure joy… whenever you face trials of many kinds, because you know that the testing of your faith develops perseverance.
  Perseverance must finish its work so that you may be mature and complete, not lacking anything (in body, mind or spirit). (NIV)
- We also rejoice in our sufferings, because we know that suffering produces perseverance; perseverance (never quitting, stopping or giving up), character (becoming mature, complete in body, mind and spirit); and character, hope (knowing the Truth). And hope (knowing the Truth in our hearts and following that Truth) does not disappoint us, because God has poured out his love (covenant blessings) into our hearts by the Holy Spirit, whom he has given us. (NIV)

Battle vs. War

- We might lose a battle but we will not lose the war.
- Make a new battle plan each day.
- For the battle is the LORD's (after we have followed our hearts with the action steps He has shown us). (NIV)

How to Win the War?

- Get to the end of yourself (your old mind).
- You must die to the flesh, to the world, to the self - the old you, to the 5 senses, to time past and time future, to the physical bound old mind.
- Listen to and obey the heart only.

- Take and keep taking the action steps in faith that the heart has shown you.
- Never ever give up or quit or stop.

Do Not Stop

- So do not throw away your confidence (knowing in the heart); it will be richly rewarded. You need to persevere so that when you have done the will of God (that which He has put in your heart), you will receive what he has promised (covenant partner blessing). But my righteous one (my covenant partner) will live by faith (believing, trusting, and relying upon the Truth spoken into your heart and taking the action steps that Truth has revealed). And if he shrinks back (goes back and follows the old world, flesh, ego, lie-filled mind instead of the Truth-filled heart), I will not be pleased with him. But we are not of those who shrink back and are destroyed, but of those who believe and are saved (made whole in body, mind and spirit). (NIV)

Suffering

- Literal meaning is "pressure."
- It is the pressure applied that makes us grow spiritually, it is what causes us to let go of the old mind filled with the world, knowledge of man, the ego, the flesh, religion, past and future, and our physical existence as we know it.
- Out of the most severe trial, their overflowing joy and their extreme poverty welled up in rich generosity. For I testify that they gave as much as they were able, and even **beyond their ability** (when they let go of their old mind, and followed their heart, they flowed supernaturally and gave beyond their physical ability). (NIV)

To grow spiritually there must be some stress applied (suffering)

Types of suffering include:
- Sickness and dis-ease
- Broken relationships - marriage, family, friends
- Foundation shaken - built on the sinking sand of the world's knowledge (lies)
- Financial crisis, job loss

Suffering: Good vs. Not Good

Good

- Good = God
- Brings you to the end of yourself, your ego, your world of knowledge = lies, your flesh, your religion, your past and future, your physical world.

■ Brings you to the point where you finally let go of (die to) the ego, the world, the lies, the flesh, religion, time, and the physical.

Not Good

■ Not good = yourself
■ Trying to hold on to your ego, your world of knowledge, your flesh, your religion, your future and past, your physical world.
■ Not willing to let go of (to put to death) your ego, your knowledge, your flesh, your religion, your past and future, your physical world.

We also rejoice in our _sufferings_, because we know that _suffering_ produces _perseverance_ (never quitting stopping or giving up); _perseverance_, _character_ (mature ,strong, complete in body, mind and spirit); and _character_, _hope_. And _hope_ (the knowing that comes from a heart of Truth) does not disappoint us, because God has poured out his _love_ (all that He IS, our covenant partner) into our hearts by the Holy Spirit, whom he has given us. (NIV)

Suffering will either make you:

■ Quit and run.
■ Stand your ground.
■ Or press forward even stronger.
■ If you stand or press forward you break all the old mind barriers, overcome the roaring lion.
■ The heart has victory and freedom.
■ The heart rules.
■ The heart is the knowing that has overcome the mind's thinking.

Fasting is the WILLFULLY brought on suffering that will break the old world/flesh/ego filled mind barrier.

Fasting is putting the old mind, the world, ego, flesh filled mind to death WILLFULLY.

The willfully brought on suffering of fasting affects the physical, mental and emotional all at the same time.

When one is whole, complete, not lacking anything in body, mind and spirit, there is no more suffering.

I Can't Do It!

- You cannot do it in your own strength but with God all things are possible.
- Self discipline vs. self control.
- God will not let you be tested beyond your ability to endure and pass your test - Job.
- Battle plan - break the task down into smaller pieces that you can do-fast one meal, then two, then one day, then 2 days and so on.
- This gives you the **confidence**, the knowing you can, not only in your heart but also in your supremeconscious mind and your conscious (thinking) mind.

Who is in control?

- When you think about the concept of fasting, your **mind** is in control if it causes you to avoid it or reason why you should not or cannot, or do not.
- When you think about the concept of fasting, your **heart** is in control if it causes you to be drawn to it, knowing you should, knowing you can and knowing you will do it.
- Your **heart/spirit** want to fast, your **mind** does not.

Self Discipline vs. Self Control

- Self discipline is a product of the mind.
- Self discipline will always fail if it is put to a strong enough test, a great amount of suffering. Why? Because it is of the conscious (thinking) mind, and the mind has limitations.
- Self Control is of the Spirit.
- Self Control will never fail no matter what the test or how great the suffering because it is God working in and through you. Why? Because once you put your old world/self/ego/flesh/religious/time/physical lie-filled mind to death the spirit (heart) and supremeconscious mind flow with the self control that never ends because it comes from the infinite and eternal God.

Fasting, Religion, Ego, Healing

■ Is this the kind of fast I have chosen, only a day for a man to humble himself? Is it only for bowing one's head like a reed and for lying on sackcloth and ashes? Is that what you call a fast, a day acceptable to the LORD? (NO! This is religion). Is not this the kind of fasting I have chosen: to loose the chains of injustice and untie the cords of the yoke, to set the oppressed free and break every yoke? Is it not to share your food with the hungry and to provide the poor wanderer with shelter--when you see the naked, to clothe him, and not to turn away from your own flesh and blood (all this when done from the Truth-filled heart/spirit, not from an ego/religion-filled mind)? Then your light will break forth like the dawn, and your healing will quickly appear (because you followed your heart, not your mind); then your righteousness (your covenant relationship with God) will go before you, and the glory of the LORD will be your rear guard. Then you will call, and the LORD will answer (because you are His covenant partner); you will cry for help, and he will say: Here am I (your covenant partner that meets ALL your needs after you have done ALL you have been shown in your heart.

If you are faithful in your part no matter how great or small that part has been revealed to you, He takes care of the rest. This is the covenant). (NIV)

■ …If I have a faith that can move mountains, but have not love (have not a covenant partnership with God), I am nothing. If I give all I possess to the poor and surrender my body to the flames (if this is done from the religion/ego-filled mind, it means nothing), but have not love (covenant partnership with God), I gain nothing. Love is patient (heart), love is kind (heart). It does not envy (old ego mind), it does not boast (old ego mind), it is not proud (old ego mind). It is not rude (old ego mind), it is not self-seeking (old ego mind), it is not easily angered (from old lie-filled mind); it keeps no record of wrongs (lets go). Love does not delight in evil (lie-filled mind) but rejoices with the truth (filled heart). It always protects, always trusts, always hopes (**knows**), and always perseveres (your covenant partner never quits, stops or gives up on you His covenant partner). (NIV)

Jesus and Fasting

■ Then Jesus was **led by the Spirit** into the desert to be tempted by the devil. After fasting forty days and forty nights, he was **hungry**. The tempter came to him and said, "If you are the Son of God, tell these stones to become bread." Jesus answered, "It is written: **'Man does not live on bread alone, but on every word that comes from the mouth of God.'"** (Every Word of Truth that is spoken into your heart brings life, health and healing more so than any physical substance) Then the devil took him to the holy city and had him stand on the highest point of the temple. "If you are the Son of God," he said, "throw yourself down. For it is written: 'He will command his angels concerning you, and they will lift you up in their hands, so that you will not strike your foot against a stone.'" Jesus answered him, "It is also written: **'Do not put the Lord your God to the test.'**"(Tests are to grow and mature us spiritually, mentally and physically in our journey of life. God cannot be tested because He is perfect, complete, not lacking anything. When the test comes, if we obey and follow our heart, take the action steps it tells us, and if we never quit, stop or give up following our heart, we always pass the test and grow. If we waiver and choose to follow our mind, the test has become the temptation and we will always fall, and fail, and have to take the test again.) Again, the devil took him to a very high mountain and showed him all the kingdoms of the world and their splendor. "All this I will give you," he said, "if you will bow down and worship me." Jesus said to him, "Away from me, Satan! For it is written: **'Worship the Lord your God, and serve him only.'**" (We worship God, our covenant partner, by doing all He has placed in our heart with all our soul, all our strength, all our ability, never quitting or giving up. We worship Him with all of our body, soul and spirit.) Then the devil left him, and angels came and attended him. (NIV)

- **MORE** - after fasting 40 days when it said He was hungry, it meant that He had come to the end of His fast and if He did not eat He would start to digest His own organs. This is starvation. This is when the tempter came to Him and hit Him with his best shot first - temptation of food. This is why fasting from food is so powerful, not only physically but also mentally and spiritually - the hundredfold blessing. When we can overcome our addiction to food, with fasting and prayer, we have overcome the best shot the tempter can hit us with. From there on you know you can do all things in your heart, in your supremeconscious mind, and even your conscious thinking mind has now been renewed with the Truth. So stand strong, never quit, stop or give up and reap the blessings your covenant partner is yearning to heap upon you.

- **When you fast**, do not look somber as the hypocrites do, for they disfigure their faces to show men they are fasting. I tell you the truth; they have received their reward in full. But when you fast, put oil on your head and wash your face, so that it will not be obvious to men that you are fasting, but only to your Father, who is unseen; and your Father, who sees what is done in secret, will reward you. (NIV)

- **MORE** - you will always be blessed when you listen to the voice of Truth spoken into your heart. Do not fast because you "think" it is the right thing to do. This just feeds the religion (the ego filled old mind that blocks the flow of the Spirit). As the old mind, flesh, religion, ego, lie-filled mind is fed, the Spirit is quenched or suppressed. So always follow your heart (not your mind) in everything you do. *This is where God speaks; this is where miracles are born.*

- While they were worshiping the Lord and fasting, the Holy Spirit said, "Set apart for me Barnabas and Saul for the work to which I have called them." (NIV) (Fasting opens the door to hear the voice of God spoken into your heart clearly).

- "Lord, have mercy on my son, for he is an epileptic and suffers severely; for he often falls into the fire and often into the water. So I brought him to Your disciples, but they could not cure him." Then Jesus answered and said, "O faithless and perverse generation, how long shall I be with you? How long shall I bear with you? Bring him here to Me." And Jesus rebuked the demon, and it came out of him; and the child was cured from that very hour. Then the disciples came to Jesus privately and said, "Why could we not cast it out?"
So Jesus said to them, "**Because of your unbelief (you went back into your 5 senses and fed your mind which produced unbelief in you)**; for assuredly, I say to you, if you have faith as a mustard seed, you will say to this mountain, 'Move from here to there,' and it will move; and nothing will be impossible for you (if you followed the Truth spoken in your heart instead of the lies spoken into your head you can do ALL things because God is doing them through you. You are an unblocked vessel through whom His Spirit can flow freely). However, this kind (of unbelief, not demon) does not go out except by **prayer and fasting**." Prayer is listened to His voice of Truth spoken into your heart, and fasting is putting the old, flesh, ego, 5 senses, religion, world, lie-filled mind to death willfully. (NKJV)

Lessons from the Greatest Tests

- Food is the greatest temptation, it is also the path to passing the greatest test>greatest victory>freedom.
- Tests are meant for us to grow spiritually, mentally and physically. We do not test God; we do not question God's infinite wisdom. His ways are not man's ways.
- God's Word spoken into our heart is the Right Word at the Right Time.
- We are to only worship God, and this worship is to be with our body, our mind and our spirit.

■ When we know Him, we can have the hope (knowing in the heart) that produces the faith that can move mountains, or raise a son from the dead.

Fasting does not move God, rather it puts to death our ego/self/flesh/world filled mind so the Spirit of Life and Truth can flow from the heart into the supremeconscious mind and into the body with healing, health and wholeness.

Hundredfold Principle

■ One fold is the physical. (1X)
■ Tenfold is the mental/emotional. (10X)
■ Hundredfold is the spiritual. (100x)
■ Everything in your life is connected to this principle.
■ In all that we do, think, say and know there is the hundredfold principle always being demonstrated.

Hundredfold Decrease

■ **1 Fold Decrease (-1X)** - if you do not fast from the American diet, then it will in time decrease the life of the body (physical).
■ **10 Fold Decrease (-10X)** - the lack of fasting causes a feeding of your ego, world, flesh filled mind. As the mind is fed the lie grows and the mental/emotional toxins increase and store in organs/glands/tissues (mental/emotional).
■ **100 Fold Decrease (-100X)** - if the lack of fasting causes you to feed the flesh (the negative mind, emotion, body energy) by either eating dead, cooked, pleasurable food, or being addicted to anything, the flow of the Spirit is blocked. If the flesh/ego/world/lie-filled mind increases, the Spirit flow decreases (spiritual).

Hundredfold Increase

■ **1 Fold Increase (1X)** - if you fast from whatever binds you, first and foremost FOOD, it will bring life, health and strength to the body (physical).
■ **10 Fold Increase (10X)** - if the fasting puts our flesh/ego/world/lie-filled mind to death, and at the same time we reprogram our conscious and unconscious mind with Truth, we bring healing and wholeness to our mind and emotions. As the old mind decreases, the heart and spirit increases (mental/emotional).
■ **100 Fold Increase (100X)** - if the fasting is offered as a worship to God—offering your **bodies** as living sacrifices, holy and pleasing to

God, this is your spiritual act of worship (NIV), and the fast is the action step that combines with faith, it brings life, health and wholeness to your whole being, when done in obedience and perseverance, never quitting, stopping or giving up (spiritual).

How to Fast

- Do it as the 100 fold blessing.
- Renew the conscious thinking mind with Truth from your heart and supremeconscious mind as you fast: thinking on whatever is true, whatever is right, whatever is pure, whatever is lovely, whatever is ...excellent or praiseworthy.... And the God of peace will be with you. (NIV)
- Press into the pain, the suffering because when you run into it instead of away from it, this is where victory and freedom are found. This is where the hope is found, this is where the knowing is found, this is where the mind barrier is broken and the heart rules with love, joy, peace and hope.
- Offer it as a worship; holy (whole = in body, mind and spirit) and pleasing to God.

Fasting

- In breaking the bondage to food, you also start to break the mind/emotion barriers, which opens the door to the Spirit of God flowing from your heart into your mind and body, His life, His healing, His wholeness.
- As the flesh decreases the Spirit increases. The flesh is one aspect of the old mind that blocks the heart/spirit.

The most powerful aspect of food fasting is not the physical but the breaking of the old mind, the flesh. When this is broken the Spirit flows unhindered bringing healing and wholeness.

The greatest addiction is food.
The greatest bondage is food.
The greatest pleasure is food.
These should only be filled by God—not by food.

Fasting breaks the mind barrier (limitations) so one can grow, to increase spiritually (limitless).

The Roaring Lion

- The roaring lion is the old mind.
- When you stand and do not run away but actually run into the roaring lion (led by the heart), you realize that the roaring lion has no teeth and no claws. The old mind/ego gives us its best shot but also puts itself on the line, because if it does not win by making us run it knows it has lost everything.
- So follow your heart, run into the suffering, the pain, the roaring lion, and see the awesome miracles of God that await you in your journey of life.

There is NO better way to put the old mind to death and unlock the door to spiritual growth and to hear and know the voice of God than by FASTING.

You must suffer the old house to build the new temple of worship, praise and thanksgiving.

Offer your bodies as living sacrifices; holy (holy = whole in body, mind and spirit) and pleasing to God (following your Truth-filled heart, not your lie-filled old mind) - this is your spiritual act of worship. Do not conform any longer to the pattern of this world (the old mind), but be transformed by the renewing of your mind (from a Truth-filled heart). Then you will be able to test and approve what God's will is (it is always revealed and known in your heart of Truth and never revealed or known in the mind) - his good, pleasing and perfect will. (NIV)

Do you not know that your body is a temple of the Holy Spirit, who is in you, whom you have received from God? You are not your own; you were bought at a price. Therefore honor God with your body. (NIV)

Worship
Reverent devotion and allegiance pledged to God, the actions by which this reverence is expressed. The English word worship comes from the Old English word worthship, a word which denotes the worthiness of the one receiving the special honor or devotion.

The two most powerful physical action steps to bring health, healing and wholeness to the body, mind, emotions and spirit are: FASTING and PRAYER.

All things are possible and all things can be changed with: FASTING and PRAYER.

A New World
- Once you have adopted the 7 basic steps to total health as a lifestyle, and your physical being becomes balanced in the present, the energy for maintaining life can turn inward and begin healing your past physical toxins, stored emotional toxins in the tissues, and negative mental thought patterns stored in your conscious and unconscious mind. As you continue to stay balanced in the present and start to balance in your past, the energy of healing turns further inward to the generational toxins of body, emotions and mind. Once these are released the body/emotion/mind/spirit enters the place of wholeness, the place of no time, the place where the physical laws can be transcended, because the Spirit of God flows unhindered in a whole human body, mind, and spirit. This is the temple of purity and holiness in which the Spirit of God makes His dwelling place.
- When you have built a temple of holiness, which is the body free from all toxins and blockages in all time periods - this is timelessness.
- When the stored emotions have been released from all organs, glands, and tissues in all time periods - this becomes the timeless spiritual states of being: love, joy, peace and hope.
- When all the stored lies from all time periods have been released from the conscious and unconscious mind and reprogrammed with only Truth so the supremeconscious mind is one with the other two - this becomes the timeless, boundless mind of God.

- When you live in a pure, holy temple, and have a timeless state of being of love, joy, peace and hope, and have the mind of God unhindered in the endless present moment, then the Spirit of God will flow out from you as a True light to the world to entrain the world around you to the frequency of Love, of Light, of Life of body, mind and spirit, being filled with the Spirit of God. All peoples and nations will be filled with the Light, the Life, the Spirit of God and "all will become one," "one with each other" and "one with Him" who created them. This is heaven come to earth.

- This is when you will "Love the Lord your God with all your heart and with all your soul and with all your mind and with all your strength." And you will "Love your neighbor as yourself" because you do **know** the Truth and the Truth has set you free in body, in mind and in spirit.

I would rather live one day in faith, obedience, and perseverance to what God has put in my heart than 75 years of mere existence being ruled by my mind, living in fear, disobeying my heart.

Enjoy the moment.
Enjoy the battle.
Enjoy the journey on your way to the Promised Land.
This is living life to the full.
This is as good as it gets because this is where God IS.

_____

_____

_____

_____

_____

_____

_____

_____

_____

_____

_____

_____

_____

Go Deeper

1. Why is it so important to lose all the "old you?"
2. How is the "new you" new in body, mind, and spirit?
3. Why do you not become deficient when you fast?
4. How does fasting release physical, and emotional toxins?
5. How does fasting promote retracing? Give an example.
6. What does the second part of the group 3 Rat study confirm?
7. What type of fasting is the quickest to clear the body of toxins?
8. What type of fasting has the greatest long-term benefits?
9. Why do you need to know what signs to expect when you fast, and the principle of retracing?
10. Why is fasting the conscious thinking mind and the negative emotions more important than fasting the physical body?
11. What is your greatest adversary in a fast, and what is that a part of?
12. What should we fast from, and why?
13. What are the 9 strongholds of the old mind, and what effect do they have on your total health?
14. Of the 9 strongholds of the old mind which are the 5 most important to fast from and why?
15. Do you know why, if fasting is not done with the hundredfold principle in your heart, its benefits will be minimal and short-lived?
16. Do you know how to turn your old house built by your old mind into a holy temple built by your heart?
17. If the battle is between your heart and your old mind, what is your battle plan to become victorious and free?
18. What is the only thing that can stop you from healing in body, mind and spirit?
19. Are you aware that any time you try to think of a solution to a situation in your life, you are suppressing the Spirit from flowing powerfully in your life, and why?
20. Why is food the greatest bondage to the entire human race, and how can you break this bondage applying the hundredfold principle?
21. Why would you want to run into the suffering in your life, and how will this affect your total health of body, mind, and spirit?
22. What is the first step in building a new world, and how will this critical first step eventually lead to the Spirit of Love filling every person on the planet?
23. What does "God's kingdom has come" mean now that you know the Truth and have been set free from the lie?
24. What does "heaven coming to earth" mean in relation to the seven basic steps to total health?
25. What is the strongest power on the earth? How will it heal/save us?

Prayer

What is Prayer?

- Prayer - communication with God, a spoken or unspoken communication with God. It may express praise, thanksgiving, confession or a request for something such as help or somebody's wellbeing.
- From Old French *preiere* from, ultimately, Latin *precarius* "obtained by entreaty," from *precari* "to entreat," plead desperately: to beg somebody for something, often repeatedly (*formal*).[91]

Prayer

is communication with God by talking and most importantly by listening.

Prayer Facts

- 82% of Americans believe in the healing power of personal prayer.
- 90% of American women and 80% of American men pray regularly.
- 54% Americans pray daily, 29% more than once per day.
- Over 130 controlled laboratory studies show that prayer or a prayerlike state of love and compassion can increase health in many living organisms from humans to bacteria.

Belief and Healing Rate

- Patients with retinal detachment at Columbia-Presbyterian Medical Center in New York City were reviewed; a 400% difference in healing time between quickest and slowest healers was found. No correlation was found in any physical factor; the most significant factors found in the healing rates were psychological factors.
- Patients who healed quickly confronted their situation directly, were trusting of the surgeon, were optimistic about the results, were confident about coping and doing things for themselves, were willing to accept their situation without special concern, and accepted the bad with the good in life.
- Patients who healed slowly tended to feel trapped in life, were suspicious of others and pessimistic. They could not cope well. They were angry about being dependent on others and avoided personal contact. They often felt helpless.
- In this study the Columbia-Presbyterian researchers concluded that some types of religious faith were healthy and some were not.
- The people that healed the quickest demonstrated a transcendent faith, were convinced that life will continue to be meaningful whether they

could see again or not. They affirm, "Whether I see or go blind, life will continue to be meaningful and rich."

■ Most patients appeared to have been taught that faith is believing that you will receive what you wish if you believe and pray sufficiently, that reality can be changed…This type of faith is usually quite brittle, easily destroyed or challenged by adverse circumstances. Any negative word about the surgeon or his methods becomes an immediate concern.

■ In this study only 1-2% of the total patients demonstrated this transcendent faith.[92]

Types of Prayers and Cancer Cells

■ Study was done on Dr. Leonard Laskow, physician and reported healer.[93]

■ Laskow reported success when he would emotionally connect with the subject, in this case the cancer cells, by adopting a generally loving attitude toward the cells. He addressed the cancer cell cultures 5 different ways:

  ■ 1. Asking that they return to the natural order and harmony of ordinary cell growth.
  ■ 2. Visualizing that only 3 cells remaining in the culture.
  ■ 3. Letting God's will flow through his hands without trying to direct the outcome.
  ■ 4. Offering unconditional love to the tumor cells, without giving specific instructions.
  ■ 5. Dematerializing the cancer cells.

■ The results were as follows:

  ■ Most effective was asking the cultures to return to the natural order and harmony of the normal cell line, 39% inhibition of tumor cell growth.
  ■ Allowing God's will to manifest showed 21% inhibition of the cancer cell growth.
  ■ Visualizing only 3 cells remaining showed 18% inhibition of the cancer cell growth.
  ■ Unconditional love appeared to be neutral.

Directed vs. Non-directed Prayer

■ Directed prayer - has a specific goal or outcome in mind. One is attempting to steer the system in a precise direction, i.e., cancer cured, pain leaves.

- Non-directed prayer - has no specific outcome kept in the mind; with this type of prayer one is not telling God what to do but more of a "thy will be done" prayer.

Spindrift Studies Results

- Spindrift organization in Oregon has, for a decade, been performing simple laboratory experiments showing that prayer works.
- In their 10 years of testing the results showed that both directed and non-directed prayers work, but in their tests the **non-directed technique** appeared quantitatively more effective, frequently yielding results that were *twice as great, or more, when compared to the directed technique.*[94]

Mold Growth Directed vs. Non-directed Prayer

- Why lower organisms? The mind factor, placebo effect and all other possible factors that the one receiving the prayer could produce to alter the results would be removed.
- Mold growth was stressed with an alcohol rinse then prayer was initiated to encourage the growth of the mold.
- When directed prayer was used nothing happen, no growth was seen; when non-directed prayer with no goal in mind was used the mold growth began to multiply.

Wound Healing and Prayer

- 44 patients with artificially created, full-skin-thickness surgical wounds.[95]
- Subjects would insert their arm through a circular opening in the wall of the testing facility through which they could not see. The arm would remain in the opening for 5 minutes. They were told this was to measure biopotentials from the surgical site with a non-contact device.
- The prayer was on the other side of the wall praying for the healing but not touching the skin.
- 23 patients received prayer, 21 patients did not.
- The results were statistically highly significant.
- Placebo effect was ruled out by telling the subjects that the purpose of putting the arm through the wall opening was to measure biopotentials of the wound healing, not the effectiveness of prayer.
- On day sixteen, in 13 of the 23 treated subjects the wound had completely healed compared to none of the group not prayed for.

Spontaneous Regression of Cancer

- Dr. Yujiro Ikemi at the Kyushu University's School of Medicine in Fukuoka, Japan studied cases of spontaneous regression of cancer (SRC).[96]
- Results showed SRC is not accidental, random, or beyond the patient's thoughts, attitudes and feelings. The results strongly suggest that there is a profound effect of prayerfulness and an indwelling spiritual sense on the cancer process.
- One of Ikemi's typical SRC cases involved Y.H., a male church worker age 64 who developed cancer of the upper jaw. The tumor was removed but the cancer reappeared 9 months later on his vocal cord. Removal of his larynx, including his vocal cords, was recommended, but Y.H. refused. He stated he preferred to continue to be a preacher for as long as he could speak rather than losing his voice to surgery. "This is God's will and I have no complaint about it, whatever should happen will just happen."
- Ten days after he received "sentence of cancer" he went to see the president of his religious organization who said, "Remember that you are an invaluable asset for our church." This left Y.H. extremely happy; he shed tears of joy all the way home. Beginning with this experience, his hoarseness improved. Four months later he began to give short speeches at his church again. Two months later he could speak up to 30 minutes and his voice was quite clear. Y.H. lived the next 13 years without any form of medical treatment or surgery. All follow up examinations showed no evidence of the laryngeal tumor. He died at 78 from unrelated causes.
- Y.H. case demonstrated certain traits evident in SRC:
    - Following his diagnosis Y.H. showed no tendency to lapse into depression, despair, lack of motivation or fear of death, which is typical of many patients.
    - He did not engage in specific prayers in which he pleaded or bargain with God to cure him.
    - He did not "fight" cancer as is often recommended.
    - His attitude was rather one of renewed commitment and gratitude to God, combined with the belief that God's will was being done, no matter what happened.
- Dr. Ikemi's findings in his study of SRC were: Often a prayerful, prayer-like attitude of devotion and acceptance, not robust, aggressive prayer for specific outcomes, including eradication of the cancer, precedes the healing.

Directed Prayer-5 Steps

- Dr. William Braud of Mind Science Foundation lists 5 powerful steps to increase our power of prayer:[97]
    - Relaxation and Quietude
    - Attention Training
    - Imagery and Visualization
    - Intentionality
    - Strong Positive Emotions

- **Relaxation and Quietude** causes a wide range of beneficial mental/emotional as well as physical effects. Quieting or stilling the mind as well relaxing the body combine to set the stage for more effective prayer.

- **Attention Training** is the ability to stay focused on the image or thing being visualized in prayer for an extended period of time. This will take practice because the mind tends to wander so quickly. According to Dr. Braud, *"Focusing attention upon any object establishes a two way communication channel with that object - a channel that can be used to gain knowledge about that object or to influence it."* After one has opened the channel, images provide the vehicles for carrying information back and forth from the prayer and the person or thing being prayed for.

- **Imagery and Visualization** both entail thinking without words, but in imagery wordless pictures appear in the mind, whereas in visualization these wordless thoughts are formed with a desired outcome or goal in mind. Imagery is a mode of communication between the prayer and the subject being prayed for.

- **Intentionality and Strong Positive Emotion** - this can vary depending on culture. The western thought is "make it happen", whereas eastern thought believes more in "it will be as it should be." **The key factor in either belief is how strong in the heart it is believed and does not waiver no matter what is physically seen.**

Those who have developed the ability to help others heal through prayer:

- They uniformly state that distance is not a factor in the healing power of prayer but love is.[98]
- They state that love heals across any distance because prayer is not time and space bound.

■ They also state that their results are in the proportion that they feel love and caring for the person they are praying for, in essence the more they become one with that person.

Prayer Studies on Lower Organisms[99]

■ Ten subjects tried to inhibit fungus growth in laboratory cultures by conscious intent focusing for 15 minutes at a distance of 1.5 yards. Of the 194 culture dishes, 151 showed retarded growth.

■ In a replication of this study the subjects were at a distance of 1 to 15 miles from the fungus culture dishes. The results were the same - fungus growth inhibition in 16 out of 16 trials.

■ Sixty subjects not known to have healing abilities were both able to impede and stimulate significantly the growth of cultures of bacteria.

■ Sixty university volunteers with no known healing abilities were asked to alter the genetic ability of a strain of bacteria E.Coli, which normally mutates from the ability to metabolize the sugar lactose (lactose negative) to the ability to use it (lactose positive) at a known rate. The students tried to influence test tubes of bacterial culture-three for increased mutation from lactose negative to positive, three for decreased mutation from lactose negative to lactose positive and three tubes as controls. The results were that the bacteria did mutate in the direction desired by the students.

■ **These and other studies show that, if genes can be altered by conscious thought, then genes cannot be the ultimate controllers that they are thought to be. Our biology is not our destiny.**

Prayer can change our destiny.

■ **MORE** - this shows that genes are not our destiny because they are physical; they are nothing more than information and energy. This information and energy can be changed by conscious awareness, and even more powerfully by the power of TRUE prayer.

■ These studies also indicate that ordinary people have the ability to bring about biological changes in living organisms. This suggests that everyone may possess the inborn ability to heal.

■ The evidence is supportive of the positive effects of prayer, not only in humans but also in mice, chicks, enzymes, fungi, yeast, bacteria, and cells of various sorts. These cannot be dismissed due to suggestion or placebo since the lower life forms that do not consciously think are presumably not susceptible to suggestion.

Relaxation and Meditation

- Dr. Herbert Benson of Harvard University Medical School was one of the first medical researchers to study the health benefits of prayer and meditation. He developed a technique called the Relaxation Response.[100]
  - 1. Pick a focus word or phrase that is firmly rooted in your belief system.
  - 2. Sit quietly in a comfortable position.
  - 3. Close your eyes.
  - 4. Relax your muscles.
  - 5. Breathe slowly and naturally, repeat your focus word, phrase or prayer silently to yourself as you exhale.
  - 6. Assume a passive attitude. Do not be concerned with how well you are doing and when other thoughts enter your mind return to the focus word or prayer.
  - 7. Do this for 10-20 minutes.
  - 8. Remain quiet for a couple of minutes allowing other thoughts to return and then to arise.
  - 9. Practice this technique 1-2 times daily.
- Dr. Benson found that 80% of patients chose to use a prayer or religious phrase (such as Heavenly Father, Lord God) reflecting the highly religious nature of Americans.
- This prayer and meditation has proven to be beneficial in the treatment of hypertension, irregular heart rhythm, chronic pain, insomnia, anxiety, depression, infertility, and the side effects from treatments from cancer and AIDS.
- Generally seen were decreased heart rate, lower metabolic rate, lower breathing rate, slowing of brain waves.

Power of Intercessory Prayer

- Dr. Randolph Byrd measured the clinical effects of intercessory prayer.[101]
- In the coronary care unit of San Francisco General Hospital 393 patients were randomly assigned to two groups. One group of 192 patients was prayed for by outside intercessors from around the country, who were told the patient's name and clinical status and who committed to pray for them until their discharge. The other group of 201 patients was the control group. They did not receive any prayer. No patient, nurse or doctor knew who was being prayed for and who was not.

- The results were statistically significant - the patients in the control group were almost twice as likely to suffer complications than the prayed-for group, 27% vs. 15%.
  - Episodes of congestive heart failure, 10% vs. 4%.
  - Use of diuretics, 7% vs. 3%.
  - Episodes of cardiopulmonary arrest, 7% vs. 2%.
  - Episodes of pneumonia, 7% vs. 2%.
  - Use of antibiotics, 9% vs. 2%.
  - Intubation/ventilation required, 6% vs. 0%.

Prayer Studies - Spoken Words

- At a rehabilitation hospital in Chicago, a group of researchers tested the effects of a spoken message on patients undergoing back surgery. The patients were unconscious, under total anesthesia, and had no awareness that a message was being spoken. The most common complication after this type of surgery is the inability to urinate, which necessitates the use of a catheter. Toward the end of the surgery, while the patient was still asleep, the surgeon spoke to the patient by name and said, "The operation has gone well. You will be flat on your back for the next couple of days. When you are waiting, it would be a good idea if you relax the muscles in your pelvic area. This will help you urinate, so you won't need a catheter." The results were amazing: not one patient spoken to needed a catheter, while more than half in the control group, who were not spoken to, needed a catheter.[102]

Study on Prayer Types

- Sociologist Margaret Poloma defined and measured four types of prayer in a 560-person survey.[103]
- The types included:
  - 1. Colloquial - talking to God informally as you would talk to your best friend.
  - 2. Petitional - asking God for something for yourself or others.
  - 3. Ritual - using/reciting formal prayers.
  - 4. Meditative - focusing the mind on an aspect of God for a period of time, calming the conscious mind and dismissing extraneous thoughts.
- The results were that the people who most often used colloquial or informal prayer reported a higher degree of happiness.
- Those who favored meditative prayer were more likely to experience satisfaction with the meaning and purpose of their lives.

- Those who used only petitionary and formal, ritualistic prayer reported less happiness and lower levels of life satisfaction.
- This study shows the more we see prayer as an expression of our personal relationship with God, the more effective it is.

Prayer to God is like talking to and listening to your most precious and adored spouse, your covenant partner.

Prayer Types

- **Talking** - informally from the heart as one best friend to another. Talking to the love of your life, the two being one, sharing your likes, dislikes, dreams, hopes and desires. Sharing your life.
- **Listening** - meditatively stilling the mind so you can hear the voice of your best friend - God, just like you would keep extreme attention and hang on every word your love speaks to you. Every word means everything to you, so you listen extremely attentively.
- **Adoring/Praise** - this prayer is like the adoring a loving couple feels when they look into each other's eyes. It is telling your spouse how much you love, adore and praise them for who they are. Telling them how you think about them all the time, that you cannot live without them and how they are the most important person in your life. It is lifting your spouse, your covenant partner, up on a pedestal.
- **Thanksgiving** - thanking your covenant partner, your other half, for all they have given you; their love, their life, their devotion, their time, their patience, they have given everything they have to meet your needs and you thank them with every part of your being.
- **Worship** - this is the giving of your body, your mind and your spirit to your covenant partner as a sign of your commitment and devotion to them. To worship is to count as worthy, as deserving of your spirit, mind and body devotion.
- **Petition** - asking for something from your covenant partner, your love, that you truly know you need in your heart and you cannot supply yourself. These are not superficial, worldly desires but heartfelt needs.
- **Intercession** - listening and praying for your love's needs and other needs that she/he brings before you. No matter where you are she/he is always before you and you lift her/him up in prayer continually. Spirit vs. mind.

- **Compassion/Lifting One Up** - This is a type of intercession that just strengthens/empowers one in the journey - Moses' hands being lifted up by Aaron and Hur.
- **Confession**-this is telling your covenant partner, your love, that you were wrong, you chose to follow your old ego, flesh, world, lie-filled mind instead of your Truth-filled heart. You are sorry and ask for her/his forgiveness (letting go) and you repent, which means taking an 180-degree about face and going in the opposite direction. This means you are now choosing to follow your Truth-filled heart instead of your lie-filled old mind.

Worship-One of the Most Powerful Prayer Types

- Yet a time is coming and has now come when the true worshipers will worship the Father in spirit and truth, for they are the kind of worshipers the Father seeks. God is spirit, and his worshipers must worship in spirit and in truth. (Truth's home is the heart; lies make their dwelling place in the mind). (NIV)
- Offer your bodies as living sacrifices, holy (holy = whole in body, mind and spirit) and pleasing to God (following your Truth-filled heart, not your lie-filled old mind) - this is your spiritual act of worship. Do not conform any longer to the pattern of this world (old mind), but be transformed by the renewing of your mind (from the Truth revealed to your heart). Then you will be able to test and approve what God's will is (His Truth shown to your heart) - his good, pleasing and perfect will. (NIV)

The Right Word
(*from the Truth-filled heart not the lie-filled old mind*)

at the Right Time
(*present moment not the past or future*)

at the Right Place brings healing.

Prayer of Saint Francis

Lord, make me an instrument of your peace.
Where there is hatred (emotion produced from old mind), let me sow love (spiritual state of being from a Truth-filled heart),
Where there is injury, pardon;
Where there is doubt (lie-filled old mind), faith (Truth-filled heart);
Where there is despair (old mind), hope (heart);

Where there is darkness (the old lie-filled, unaware of the Truth mind), light (total awareness of the Truth revealed from the heart and supremeconscious mind);
Where there is sadness (emotion produced from old mind), joy (spiritual state of being from a Truth-filled heart).
O divine Master, Grant that I may not so much seek to be consoled, as to console,
To be understood, as to understand
To be loved, as to love,
For it is in giving that we receive;
It is in pardoning that we are pardoned;
It is in dying (to our old ego, self, world, flesh, religion, lie-filled mind) that we are born to eternal life (which flows from the Truth-filled heart).

Prayer is not confined to time or space. It can transcend both.

What is prayer really?
Is prayer just focusing on what you or another need or want?
Prayer is not just focusing the mind with the intention of getting an expected result - this is the power of the mind.

Is prayer letting go of the needs and wants and letting God be God and you be a vessel of His love, joy, peace and hope, whether it is for one moment, one day, one year, or as long as He fills your lungs with the breath of life?

Your purpose in life is to love the Lord your God with all your heart and with all your soul and with all your mind and with all your strength and to love your neighbor as yourself.

**In life, in healing, in wholeness
our purpose is to receive from Him and give
to the world as He directs us to give.
Not to receive only.
Not to give only,
but to receive for the purpose
of God-directed giving.**

**Does God ever answer worldly, ego, flesh filled
prayers?
Yes.
Israel prayed for a king in order to be like the other
nations; this was a big mistake but God granted their
request.**

**So be careful to pray from a Truth-filled heart, not a
world/ego/flesh-filled old mind, otherwise you might
be bringing more pain and suffering upon yourself
and those you are praying for.**

**The biblical prophets prayed and heard the voice of
God. Their accuracy in foretelling future events was
100% because they listened to God speak to their
heart and supremeconscious mind. If they were not
100%, they were stoned.**

MORE - when you still the mind completely, then you can hear the voice
of Truth, the voice of God clearly. When you train yourself to hear the
voice of Truth you will know, that you know that you know that God has
spoken to your heart and filled your supremeconscious mind (mind of
God) with wisdom, understanding, revelation and KNOWING. This is
what the prophets had and they were always RIGHT, because God's
voice is always RIGHT. You can operate in this also if you just learn to
still your mind and listen to your heart.

Always remember when you follow your heart/spirit, the Spirit of God speaking to your heart, you always make the Right decisions, because you are always following the Truth no matter what the outcome is, because there is no mind involvement.

God's ways are not man's ways.

Prayer - Mind or Spirit Power?

■ **If a so called prayer is conceived in the mind, as most if not all prayer studies are, then the power is of the mind; the dilemma exists in that if we feed the mind we are suppressing the heart/spirit where the true power of God flows from, and where the place of miracles are born. Mind power can cause positive changes and improvements, but Spirit power causes complete transformations, healings and miracles.**

■ **Is it your mind or your heart/spirit that will change you and the world?**

"If God had granted all the silly prayers I've made in my life, where should I be now?"- C.S. Lewis[104]

The Missionary's Revelation

■ A true story of a missionary who was captured by soldiers. They told him to dig his own grave and, when he was done he would be shot and buried. At first he was filled with fear, thoughts went through his mind, "what about my family, Lord, what about my mission?" But as he continued to dig God gave him a revelation of being with him in heaven today (living in the eternal present moment where God lives). This revelation was so powerful that the man was transformed and joyfully began to dig as fast as he could. Upon seeing this, the soldier questioned him about why he was so happy when he was about to die?

He shared his revelation with them, and his faith with them and not only did they not kill the missionary they gave their hearts to God that day (entered into a covenant partnership with the Living God).

Lessons from Life

- When we die to our self, our flesh, our ego, our old mind, that is when we truly begin to live life to the full in body, mind and spirit.
- When we have no fear (faith is the opposite of fear), our old mind, ego, flesh have no more hold on us.
- Fear is believing, trusting and relying upon the world system, the words of man, in the lie.
- Faith is believing, trusting and relying upon the Truth God has put in your heart and taking the action steps the Truth has revealed.
- Fear was the first emotion to come (began in the Garden of Eden) and it is the last one to leave in becoming whole, but when it is gone the chains of the old mind have been broken and can no longer hold us.
- There is no fear in love. But perfect love (being in covenant relationship with God) drives out fear. (NIV)

Two Types of Healing

- 1. **Completely letting go**, being led by the heart/spirit, letting God's will be done. Thankful for each moment of life. "If I die I die for the glory of God and if I live I live for the glory of God because I live from my Truth-filled heart." In letting go of life you regain it.
- 2. **Righteous anger** that is heart/spirit directed. One will not quit, stop or give up. "I must heal, I have more to do for God, I am not done yet with what He has called me to do!" I will not die but live and proclaim the works of the Lord. (NIV)

A Prayer Life without Options

- We need to live life without options, because options are opportunities for the old world/lie-filled mind to be empowered, to rule over our body, mind and spirit.
- Whose prayer has the most power: the woman in America who prays that God heal her cancer (and if He doesn't she goes ahead with surgery, radiation and chemotherapy) or the woman living in the jungle who has no contact with doctors or hospitals? There is no option but to be healed by the power of God, or die. If I live or die I do it all for the glory or God.

The mind heals no one, it is the heart/spirit where healing flows from. The mind is the place of temporary cures but the heart/spirit is the place of forever healing.

The Power of the Spoken Word

■ The Truth spoken resonates as the Right frequency to positively entrain every cell in your body, every thought in your conscious and unconscious mind into health, healing and wholeness.

■ Just like a tuning fork brings everything it touches into the same frequency, the Truth spoken does the same for your body, your mind and your spirit.

Words-the Containers of Energy

■ God's Word spoken into your heart - the most powerful, miraculous and life-changing of all energy.

■ Man's positive words can cause positive changes in the environment but they are still of the old mind and can quickly change to the negative. You speak positive words, and the people around you become more positive, you can also speak negative words, and the people around you become more negative - this is entrainment.

■ Man's words, unless they come from the heart/spirit, are a product of the tree of the knowledge of good and evil. This feeds the happy/sad, good/bad cycle. This feeds the old mind.

God said, "Let there be light" and there was light.

God's Word, the Word of Truth that is received in the heart and spoken out of the mouth, is a spiritual energy that has the power to transform, heal and create all things.

God's Word in essence is God.
His Word spoken is entraining the environment to His nature of love, joy, and peace, which brings healing, health and wholeness to every part of your being.

Your voice is heard by every cell in your body, every part of your conscious and unconscious mind and all of your spirit.
It entrains them all to the Truth or to the lie.

Spoken Truth vs. Lie

- If Truth is spoken the body, mind and spirit align with it - all are one.
- If lies are spoken the body and mind align with it, but the spirit does not.
- **Just as the body without the spirit is dead, the spirit without the Truth-filled mind and body is suppressed, it cannot flow freely and powerfully until all three, the body, mind and spirit are in agreement, until all are one.**

Proclaiming His Word

- Whatever God puts in your heart should be proclaimed out of your mouth as worship, as praise, as thanksgiving.
- All the cells of your body, all the thoughts of your mind, all of your spirit resonate/entrain with this Truth that has come from what God put in your heart.
- If we think and say some Truth and some lies, the body, mind and spirit are not in one accord. Each is following a different frequency; this leads to eventual disharmony, imbalance, and dis-ease.

God's Word in You

- God's Word creates, heals, sets free, transforms, produces miracles.
- When you still your mind and listen to your heart, this is where God speaks with love, joy, peace and hope.
- His Word in you becomes just that, it creates life in you, it heals you, it sets you free, it transforms your body, mind and spirit, it produces the miracle of eternal life - God filled abundant life in body, mind and spirit.
- His Word spoken from your heart is Truth and it produces life, any other word spoken from your mind is a lie and produces sin and death - separation from God. Anything that is not of faith (Truth-filled heart, and the actions the Truth has revealed to you) is sin (separating from God). (NIV)

Do You Know God's Phone Number?

- How can you talk to anyone in the entire world? Dial the right numbers, in the right sequence (phone number) at the right time and you can communicate with anyone on the planet.
- To talk to God and bring Him into your life situation you need:
    - The Right numbers - His Truth Spoken into your heart.
    - The Right sequence - the right priorities - balance the body, and then the mind so the spirit can flow unhindered.
    - The Right time - the Truth received NOW for this present moment, not the right Word at the wrong time.

- Communicating = talking to and listening to God. Receiving His light and love, His joy and peace, His hope and faith, His healing and wholeness.

Spoken vs. Silent Prayer

Spoken

- Every part of your being aligns/resonates/entrains with the frequency of Truth spoken.
- All are one.
- Like a siren that all the cells of your body, all the thoughts of your mind, every part of your spirit can hear and become one with. All entrain to this sound.

Silent Prayer

- Every part of your being does not align/resonate/entrain with the frequency of Truth.
- All are not one; all are different.
- Not all the cells of your body, not all the thoughts of your mind will hear and become one. Not all of your body, mind and spirit will entrain to this prayer.

Energy

- Sound is energy.
- Light is energy.
- Energy and matter are interchangeable. E=mc2.
- So light and sound can be condensed into matter.
- Which came first, sound or light? God said, "Let there be light" and there was light.
- Words of Truth received in the heart and spoken out of the mouth can become physical and can change the physical.

Spoken Word of Truth Reprograms the Conscious and Unconscious Mind

- When you speak the Words of Truth that have been placed in your heart by God, these Words are powerful and alive; not only do they do they resonate at the Right frequency to entrain/align the body, mind and spirit into life, healing and wholeness, but they also reprogram or renew the conscious and unconscious mind.
- Do not conform any longer to the pattern of this world (world/ego/flesh-filled old mind), but be transformed by the renewing of your mind (your heart of Truth flows into your supremeconscious mind - mind of God, which starts to reprogram your conscious - thinking and unconscious - stored thoughts mind.) Then you will be able to test and approve what God's will is - his good, pleasing and

perfect will (His will is always spoken into your heart. Listen to and follow your heart and you are always doing His will). (NIV)

Prayer is not so much something I do as much as an expression of who I AM.
One who is in communion with God.
One who is in covenant with God.
One who is one with God.

Communion with God

■ Communion - intimacy: a feeling of emotional or spiritual closeness connection: an association or relationship, an act of sharing.

■ From, ultimately, Latin *communis*, literally "duties together," from *munia* (plural) "duties." Mutual participation. Ultimately from an Indo-European word meaning "exchange."[105]

■ When we commune with God in prayer we celebrate our oneness with Him, our covenant with Him, our doing everything together with Him, our being exists only through Him, and cannot exist separate from Him.

■ The two have become one, knowing each other's thoughts, feelings, desires, and needs. No longer individual.

Prayer

■ May my prayer be set before you like incense; may the lifting up of my hands be like the evening sacrifice. Set a guard over my mouth, O LORD; keep watch over the door of my lips. (NIV) (So I only speak words from a Truth-filled heart not a world, ego, flesh, lie-filled old mind.)

■ Come and listen, all you who fear (revere, hold in awe) God; let me tell you what he has done for me (my covenant partner). I cried out to him with my mouth; his praise was on my tongue. If I had cherished sin (separation from Him by obeying my old ego/flesh/lie-filled mind) in my heart, the Lord would not have listened; but God has surely listened and heard my voice in prayer. Praise be to God who has not rejected my prayer or withheld his love (covenant partner blessings) from me! (NIV)

■ By day the LORD directs his love (covenant blessings), at night his song is with me - a prayer to the God of my life. (NIV)

■ 'My house will be called a house of prayer,' but you are making it a 'den of robbers.' (NIV) (Our house or body is a temple of His Spirit, let us not let anyone or anything in our temple that would steal, kill or destroy.)

- Do not be anxious (product of the old mind) about anything, but in everything, by prayer and petition, with thanksgiving, present your requests to God (talk to and listen to God). And the peace of God (which fills your heart), which transcends all understanding (of the mind), will guard your hearts and your minds (1st, supremeconscious mind - the mind of God and extension of your heart; 2nd, conscious mind - the thinking mind; 3rd, unconscious mind - the storage, memory mind). (NIV)

- Devote yourselves to prayer (listening to the voice of Truth being spoken into your heart of Truth), being watchful and thankful. (NIV)

- The prayer of a righteous man (one who is in covenant with God and listens and obeys his heart) is powerful and effective. (NIV)

- And pray in the Spirit (God led and directed from the heart, not from the head) on all occasions with all kinds of prayers and requests. With this in mind, be alert (listening to the Truth-filled heart) and always keep on praying. (NIV)

- Be joyful always; pray continually; give thanks in all circumstances, for this is God's will for you…(NIV) (All this is a product of being one with God and listening to and obeying your Truth-filled heart instead of your religion/world/ego/flesh/5senses/lie-filled old mind.)

- Is any one of you in trouble? He should pray (listen to the Truth spoken into your heart, it will reveal the action steps to victory and freedom). Is anyone happy? Let him sing songs of praise. (NIV)

- Beloved, I pray that you may prosper in all things and be in health (of body, mind and spirit), just as your soul prospers (**your will -**choosing the Truth instead of the lie, **your mind** - supremeconsious filling conscious, **your emotions** - set free from them as they are replaced with the spiritual states of being: love, joy, peace and hope). (NKJV)

- But you, dear friends, must continue to build your lives on the foundation of your holy faith (holy=whole - with your body, mind and spirit - believing, trusting and relying upon the Truth that was spoken into your heart). And continue to pray as you are directed by the Holy Spirit. Live in such a way that God's love (covenant partner relationship) can bless you as you wait for the eternal life (revealed into your Truth-filled heart). (NLT)

How to Pray

- And when you pray, do not keep on babbling like pagans, for they think they will be heard because of their many words. Do not be like them, for **your Father knows what you need before you ask him.**

- This, then, is how you should pray:

"Our Father in heaven,
hallowed be your name,
your kingdom come,
your will be done
on earth as it is in heaven.
Give us today our daily bread.
Forgive us our debts,
as we also have forgiven our debtors.
And lead us not into temptation,
but deliver us from the evil one." (NIV)

- **Our Father in heaven** - "the kingdom of God (heaven) is within you." (NIV) The kingdom of God and the kingdom of heaven are used interchangeably. *Heaven is in your heart.* God lives in our heart once we enter covenant with Him. The prayer says Father God of my heart.

- **Hallowed be your name** - holy, consecrated and set apart is your name. I will bow down toward your holy temple and will praise your name for your love and your faithfulness, for you have exalted above all things your name and your word. (NIV) *God's very essence; is in His name - I AM, God of the eternal present moment.*

- **Your kingdom come** - giving full consent for the Spirit of God to rule from your heart, a prayer that ushers in the new heaven and new earth where the Spirit of God rules from the hearts of the people instead of the spirit of the world ruling from the minds of the people.

- **Your will be done on earth as it is in heaven** - when we follow our heart/spirit, not our old world/flesh/ego/lie-filled mind, God's will is done and the Spirit of God reigns in the physical realm.
  I have set before you life and death, blessings and curses. Now choose life, so that you and your children may live and that you may love (be in a covenant relationship with God) the LORD your God, listen to his voice, and hold fast to him. *For the LORD is your life.* (NIV)

- **Give us today our daily bread** - the Word of Truth spoken into our hearts. Man does not live on bread alone, but on every word that comes from the mouth of God. (NIV) (The Truth sustains our body, mind, spirit far more than physical substance.)

- **Forgive us our debts, as we also have forgiven our debtors** - thanking God that He has forgiven or let go of all our sins (separations from Him with our ego/world/religion/flesh/lie-filled old mind). I will put my laws in their hearts, and I will write them on their minds (supremeconscious mind 1st, then this will renew the conscious thinking mind 2nd, and then this will reprogram the unconscious stored memory mind 3rd)." Their sins (separations from God because of following the old mind) and lawless acts I will remember no more. (NIV)

- **And lead us not into temptation** - God tests us to help us grow in body, mind and spirit. Tests are of God and are passed from obeying the heart. The test becomes a temptation to sin (separate from God) when we try to pass it from the old world/flesh/ego/lie-filled mind.
- **But deliver us from the evil one** - what is Satan's name? The father of lies, the prince of this world. Where is his kingdom? Your old world/flesh/ego/lie-filled mind. To be delivered from him **one must break the mind barrier, the roaring lion, and listen to and follow only the heart/spirit.**

Prayer and Faith

- Faith is believing, trusting and relying upon the Truth spoken into your heart and taking the physical action steps that the Truth has revealed.
- Prayer and faith cannot be separated, they are the two that have become one.
- As he thinks in his heart (not his mind), so is he. (NKJV)
- I tell you the truth, if you have faith (believe the Truth that has been revealed in your heart and take the action steps that Truth leads you into) as small as a mustard seed, you can **say** to this mountain, "Move from here to there" and it will move. Nothing will be impossible for you. (NIV)
- I tell you the truth, if you have faith (trust in the Truth revealed in the heart and follow that Truth) and do not doubt (product of the old mind), … you can say to this mountain, "Go, throw yourself into the sea," and it will be done. If you believe, you will receive whatever you ask for (that is a product of a Truth-filled heart, not a world/ego/flesh/lie-filled old mind) in prayer. (NIV)
- Therefore I tell you, whatever you ask for in prayer, believe (know in your heart) that you have received it, and it will be yours. And when you stand praying, if you hold anything against anyone, forgive him (let go of the blockage, otherwise you will not be able to hear the voice of Truth that is speaking into your heart). (NIV)
- Be joyful in hope (knowing the path God has shown you), patient in affliction (knowing it will grow and mature you and that God; your covenant partner, is in it with you, that He will not allow anything in your life that you cannot overcome and grow stronger from), faithful in prayer. (NIV)
- And the prayer offered in faith (taking the action steps the heart of Truth has revealed to you) will make the sick person well (in body, mind and spirit); the Lord will raise him up. (NIV)
- Faith without action steps is dead and produces death.
- Faith with action steps is life and produces life.

- Those who all their lives were held in slavery by their fear of death (a product of the old lie-filled mind). (NIV)
- Where, O death, is your sting? (words spoken from a Truth-filled, knowing, heart). (NIV)
- *There is no fear in love.* But perfect love (covenant partnership with God, He meets you with ALL that He IS, once you do ALL that He has put in your heart) drives out fear. (NIV)
- **MORE** - once you die to your old mind, die to your ego, die to your flesh, die to the world system, die to religion, die to the 5 senses feeding the old mind, die to time past and time future, die to the physical reality, and are willing to physically die for the Truth, the path, the journey that has been placed in your heart, this is when the old mind barrier is broken and the heart/spirit rule supreme. This is when the love, joy, peace, and power of God can flow unhindered, can produce miracles every moment of your life.
- Everything that does not come from faith (following the Truth in your heart instead of the lie in your mind) is sin (causing you to separate from God, this is a product of the old lie-filled mind). (NIV)
- So then faith comes by hearing (hearing the voice of Truth spoken into your heart, into your supremeconscious mind and into your body), and hearing by the word of God (the Truth). (NKJV)
- By faith we understand that the worlds were framed by the word of God (the Truth, not the lie), so that the things, which are seen were not made of things which are visible (the physical was made from the spiritual, not from the physical). (NKJV)
- A large crowd followed and pressed around him. And a woman was there who had been subject to bleeding for twelve years. She had suffered a great deal under the care of many doctors and had spent all she had, yet instead of getting better she grew worse. When she heard about Jesus, she came up behind him in the crowd and touched his cloak, because she thought, "If I just touch his clothes (**knowing** in the heart), I will be healed." Immediately her bleeding stopped and she felt in her body that she was freed from her suffering. At once Jesus realized that power (spiritual energy) had gone out from him. He turned around in the crowd and asked, "Who touched my clothes?"…. Jesus kept looking around to see who had done it. Then the woman, **knowing** what had happened to her, came and fell at his feet and, trembling with fear, told him the whole truth. He said to her, "Daughter, your faith (following your heart) has healed you. Go in peace and be freed from your suffering." (NIV)
- **MORE** -spiritual energy can only be accessed from a pure Truth-filled heart, never a self/ego/world/religion/flesh/lie-filled mind. When you know it in your heart (like you know you are in love) then

you press on forward no matter what consequences your old lie-filled mind tells you, never quitting, stopping or giving up; this is how you will always access the spiritual power of miracles in your life.

- "Lord, have mercy on my son, for he is an epileptic and suffers severely; for he often falls into the fire and often into the water. So I brought him to Your disciples, but they could not cure him." Then Jesus answered and said, "O faithless and perverse generation, how long shall I be with you? How long shall I bear with you? Bring him here to Me." And Jesus rebuked the demon, and it came out of him; and the child was cured from that very hour. Then the disciples came to Jesus privately and said, "Why could we not cast it out?" So Jesus said to them, "**Because of your unbelief** (product of the old mind); for assuredly, I say to you, if you have faith (taking the action steps that have been revealed to your heart) as a mustard seed, you will say to this mountain, 'Move from here to there,' and it will move; and nothing will be impossible for you. However, this kind (of unbelief) does not go out except by **prayer** (listening and being directed by God) **and fasting** (willfully putting the old mind to death)." (NKJV)

Faith

- So then, as the body without the spirit is dead, also faith without actions is dead. (TEV)
- Everything that does not come from faith (believing, trusting and relying upon the Truth spoken into your heart, not your head, and taking the action steps that Truth shows you) is sin (separation from God because you believed the world/ego/flesh/lie-filled old mind instead of the Truth-filled heart). (NIV)
- And without faith it is impossible to please God. (NIV)
- ".... But my righteous one (covenant partner) will live by faith (the heart and the action steps the Truth-filled heart reveals). And if he shrinks back, I will not be pleased with him (one who goes back and follows the old mind instead of the Truth-filled heart)." But we are not of those who shrink back and are destroyed, but of those who believe and are saved (healed, set free, made whole in body, mind and spirit). (NIV)
- They overcame him (father of lies, the prince of this world) by the blood of the Lamb (the covenant) and by the word of their testimony (the word of Truth spoken from their heart to positively entrain the world around them); they did not love their lives (were not bound to the physical, only bound to the spiritual covenant of love) so much as to shrink from death. (NIV)

Faith or Fear?

- Faith is to believe, trust and rely upon the Truth spoken into your heart - the Word of God.
- Fear is to believe, trust and rely upon the words of a lie-filled world - the words of man.
- There is no fear in love. But perfect love (covenant partnership with God, He meets you with ALL that He IS, once you do ALL that He has put in your heart) drives out fear. (NIV)
- **What you fear the most will come upon you and when it does it is your greatest opportunity to break the old mind barrier (ego/world/flesh/lie-filled).**
- **You can only break this barrier when you are willing to DIE, willing to give it all up. When you are willing to let it all go is when your greatest fear becomes your greatest victory.**
- **Where will you be tested? The place you fear the most - pain where the cancer is. It is then that you must choose to either believe and follow the heart, or the old mind.**

Faith without action steps (not following your heart) is dead and produces death, separation from God. Faith with action steps (put in your heart) is life and produces life, oneness with God.

Faith and Hope

- If faith is believing, trusting and relying upon the Truth spoken into your heart and taking the physical action steps that the Truth has revealed, then
- Hope is the knowing in the heart that allows you to take those action steps.
- Hope is the knowing that allows faith to be the doing.
- Now faith is the substance (physical manifestation) of things hoped for (revealed and know in the heart), the evidence of things not seen. (NKJV)
- The faith and love that spring from the hope (the knowing the Truth in your heart). (NIV)
- If you continue in your faith, established and firm, not moved from the hope (the knowing in your heart). (NIV)
- A faith and knowledge resting on the hope of eternal life (a life of total balance, with all blockages removed, a life of total health in body, mind and spirit). (NIV)

- Against all hope (trusting in the knowledge of the mind), Abraham in hope, (trusting in the knowing in the heart) believed and so became the father of many nations. (NIV)
- For in this hope (knowing the Truth in the heart) we were saved (healed, set free, made whole in body, mind and spirit). But hope that is seen is no hope at all. Who hopes for what he already has? But if we hope for what we do not yet have, we wait for it patiently (knowing in our heart that it has already been given to us by our covenant partner). (NIV)
- **MORE** -if you are waiting for the tumor to go away to know you are healed, you never will be. Healing is knowing the Truth and the path that God has spoken to your heart, walking it out, never quitting or giving up. You will KNOW you are healed long before the tumor goes away. You will know it in your heart/spirit first, then it will flow into your supremeconscious mind, which will then fill your conscious (thinking) mind, and then you will feel it in your body. All this comes long before the tumor leaves.
- Now faith is the substance (the physical action steps) of things hoped for (known in the heart), the evidence of things not seen. (NKJV)
- And now these three remain: faith, hope and love. But the greatest of these is love (our covenant with God, our covenant with ourselves - body, mind, spirit covenant, our covenant with our neighbor-which flows out of our body, mind, spirit covenant - "all are one"). (NIV)
- We have this hope (knowing in the heart) as an anchor for the soul (the **will** - to choose to follow your Truth-filled heart, the **mind** - first the **supremeconscious mind** filled with the Truth from the heart/spirit, then second the **conscious mind** which has been reprogrammed with the Truth from the supremeconscious mind, then the **emotions** are replaced with spiritual states of being: love, joy, peace and hope) firm and secure. It enters the inner sanctuary (the heart) behind the curtain. (NIV)

After Listening comes Doing
- Get to the end of yourself.
- You must die to the flesh, to the world, to the self - the old you, to the 5 senses, to time past and time future, to the physical bound mind.
- Listen to and obey the heart.
- Take and keep taking the action steps in faith that the heart has shown you.
- Never ever give up or quit or stop.

Letting go is a key ingredient in prayer and healing, just like a bow string is pulled back with all the power to propel the arrow, this power is only manifested once one lets go of the string.

How do we Pray when we are in Pain and Suffering?

- How does one withstand the pain and intense suffering of mind and body?
- You can only stand when you stand in the heart/spirit, you cannot stand in the mind.
- By knowing God is in everything, and everything is designed to strengthen you in your journey so that you become complete, mature, not lacking anything.
- Knowing God is faithful; he will not let you be tempted (tested) beyond what you can bear. But when you are tempted (tested), he will also provide a way out (up - climbing the mountain to total health) so that you can stand up under it. (NIV)
- Realizing that you are not the pain and suffering, and that they do not have to leave, but you will not feed them; without being fed mentally and emotionally the pain will begin to decrease.
- By staying in the present moment where God is. Pain and suffering are magnified/empowered when we step into the future or past - we must stay in the I AM present moment.
- Remember you do not stand alone; your covenant partner is holding your hand, He will never leave you or forsake you.
- **By thanking, praising and worshipping God - first standing in the pain, then going into the suffering. This breaks the mind barrier. The battle has been won, you have the victory - this is the place of miracles.**
- **MORE** - pain can be physical, mental/emotional, or spiritual. Physical pain is either the body/mind/spirit covenant telling you that you are going further out of balance and you need to change your lifestyle (with the 7 basic steps to total health), or you are going further into balance (if you are following the 7 basic steps). Mental/emotional pain is from the stored lies of the old world/ego/flesh/religion/time future and past bound/physical limitation bound mind. These stored lies produce negative energy (emotional toxins) that stores in the organs, glands, tissues, and body parts of the body. Mental/emotional pain can also be caused as these lies are being released, as you follow the 7 basic steps, because the old mind is dying and it does not die without a fight. How do you know if the mental/emotional pain is you going further out of balance (getting

worse), or you going further into balance (getting better, healing)? You know that if you are living a normal American lifestyle, you are definitely getting worse, and if you are following the 7 basic steps to total health with all of your heart, you are healing. Spiritual pain is primarily caused when the Truth that has been placed in the heart/spirit is imprisoned by the old, lie- filled mind. The Truth was placed in our heart/spirit to set us free in body, mind, and spirit. When we live a life that is less than what God created us for, there is going to be pain and suffering as the Truth-filled heart/spirit tries to break free from the bondage of the old, lie-filled mind. This is like a woman in labor pains, the baby wants to be born; so also is the Truth in our heart/spirit that wants to come forth and heal our spirit, mind, and body. The other type of spiritual pain is produced when your spiritual gifts are suppressed by the old, lie-filled mind. If you have a gift of discernment of the Truth versus the lie, you will hunger for what is Right (Truth led heart/spirit as opposed to the lie-filled, led old mind). If you are not balanced in body, mind, and spirit yourself then your gifts are suppressed (by the old mind) and you might be hungry all the time even when you eat plenty of food. Until you become balanced in body, mind, and spirit, letting go of the lies and following the Truth-filled heart/spirit, your spiritual gifts are quenched and this can produce pain. The other way spiritual pain is produced is when you weep in the Spirit for those that are in bondage to the old, lie-filled mind and are living a life in total darkness, completely unaware of the Truth that is in their heart/spirit waiting to set them free.

Why do bad things happen to good people?
To make them better, to grow them stronger.

How to Pray
- **Talking** - informally from the heart as one best friend to another. Talking to the love of your life, the two being one, treat God just as He is your best friend, your covenant partner. Talk to Him about everything in your day, everything in your life.
- **Listening** - meditatively stilling the mind so you can hear the voice of your best friend - God. God will speak to you with love, joy, peace, hope, words, images, ideas, once you have trained your self to still your mind and listen to His voice.
- **Adoring/Praise** - this prayer is like the adoring a loving couple feels when they look into each other's eyes. It is telling your spouse how

much you love, adore and praise them for who they are. Telling them how you think about them all the time and cannot live without them and how they are the most important thing in your life. The same is done with God. Praise Him for who He is, the awesome creator and sustainer of all things, and for becoming your covenant partner. This can be with words, writing, song, or dance.

- **Thanksgiving** - thanking your covenant partner, God your other half, for all He has given you; His love, His life, your life, your breath, this moment. That He is there meeting all your needs above and beyond what you could possibly imagine. This can be with words, writing, song, or dance.

- **Worship** - this is the giving of your body, your mind and your spirit to you covenant partner, God, as a sign of your commitment and devotion to Him. To worship is to count as worthy, as deserving of your spirit, mind and body devotion. In everything you do, you do it to lift up your covenant partner, God.

- **Petition** - asking for something from your covenant partner, God, that you truly know you need in your heart and you cannot supply yourself. These are not superficial, worldly desires but heartfelt needs.

- **Intercession** - listening and praying for how God, your covenant partner, can use you. No matter where you are He is always before you and you lift up Him or those He has put in your heart, in prayer continually. Spirit vs. mind.

- **Compassion/Lifting One Up** - this is a type of intercession that just strengthens/empowers one in the journey, knowing you cannot change it, but can lift them up in it.

- **Confession** - this is telling your covenant partner, God, that you were wrong, you chose to follow your old ego, flesh, world, lie-filled mind instead of your Truth-filled heart. You are sorry and ask for His forgiveness (letting go) and you repent, which means taking a 180-degree about face and going in the opposite direction. This means you are now choosing to follow your Truth-filled heart instead of your lie-filled old mind.

As Your Prayer Life Grows

As your communion with Him develops

- You will rest in Him in all things, rest in His love, His joy and His peace in all situations, in sickness and dis-ease, in tests and trials.
- You will rest in Him because you know that you know that you know that He is your source, your life, your covenant partner, your best friend who will never leave you or forsake you - not

"God take it away" but "God show me the way that this can become a great blessing."

- You will rest in Him because you know that whatever has been put in your path of life, you will overcome it, you will become better for it as the two become more and more one.

Prayer is breathing the breath of life of God, as we inhale we are taking in/receiving His Truth. As we exhale we are pouring out His love, joy, peace and hope into our body, mind and spirit and into the others He leads us to.

Prayer of an Unknown Confederate Soldier[106]

I asked God for strength that I might achieve
I was made weak that I might learn to obey
I asked for health that I might do great things
I was given infirmity, that I might do better things
I asked for riches that I might be happy
I was given poverty that I might become wise
I asked for power that I might have the praise of men
I was given weakness that I might feel the need of God
I asked for all things that I might enjoy life
I was given life that I might enjoy all things
I got nothing that I asked for,
but everything that I ever hoped for
Almost despite myself my unspoken prayers were answered
I am among men most richly blessed

How to Hear the Voice of God

- Still the ego/self/world/lie-filled old mind by staying in the eternal present moment. This is where God, the I AM lives.
- Let go of the past and the future bound thinking.

- Be and stay in the present moment. This is the place of no time; this is the place of God (the I AM). It is the only place that love, joy and peace exist.
- Be patient, this comes from listening to the heart, which "knows" instead of the mind, which "thinks."
- Have no expectation of results or outcome. What you need you do not get until you do not need it anymore, then it comes.
- Let go of all resistance to "what is" and allow it "to be."
- Go to the place of No-thing (the stillness where God, the I AM, lives in the heart). This is the place of Truth/Spirit.
- Listen to the silence. It is where the still quiet voice of God is heard.
- Be open (this is your free will choice) to change your perceptions (change the way you see life, from an old lie-filled mind view to a Truth-filled heart knowing).
- Have a pure heart. The heart is pure once the old mind has been put to death. Remove the blockages or coatings that the old mind has covered the heart with. Remove the artificial heart (old, ego mind built to show how good you are).
- Remember God is Spirit and Truth. God speaks to the pure heart with love, joy and peace, never fear. God does not speak to the ego/self/world lie-filled mind.
- "All are one" – seeing everyone as a creation of God and all apart of the same family, the human race. This helps you to let go of the ego, the "I against them," and become a "we," God, me and the rest of the family.
- Know your purpose in life and fulfill it – it is LOVE (enter the covenant with God, the covenant with oneself – body, mind, spirit covenant, and with your other half, your spouse, and the covenant with your neighbor – all are one, all being led by the heart/spirit).
- Always trust God, your covenant partner by "letting go." You were never in control anyway; He was, is and always will be.
- See the big picture in life as God sees it – don't major on the minors. You never know what the tide of life will wash in the next moment.
- Be loved and love God, love yourself and your neighbor – the covenants of Life.
- Still your mind – Be still, and know that I am God. (NIV)
- "For I know the plans I have for you," declares the LORD, "plans to prosper you and not to harm you, plans to give you hope (knowing in the heart) and a future. Then you will call upon me and come and pray to me, and I will listen to you (when you pray from a Truth-filled heart, not a world, ego, flesh, lie-filled old mind). You will seek me and find me when you seek me with all your heart (not mind)." (NIV)

How to Know the Voice of God

- Be still – quiet the conscious, thinking mind, and put the old, lie-filled mind to death so you can hear the heart/spirit.
- Go to the place of No-thing – release the thought bubbles (conscious thinking, mental chatter).
- Focus on a word or phrase that God puts in your heart – repeat it over and over.
- Breathe the breath of Life over the word or image that your heart has shown you. Inspire – receiving the Spirit, the power from God. Expire – pouring out the Spirit, the power of God into the word or image God has shown you in your heart (praying in the breath).
- God's spoken Word then comes spontaneously into your heart and supremeconscious mind, and you know when it is from Him – it brings love, joy, peace and hope.
  It does not come from your thinking; it is just there, a revelation from God that comes in the heart when the mind is stilled.
- His Word comes first, and then your mind tries to talk you out of what your heart knows.
- If it makes no sense to your mind, you are right where you want to be.
- The path will almost always be the one less traveled.
- **MORE -** a very powerful tool in growing spiritually for someone who hasn't developed their spiritual listening to the Truth, the love, the joy, the peace, the voice of God spoken into their heart, is to do the opposite of what the mind tells you. If one is imprisoned by the ego, by the flesh, by the world system of lies, by religion, by future and past thinking, by physical limitation bound thinking, by the old mind, then the best thing to do when you do not know what to do, is not to feed the mind by doing what it tells you. This will not only cause the Spirit to increase as the old mind is suppressed, but it usually is the direction the heart/spirit would have led you if they were not imprisoned by the old mind. How do you know you are hearing the Truth-filled heart/spirit and not the lie-filled-old mind? By the language they speak. God always speaks to the heart with love, joy, and peace. God never ever speaks with fear. So if fear is involved in the decision, it is not of God, it is not the Truth, it is from the lie-filled old mind. If you are led by the Truth in your heart to do the 7 basic steps to total health instead of more drugs, and surgeries, how does the lie-filled old mind retaliate? By saying, "If you do not get medicine and have surgery you will die!" This evokes fear. This is not from God. This is from the lie-filled old mind. If you were supposed to take the medicine or have the surgery God would speak to your heart with

peace, and there would be NO FEAR. This is how you will know His voice.

- Nothing ever ventured, nothing ever gained – it is better to try and fail than not to try at all. If at first you don't succeed try, try again. In time with persistence and perseverance you will train yourself to know His voice. Does a baby know its parents voices the first time it hears them? No, it comes with listening to them each and every day. Training his ears to hear his parents' particular frequencies. It is the same with us. We need to train our spiritual ears to hear the voice of God, the frequency of Truth.

- My sheep know my voice. Your children know your voice. Why? Because they have been listening to it their whole lives.

- God ALWAYS speaks with love, joy, peace and hope (knowing in the heart). These are of the heart/spirit. God NEVER speaks with fear, this is the voice of the old world, flesh, ego, lie-filled mind.

- Start listening to His voice and as you develop your spiritual ears you will have the confidence and hope that you know that you know that you know.

- No matter how bad the life situation or world gets, you are on a journey into wholeness with Him, He is always with you. He said He would never leave us or forsake us and that we would never be put in a situation that we could not handle.

- Just let go (of your minds) and fly on wings of eagles (following your heart/spirit). The sun always shines once you get above the clouds.

- Give God the opportunity to produce miracles in your life. Faith is following the heart into the seemingly impossible. That is where God is. All things are possible for him who believes (the Truth in the heart, not the lies of the mind).

- Do not be afraid to fall, God is in control, you are not, never were, and never will be. He will catch you just like the mother eagle teaches her eaglets to fly. She throws them out of the nest and waits for them to fly and if they do not, she catches them, and does it again until they learn; she does not abandon them.

- Break the mind barrier, run into the suffering, run into the roaring lion, because when you do, the Spirit is magnified/empowered and flows freely because you have broken the old ego, flesh, lie-filled mind.

- How do you know you are hearing God's voice? The same way you know you're in love. Does your mind tell you or your heart? Do you figure it out or do you just know that you know? God speaks in the language of love, joy, and peace filling your heart.

- When you fall in love your body tells you and your heart/spirit tells you. They are all in one accord, in agreement, when you are in love.

- When we are in love (in covenant relationship) with God, when we are in love with ourselves (the body/mind/spirit covenant balanced), when we love our spouse (an extension of loving God, and loving ourselves), then we are ready to love the world (our fellow human being) and be the True shining Light that brings the Truth that will set them free in body, mind, and spirit.

How do you know you are healed?

- You know it in your heart/spirit.
- You know it in your mind (supremeconscious).
- You know it in your body (you can feel the signs).
- And eventually you know it in your conscious and unconscious mind (by reprogramming the lie with Truth).

All things are possible, and all things can be changed with PRAYER and FASTING.

I would rather live one day in faith, obedience, and perseverance to what God has put in my heart than 75 years of mere existence being ruled by my mind, living in fear, disobeying my heart.

Enjoy the moment. Enjoy the battle.
Enjoy the journey on your way to the Promised Land.
This is living life to the full.
This is as good as it gets, because this is where God IS.

Go Deeper

1. If genes can be altered by conscious thought, and even more powerfully by True prayer, what does this say about the physical being affected by the spiritual, about "all things are possible" for the one who believes in the Truth placed in his/her heart?

2. Why are petitional/ ritualistic prayers less apt to change our life?

3. Have you started to get a deeper revelation of the prayer types apart from a religion mindset? If you feed the old religion mind, what do you do to the Spirit?

4. What is one of the most powerful types of prayer and why?

5. Why does the Right Word at the Right Time bring healing and why does the Right Word at the wrong time not bring healing?

6. What are the differences between the power of the mind and the power of prayer?

7. How life changing is prayer that is mind-led, and why?

8. What type of prayer is the only one that should be used when you see someone suffering in his/her life journey, and God has not put it in your heart to say, do or give something to him/her?

9. If God put something in your heart that you are healing, and you go in for lab tests and they say you are getting worse, do you question your heart, thinking the physical test must be right, or do you question the physical test, knowing the heart is Right?

10. What are you going to use to change the world around you, your heart or your mind, and why?

11. Which type of healing is best, the "completely letting go" or the "Righteous anger" type, and why?

12. Why do you think more people are healed by prayer in remote regions of underdeveloped countries than in America, and why do you think more miracles are seen there?

13. What are the effects of positive thinking and speaking on the body, mind, and spirit, and how do they affect the hundredfold principle?

14. What is the most important thing to do when dialing God's phone number for your life situation, and why?

15. When you speak the Words of Truth at the Right Time, this starts to reprogram the conscious, and unconscious mind. Why is this vital to your total health and healing of body, mind, and spirit?

16. Why do you think, as you choose to follow the Truth God has placed in your heart to take the action steps He has shown you, that you can have an increase in pain and symptoms in your health-challenged areas (increased pain in the dis-eased organ/gland/tissue or tumor)?

17. If bad things happen to good people to make them better, what does better mean? Aren't good things are supposed to happen instead?

How to Hear and Know the Voice of God

God's voice comes in the stillness. It is always Truth and attached to the Truth is the Right answer, at the Right Time for your life situation. This first flows into the Truth-filled heart, and then into the supremeconscious mind. To access the Truth you must practice stilling your conscious thinking mind, which is a part of the world/ego/flesh/personality/religion/5 sense/time future and past/physical limitation bound, lie-filled old mind. To do this you can focus on your breathing. Breathing in (filling the heart with Truth), and breathing out (filling the supremeconscious mind with that Truth). When you are receiving Truth from God, it ALWAYS brings love, joy, and peace. It NEVER, EVER brings fear. This is a product of the old lie-filled mind. You will know it is from God because it just "comes," the "I got it" revelation as if someone (God not you) has just turned on the light and you can see clearly now. This never comes from thinking, or trying to figure the situation out. It was created by God in the *no-thing* stillness where everything is created. You can never hear the Truth, the "knowing all things," unless you still the conscious thinking mind, and the old, lie-filled mind.

Once you listen to and obey the Truth that has been placed in your heart, it fills your supremeconscious mind, and then it always brings God's peace, God's joy, because it is coming from God's covenant love relationship with you. He will never leave you or forsake you. *When you get to the end of yourself* (the end of your thinking, old, lie-filled mind) *that is where He begins to pour out all wisdom, all knowing, all Truth, all power into you.* You always know it is Him, not you, because you came to the end of yourself, your ability, your strength, your thinking. When you hear His voice of Truth spoken into your heart and supremeconscious mind you will know it came from Him because it is so True, so Right, so pure, so powerful that you could never have thought of this. This is "knowing the Truth that will set you free," and heals you in body, mind, and spirit. This is the Way, the Truth, the path to Life. It is all accessed from the Truth-filled heart where God speaks, once the mind has been stilled. Until you have learned to still your mind enough to hear, and feel the love, joy, and peace that God confirms His Truth with, you can choose by your free will to do the OPPOSITE of whatever the old, lie-filled, thinking mind tells you. When you do the exact opposite that the world/ego/flesh/personality/religion/5 sense/time future and past/physical limitation bound, lie-filled, old mind tells you to, you are suppressing and step-by-step putting to death the old mind. When the old mind is suppressed, and progressively put to death, the Spirit is magnified and can flow freely.

The opposite also holds true, feed the old, lie-filled mind (by believing it and doing what it tells you), and you quench or stop the flow of the Spirit of God in you and through you into the world around you. You stop the flow of the Truth, you stop the flow of the "all knowing," that He desires to pour into you. Remember the language of God is always love, joy, peace, Truth, and Right. God does not speak by evoking fear. Fear is a product of the old, lie-filled mind. Perfect love (covenant with the Living God) drives out fear. So when situations in life arise that need an answer, first still your mind, listen to and obey your heart, the answer will always come from the stillness, the something from the no-thing, and when it comes you will know it is the Truth; then it is your choice to obey the Truth and take the action steps to carry it to completion, never quitting, stopping or giving up no matter what the cost. *This is the place of miracles, the place of God.* If you cannot feel His love, joy, and peace at first then just do the opposite of what your mind tells you, go into the pain and suffering, go into the fear instead of running away from it, this is when you see that the roaring lion has no teeth or claws, he has no more power over you, you have been set free from his domain – the old lie-filled mind. This is the end of the old you and the beginning of the new you. The "all things are possible with God" you, the you that you were created to be, a spirit being created in the image of God, who lives in a physical body, and rules over a physical world.

How to Hear the Voice of God

- Still the ego/self/world/lie-filled old mind by staying in the eternal present moment. This is where God, the I AM lives.
- Let go of the past and the future bound thinking.
- Be and stay in the present moment. This is the place of no time; this is the place of God (the I AM). It is the only place that love, joy and peace exist.
- Be patient, this comes from listening to the heart, which "knows" instead of the mind, which "thinks."
- Have no expectation of results or outcome. What you need you do not get until you don't need it anymore, then it comes.
- Let go of all resistance to "what is" and allow it "to be."
- Go to the place of No-thing (the stillness where God, the I AM, lives in the heart). This is the place of Truth/Spirit.
- Listen to the silence. It is where the still quiet voice of God is heard.
- Be open (this is your free will choice) to change your perceptions (change the way you see life, from an old lie-filled mind view to a Truth-filled heart knowing).

- Have a pure heart. The heart is pure once the old mind has been put to death. Remove the blockages or coatings that the old mind has covered the heart with. Remove the artificial heart (old, ego mind built to show how good you are).
- Remember God is Spirit and Truth. God speaks to the pure heart with love, joy and peace, never fear. God does not speak to the ego/self/world lie-filled mind.
- "All are one" – seeing everyone as a creation of God and all apart of the same family, the human race. This helps you to let go of the ego, the "I against them," and become a "we," God, me and the rest of the family.
- Know your purpose in life and fulfill it – it is LOVE (enter the covenant with God, the covenant with oneself – body, mind, spirit covenant, and with your other half, your spouse, and the covenant with your neighbor – all are one, all being led by the heart/spirit).
- Always trust God, your covenant partner by "letting go." You were never in control anyway; He was, is and always will be.
- See the big picture in life as God sees it – don't major on the minors. You never know what the tide of life will wash in the next moment.
- Be loved and love God, love yourself and your neighbor – the covenants of Life.
- Still your mind – Be still, and know that I am God. NIV
- "For I know the plans I have for you," declares the LORD, "plans to prosper you and not to harm you, plans to give you hope (knowing in the heart) and a future. Then you will call upon me and come and pray to me, and I will listen to you (when you pray from a Truth-filled heart, not a world, ego, flesh, lie-filled old mind). You will seek me and find me when you seek me with all your heart (not mind)." (NIV)

How to Know the Voice of God

- Be still – quiet the conscious, thinking mind, and put the old, lie-filled mind to death so you can hear the heart/spirit.
- Go to the place of *No-thing* – release the thought bubbles (conscious thinking, mental chatter).
- Focus on a word or phrase that God puts in your heart – repeat it over and over.
- Breathe the breath of Life over the word or image that your heart has shown you. Inspire – *receiving the Spirit, the power from God.* Expire – *pouring out the Spirit, the power of God into the word or image God has shown you in your heart* (praying in the breath).
- God's spoken Word then comes spontaneously into your heart and supremeconscious mind, and you know when it's from Him – *it brings love, joy, peace and hope.*

It does not come from your thinking; it is just there, a revelation from God that comes in the heart when the mind is stilled.

- His Word comes first, and then your mind tries to talk you out of what your heart knows.
- If it makes no sense to your mind, you are right where you want to be.
- The path will almost always be the one less traveled.
- **MORE** - a very powerful tool in growing spiritually for someone who hasn't developed their spiritual listening to the Truth, the love, the joy, the peace, the voice of God spoken into their heart, is to do the opposite of what the mind tells you. If one is imprisoned by the ego, by the flesh, by the world system of lies, by religion, by future and past thinking, by physical limitation bound thinking, by the old mind, then the best thing to do when you do not know what to do, is not to feed the mind by doing what it tells you. This will not only cause the Spirit to increase as the old mind is suppressed, but it usually is the direction the heart/spirit would have led you if they were not imprisoned by the old mind. How do you know you are hearing the Truth-filled heart/spirit and not the lie-filled-old mind? By the language they speak. God always speaks to the heart with love, joy, and peace. God never ever speaks with fear. So if fear is involved in the decision, it is not of God, it is not the Truth, it is from the lie-filled old mind. If you are led by the Truth in your heart to do the 7 basic steps to total health instead of more drugs, and surgeries, how does the lie-filled old mind retaliate? By saying, "If you don't get medicine and have surgery you will die!" This evokes fear. This is not from God. This is from the lie-filled old mind. If you were supposed to take the medicine or have the surgery God would speak to your heart with peace, and there would be NO FEAR. This is how you will know His voice.
- Nothing ever ventured, nothing ever gained – it is better to try and fail than not to try at all. If at first you don't succeed try, try again. In time with persistence and perseverance you will train yourself to know His voice. Does a baby know its parents voices the first time it hears them? No, it comes with listening to them each and every day. Training his ears to hear his parents' particular frequencies. It is the same with us. We need to train our spiritual ears to hear the voice of God, the frequency of Truth.
- My sheep know my voice. Your children know your voice. Why? Because they have been listening to it their whole lives.
- *God ALWAYS speaks with love, joy, peace and hope* (knowing in the heart). These are of the heart/spirit. God NEVER speaks with fear; this is the voice of the old world, flesh, ego, lie-filled mind.

- Start listening to His voice and as you develop your spiritual ears you will have the confidence and hope that you know that you know that you know.
- No matter how bad the life situation or world gets, you are on a journey into wholeness with Him, He is always with you. He said He would never leave us or forsake us and that we would never be put in a situation that we could not handle.
- Just let go (of your minds) and fly on wings of eagles (following your heart/spirit). The sun always shines once you get above the clouds.
- Give God the opportunity to produce miracles in your life. Faith is following the heart into the seemingly impossible. That is where God is. All things are possible for him who believes (the Truth in the heart, not the lies of the mind).
- Do not be afraid to fall, *God is in control*, you are not, never were, and never will be. He will catch you just like the mother eagle teaches her eaglets to fly. She throws them out of the nest and waits for them to fly and if they do not, she catches them and does it again until they learn; she does not abandon them.
- Break the mind barrier, run into the suffering, run into the roaring lion, because when you do, the Spirit is magnified/empowered and flows freely because you have broken the old ego, flesh, lie-filled mind.
- How do you know you are hearing God's voice? The same way you know you are in love. Does your mind tell you or your heart? Do you figure it out or do you just know that you know? *God speaks in the language of love, joy, and peace filling your heart.*
- When you fall in love your body tells you and your heart/spirit tells you. They are all in one accord, in agreement, when you are in love.
- When we are in love (in covenant relationship) with God, when we are in love with ourselves (the body/mind/spirit covenant balanced), when we love our spouse (an extension of loving God, and loving ourselves), then we are ready to love the world (our fellow human being) and be the True shining Light that brings the Truth that will set them free in body, mind, and spirit.

A New World

- Once you have adopted the 7 basic steps to total health as a lifestyle, and your physical being becomes balanced in the present, the energy for maintaining life can turn inward and begin healing your past physical toxins, stored emotional toxins in the tissues, and negative mental thought patterns stored in your conscious and unconscious mind. As you continue to stay balanced in the present and start to balance in your past, the energy of healing turns further inward to the generational toxins of body, emotions and mind. Once these are released the body/emotion/mind/spirit enters the place of wholeness, the place of no time, the place where the physical laws can be transcended, because the Spirit of God flows unhindered in a whole human body, mind, and spirit. This is the temple of purity and holiness in which the Spirit of God makes His dwelling place.

- When you have built a temple of holiness, which is the body free from all toxins and blockages in all time periods - this is *timelessness*.

- When the stored emotions have been released from all organs, glands, and tissues in all time periods - this becomes the timeless spiritual states of being: love, joy, peace and hope.

- When the all the stored lies from all time periods have been released from the conscious and unconscious mind and reprogrammed with only Truth so the supremeconscious mind is one with the other two - this becomes the timeless, boundless mind of God.

- When you live in a pure, holy temple, and have a timeless state of being of love, joy, peace and hope, and have the mind of God unhindered in the endless present moment, then the *Spirit of God will flow out from you as a True light to the world to entrain the world around you to the frequency of Love, of Light, of Life of body, mind and spirit, being filled with the Spirit of God*. All peoples and nations will be filled with the Light, the Life, the Spirit of God and "all will become one," "one with each other" and "one with Him" who created them. This is heaven come to earth.

- This is when you will "Love the Lord your God with all your heart and with all your soul and with all your mind and with all your strength." And you will "Love your neighbor as yourself" because you do **know** the Truth and the Truth has set you free in body, in mind and in spirit.

I would rather live one day in faith, obedience, and perseverance to what God has put in my heart than 75 years of mere existence being ruled by my mind, living in fear, disobeying my heart.

Enjoy the moment, Enjoy the battle
Enjoy the journey on your way to the Promised Land
This is living life to the full
This is as good as it gets, because this is where God IS

Appendix—*The Physical Environment for Healing*

Environment is EVERTHING

French microbiologist Louis Pasteur believed in the theory of *monomorphism* which states that microorganisms are non-changeable and are the primary cause of disease. This theory states that disease is caused by the bacteria or microorganisms that invade the body from *outside* of the body. French microbiologist Antoine Bechamp believed in the theory of *pleomorphism* which states that microorganisms can change into other forms and organisms depending on the environment. This theory states that disease is caused from *inside* of the body depending on the **environment.** Claude Bernard said that it is the **ENVIRONMENT** that caused the disease, not the microbes. In certain environments non-pathological bacteria can ***change*** into pathological or disease forming bacteria. What is the most important internal environmental factor that will cause the change from non-disease forming to disease forming? Low oxygen and low pH (acidity). Interestingly on his deathbed Pasteur said, "Bernard was correct, *the microbe is nothing, the terrain (**environment**) is everything*."

The cancer virus which was isolated by Royal Rife, and which he termed BX virus, induced cancer growths in 104 successive generations of albino rats. During the course of extensive experiments performed with this virus, it was found that with a **slight change in the chemical media** for the culture, a larger virus resulted, termed BY. Another slight change in the chemical media, and the virus transformed into a monocyte. With still another change in the chemical environment, the monocyte becomes a fungi, and with still further slight change, the fungi turns into Bacillus Coli. Then if the Bacillus Coli is kept in a certain media for a year (the time required for metasteses), the BX virus appears again. The changes in the chemical environment required to effect these transformations are very slight – in fact it is stated that an alteration of 4 parts per million in the media will transform the harmless Bacillus Coli into the deadly Bacillus Typhosus. These changes can be made to occur in as short a period as 48 hours. Rife believed that non pathogenic organisms could be transformed into pathogenic organisms by changing the chemical environment as little as 2 parts per million.

Garbage and Flies

If you have a pile of garbage that attracts flies, how do you get rid of the flies? Do you spray fly insecticide to kill all the flies, will this end the flies on the garbage? Never! The flies will keep coming, you will never ever be able to stop the flies from being attracted to the garbage, no matter how many you kill, there will always be more. So what is the answer? Remove the garbage and the flies will no longer come. In this illustration the flies are the microbes, the pathogens – bacteria, viruses, parasites, fungi, and cancer cells. The garbage is the environment, the terrain that is produced with cooked food – it becomes non-digested, toxic garbage in the body (food for pathogens). Cooked food also is low oxygen, acid pH, and sugar forming. When you eat living/raw enzyme rich food that is alkaline in the body, it is totally digested and maintains the proper pH so there is no garbage (dead, cooked food) for the pathogens to feed on. Maintain the environment and you maintain your health

What Environment Causes Dis-ease?

Low Oxygen caused by: 1. Poor breathing technique – lack of deep diaphragm breathing, 2. Animal protein – as protein goes up in the blood and tissues the oxygen levels in the blood drop as much as 60%. Dr. OttoWarburg Nobel prize winner showed that when oxygen supply is decreased as little as 30%, our excess protein filled cells (from our high protein diets) can become malignant cancer cells **and that with a steady supply of Oxygen to all cells cancer could be prevented indefinitely**, 3. Animal fat – decreases blood flow and oxygen by 20% for up to 8 hours after a meal, **4.** Sugar – as the sugar content (cooked food) goes up in the blood the oxygen goes down proportionately. Lack of living/raw green plants for food =lack of oxygen, and chlorophyll= dis-ease.

Acidic/low pH produced by: 1. Cooked animal products.2. Cooked refined, processed grains and starches, **3.** Sugar, **4.** Low oxygen/poor breathing (respiratory acidosis), 5. Mental/emotional stress (anxiety, depression, fear, anger, bitterness, resentment, self criticism, etc.), 6. Spiritual stress (lack of love, joy, peace and hope).

Trapped blood proteins caused by: *Cooked animal products, Cooked refined, processed grains and starches, Sugar, Low oxygen/poor breathing* (respiratory acidosis), *Lack of rebounding cellular exercise, Free radicals formed by cooked animal fats, hydrogenated fats and oil, Overexposure to chemicals, toxins, drugs, and Alteration in the electrical/energetic field of the body-EMFs, geopathic, microwave, computer, TV.*

Trapped Blood Protein

Water follows blood protein, if there is **too much protein** (from high protein cooked animal food diets) and it leaks out into the interstitium (the space between the individual cells) then the spaces between the cells become flooded, to be in health these spaces must be dry. In order for your cells to get oxygen the cells must be in a dry state-no fluid in the interstitium. Any blood protein that seeps out into interstitium needs to removed by the lymphatic system. All oxygen and nutrients pass from the blood into the cells. All waste products and trapped blood proteins are removed by the lymphatic system. The cell could live forever if these three were maintained, oxygen and nutrients going into the cells and waste products being removed from the cells. Cooked animal protein causes the blood to become sticky (the red blood cells clump together like stacked coins instead of free flowing) or sludgelike. Not only does this slow the flow of blood, the flow of life, greatly decreasing the flow of oxygen and nutrients into the cells and waste products removed out of the cells, but this excessive undigested protein leaks into the interstitial spaces where it causes excessive fluid to surround the cells causes them to suffocate and starve, dying in their own waste that could not be removed.

What Changes the Environment?

1. Diet – cooked food is acidic, worst being animal products, then refined starches and sugars, living/raw plant based diet is alkaline, your blood is alkaline, when you eat the food that maintains the pH of the blood health is maintained or regained. **2.Oxygen** from breathing and from the right food (living/raw) which adds oxygen, not wrong food (cooked) which depletes oxygen, **3. Water** – decreased amount causes electrolyte stress and the blood to sludge, **4. Mental/emotional stress or peace** – lack of knowing the Truth and choosing to believe the lie causes the blood to become acidic, the body to become sympathetic driven (adrenal glands are over secreting adrenaline causing decreased blood flow to the intestinal tract which in turn causes maldigestion/malabsorption of everything one eats which results in low oxygen, high acid, high toxin environment) which is dominant in survival mode instead of parasympathetic driven which is dominant in healing, prayer, meditation and relaxation. **5. Spiritual stress or peace** – lack of love joy and peace causes the blood to become acidic, the body becomes sympathetic dominant instead of parasympathetic dominant. Your blood is alkaline, highly oxygenated, very fluent and to be in health you must maintain these three.

What Affects the Environment?

Oxygen levels in the blood and tissues, alkaline/acid pH of the blood and tissues, water/electrolyte/solute levels in the blood, and sympathetic/parasympathetic nervous system balance.

Enzymes and the Blood

Cooked food is devoid of enzymes that are critical for digestion. If the food has no enzymes there is never complete digestion. Incomplete digestion leads to undigested proteins, sugars and fats entering the blood stream causing the blood to sludge, carry low oxygen levels and cause acid stress to the body.

The Living/Raw Food Superhighway

When you eat living/raw food filled with enzymes and bioelectricity your blood moves at lets say 700 mph. When you eat cooked, refined, processed foods that are devoid of enzymes the blood moves at 50 mph because the undigested proteins are sticky and cause the blood to sludge or stick together. The undigested fats do the same; they decrease blood flow by clogging and congesting the blood vessels. The undigested sugars and starches cause all forms of pathogens to grow in your blood

What would happen if the national speed limit was 5 mph?

Not enough food would make it to the grocery store-people would begin to starve. Not enough garbage could be collected-disease would run rampant. This is what happens to us when we slow our blood with cooked food-our blood sludges and we become deficient and toxic at the same time opening the door to any sickness and disease. We cannot heal, we cannot thrive only exist for a while.

Living/Raw Food Keeps the Blood Moving at the Highest Speed

This increases the oxygen to all cells, this increases the nutrients to all cells, this decreases the toxins in the cells and blood; this allows our body to heal, to live, to thrive.

As cooked foods and animal products increase in the body

oxygen decreases, nutrients decrease, toxins increase, bacteria, viruses, parasites, fungi and cancer cell growth increase, symptoms, conditions, dis-eases increase, balance, harmony, homeostasis decrease.

The Secret to Long Life

The secret of long life lies in keeping the blood and bodily fluids pure and free of toxic material. Dr. Alexis Carrel of the Rockefeller Institute stated, "the cell is immortal. It is merely the fluid that it floats in that degenerates. Renew this fluid at proper intervals, and give the cell nourishment upon which to feed, and so far as we know, the pulsation of life may go on forever."

Dr. Carrel confirmed his idea of immortality of the cell through an experiment in which he kept a chicken heart alive for 28 years. This is quite amazing since the lifespan of a chicken is 8 to 10 years. Dr. Carrel stated that as long as the nutrients to the chicken heart were pure, and the metabolic waste was constantly removed, the heart would never have to die. The experiment was ended when an attendant in the lab forgot to change the fluids causing the heart to die.

Get the Good in your body and mind; Get the Bad out of your body and mind and healing, health and life always flow.

References

Air

[1]Otto Warburg, *The Prime Cause and Prevention of Cancer* (Wurzburg:K. Triltsch, 1966)

[2]Judith Kravitz, *Breathe Deep, Laugh Loudly* (Free Press, Ink, West Hartford, CT 1999), p.61

[3]Nathaniel Altman, *Oxygen Healing Therapies* (Healing Arts Press, Rochester, VT 1995), p.10

[4]Judith Kravitz, *Breathe Deep, Laugh Loudly* (Free Press, Ink, West Hartford, CT 1999), p.61

[5]Robert C. Fulford, D.O. with Gene Stone, *Dr. Fulford's Touch of Life* (Pocket Books, New York, NY 1996), pp.37-42.

[6]Kravitz, p.77.

[7]Ibid, p.67.

[8]Ibid, pp.42-44.

Water

[7]William D. Holloway,Jr. and Herb Joiner-Bey, N.D., *Water The Foundation of Youth, Health, and Beauty* (IMPAKT Health, New York, NY 2002), p.5.

[8]Ibid, p.6.

[9]Ibid, pp.7-8.

[10]Ibid, pp.8-9.

[11]Ibid, p.10

[12]Ibid, p.10

[13]Ibid, p.11

[14]Ibid, p.13

[15]Ibid, p.

[16]Holloway, Jr., p.75

[17] Brian R. Clement with Theresa Foy Digeronimo, *Living Foods for Optimum Health* (Prima Publishing, Rocklin, CA 1996), p.36.

[18]Holloway, Jr., p.75

[19] Masaru Emoto, *Messages from Water* (I.H.M. General Research Institute, HADO Kyoikusha Co., Ltd. 1999)

[20]Microsoft® Encarta® Reference Library 2003.

[21]Microsoft® Encarta® Reference Library 2003.

[22](from International Standard Bible Encyclopaedia, Electronic Database Copyright (c)1996 by Biblesoft) (from Nelson's Illustrated Bible Dictionary, Copyright (c)1986, Thomas Nelson Publishers) (from The New Unger's Bible Dictionary. Originally published by Moody Press of Chicago, Illinois. Copyright (c) 1988.) (from Fausset's Bible Dictionary, Electronic Database Copyright (c)1998 by Biblesoft)

[23]Microsoft® Encarta® Reference Library 2003.

Food

[24]Brian R. Clement with Theresa Foy Digeronimo, *Living Foods for Optimum Health* (Prima Publishing, Rocklin, CA 1996), p.36.

[25]Clement with Digeronimo, p.164.

[26]Microsoft® Encarta® Reference Library 2003.

[27]Keith Nemec, *Total Health = Wholeness A Body, Mind, and Spirit Manual* (Total Health Institute, Wheaton, IL 2000), pp.167-168.

[28]Nemec, p.171

[29]Humbart Santillo, *Food Enzymes:The Missing Link to Radiant Health* (Prescott, AZ Hohn Press, 1991), pp.34-35.

[30]C. Louis Kervran, *Biological Transmutations* (Happiness Press, Ashville NC 1998)

[31]Santisteban, GA, *Biochem. & Biophys. Res. Comm.*, vol.132, no.3, p.1174, Nov.1985

[32]Lita Lee, Ph.D., and Lisa Turner, with Burton Goldberg, *The Enzyme Cure* (Future Medicine Publishing, Inc., Tiburon, CA, 1998), p.55.

[33]Microsoft® Encarta® Reference Library 2003.

[34]Microsoft® Encarta® Reference Library 2003.

Sleep

[35]National Sleep Foundation, University of Chicago

[36]T.S.Wiley with Bent Formby, Ph.D., *Lights Out Sleep, Sugar, and Survival* (Pocket Books, New York, NY 2000), p.4